An Essay on
THE ORIGINS OF THE
HOUSE OF COMMONS

An Essay on
THE ORIGINS OF THE
HOUSE OF COMMONS

by
D. PASQUET

Docteur ès lettres
Directeur d'études à l'École des Hautes Études

Translated by
R. G. D. LAFFAN, M.A.

Fellow of Queens' College, Cambridge

With a Preface and
Additional Notes by
GAILLARD LAPSLEY, M.A., Ph.D. (Harv.)

Fellow and Lecturer in Trinity College, Cambridge

CAMBRIDGE
AT THE UNIVERSITY PRESS
MCMXXV

CAMBRIDGE
UNIVERSITY PRESS

University Printing House, Cambridge CB2 8BS, United Kingdom

Published in the United States of America by Cambridge University Press, New York

Cambridge University Press is part of the University of Cambridge.

It furthers the University's mission by disseminating knowledge in the pursuit of education, learning and research at the highest international levels of excellence.

www.cambridge.org
Information on this title: www.cambridge.org/9781107425859

© Cambridge University Press 1925

First published 1925
First paperback edition 2014

A catalogue record for this publication is available from the British Library

ISBN 978-1-107-42585-9 Paperback

PREFACE

Dr PASQUET'S essay, which is now presented to English readers, is one of a series of unrelated works which taken together have profoundly modified our conception of the origin of the English parliament and the place it occupied in the constitutional development in the middle ages. Dr Pasquet's work can best be appreciated by situating it in the perspective of that series. In 1885 the received doctrine was that of Stubbs which in turn was derived from or at least strongly influenced by Hallam. This has been carefully stated by Dr Pasquet[1]. What it comes to is that Edward I deliberately created a parliament composed of three estates, one of them based on popular representation in order to "give to all alike their direct share and interest in the common weal[2]"; that he was so successful in this that by his death "the machinery is now completed, the people are at full growth[3]." Thereafter to display the struggle of parliament to organize and equip itself to control the crown and reduce the prerogative is the main business of the constitutional historian.

In 1885 a young German scholar, Dr Ludwig Riess, published a little book on English electoral law in the middle ages[4], in which by way of an introduction he outlined a theory of Edward I's purpose quite at variance with the accepted view. Dr Riess argued that the king did

[1] *Inf.* p. 171 ff.
[2] Stubbs, *Const. Hist.* II, 3rd ed. p. 110.
[3] *Ibid. Select Charters*, 9th ed. p. 56.
[4] *Geschichte des Walhrechts zum englischen Parlament.* Leipzig, 1885.

not intend to surrender any of his authority, that he summoned representatives to supply such direct information
from the localities as would enable him to control the
administrative machinery in general and the sheriffs in
particular and that he intended to facilitate taxation and
local administration by employing as his agents those
whom he had summoned to his council. This hetero-
doxy seems to have been overlooked in view of the skill
and success with which the main enquiry was conducted,
and in particular the brilliant and acute treatment of the
very obscure question of borough representation. The
next year Gneist published his popular history of
parliament[1] in which he incorporated Riess's views with
regard to this last point. Stubbs in the third edition of
his second volume alludes to Riess's "thoughtful argument[2]." By 1890, when the fourth edition of his third
volume appeared, he incorporated a long footnote on
Riess's theory of borough representation[3] and somewhat modified his text "out of respect for Dr Gneist's
authority." Meanwhile Dr Riess had developed his
view of Edward I and his policy in an article which
appeared in the *Historische Zeitschrift* in 1888[4]. This
is a working out of the points made in his intro-
ductory chapter and is directed principally against
Gneist. In 1890 both works were reviewed by the late
Sir George Prothero, who dismissed Riess's theory as
untenable[5]. Thus, though the works were backed with

---

[1] *Das englische Parlament in tausendjährigen Wandelungen.*
Berlin, 1886.
[2] p. 224 ff.   [3] p. 465–466.
[4] *Der Ursprung des englischen Unterhauses.* See Dr Pasquet's
discussion below, p. 171 ff.
[5] *English Hist. Review*, v, p. 146–156. See App. III, note A, for
a discussion of the argument.

strong and scholarly arguments, they received little attention until a later period. Maitland naturally had read them but, as far as I know, mentioned them once only, when he alluded to them as having raised the issue of whether the house of commons was the child of authority or rebellion[1]. Meanwhile he himself approached the problem from a different angle. In the introduction to the parliament roll of 1305 which he published in 1893[2] he investigated the nature of parliament at the end of Edward I's reign, its relation to the council and the law-courts and the actual working of the institutions together and separately. The chief result was to emphasize the judicial character of the parliament of that time, its appearance as a session of the *curia regis* reinforced for special purposes.

There the matter rested until 1910 when Professor McIlwain published an essay of which the tendency is well set out in the title "The high court of parliament and its supremacy: an historical essay on the boundaries between legislation and adjudication in England[3]." With the main thesis of this work we are not concerned here. What is important for our purposes is the emphasis which Professor McIlwain very properly laid on a neglected aspect of the medieval parliament. Throughout its history it was a court, the king's court, and therefore the highest tribunal in the land[4]. How and why, then, had it acquired the national representative

[1] *Memoranda de Parliamento*, ed. F. W. Maitland, Rolls S. 1893, p. lxxv–lxxvi.
[2] *Ibid.*
[3] C. H. McIlwain, New Haven, 1910.
[4] Most terms give too much precision to the early history of institutions. The king's court was originally a feudal court, it long retained its feudal character and no one concerned with the early history of the house of lords can afford to lose sight of this fact.

character which many of its sessions undoubtedly exhibited? This question had been occupying the attention of two other American scholars. In 1912 Professor G. B. Adams published a volume of studies in which (for purposes of his own) he examined some aspects of it[1]. In the summer of 1914 Professor A. B. White published in an American periodical an important essay on the development of the representative system in the thirteenth century[2]. Both these writers show how easily and naturally the arrangements found at the end of the century grew out of the practice of afforcing the king's court with representatives (whether elected or not) sent down to give information and "bear the record of the county."

Then, also in 1914, Dr Pasquet reviewed the whole question in the original edition of the essay which is here translated. Since that time we have had Professor Pollard's vivacious treatment of the subject[3]. Dr Pasquet has in his revision dealt with the points on which he dissents from Professor Pollard.

We may ask then how the matter stands at present. On the question of origin there would be pretty general agreement that in so far as Maitland's dilemma is a fair statement of the case we must accept the authoritarian horn[4]. The crown extended and developed a familiar administrative device for purposes of its own. One of these purposes, it may be thought, is somewhat understated in Dr Pasquet's essay. This is what appears

[1] G. B. Adams, *The Origin of the English Constitution*. New York, 1912.
[2] *American Hist. Review*, XIX, p. 735 ff.
[3] A. F. Pollard, *The Evolution of Parliament*. London, 1920.
[4] But see below, App. III, note O, where an account is given of Leicht's attempt to defend the view of Stubbs.

to be the deliberate attempt of the crown to secure at moments of danger the support of one class or another which was recognized as having considerable political as well as economic possibilities. The method proposed is clearly stated in Henry III's well-known directions to the sheriffs in 1261[1]. This is manifestly the plan of moulding public opinion through elected representatives, to whom the case for the crown could be put, *viva voce*. This obligation, indeed, had been laid on the sheriffs by the writ of 1254[2]. It is probable that the political exhortations of the writs of 1264 and 1295 were intended to reach the knights and burgesses either through the sheriffs or town officials at the time of the election or through the lips of the prelates speaking in parliament[3]. Again the circumstances of the year 1275 were such that it was extremely desirable that the king

---

[1] "*Sed eos* [sc. *tres milites de singulis comitatibus*]...*venire facias coram nobis...nobiscum super praemissis colloquium habituros, ut ipsi per effectum operis videant et intelligant, quod nihil attemptare proponimus nisi quod honori et communi utilitati regni nostri noverimus convenire.*" Stubbs, *Select Charters*, 9th ed. p. 395.

[2] *Ibid.* p. 366.

[3] *Ibid.* p. 403, 480. The terms of the record in 1264 leave it doubtful whether the political considerations were introduced into the writs to the sheriffs. "*Item mandatum est singulis vicecomitibus... quod venire faciant,*" etc. are the words, while in the case of the towns and the Cinque Ports another form was used, "*In forma praedicta scribitur,*" which would suggest that the writ contained all that is found in the one addressed to the prelates and barons. It is not clear however that this was the case. The writ addressed to the bailiffs of the ports speaks only of the liberation of the king's son and other things touching the community of the kingdom, and this reappears (slightly modified) in the writ directed to the sheriff of Shropshire and Staffordshire who had neglected to send knights (*Reports on the Dignity of a Peer*, App. I, p. 34–35). In 1295 the rhetoric of the writ addressed to the clergy was reduced to a reference to the dangers overhanging the kingdom in that sent to the lords and the sheriffs. It is natural to suppose that some of the prelates would be put up to explain the nature of those dangers.

should be able to secure support by explaining and
justifying his policy in a way that would reach directly
or indirectly all classes affected.

It was hinted just now that Maitland's dilemma,
the suggestion that we might have to look for the
origin of the representative system either to authority
or rebellion, might not be a fair, or at least an ex-
haustive statement of the case. It is worth remembering,
therefore, that there is a social and economic as well
as a political side to the matter. The towns had grown
rich by their own efforts and the rise of the country
gentlemen had been independent of royal encourage-
ment. He would be a bold man who would venture to
attribute to either of these groups a desire to take part
in the government of the country at large in the thirteenth
century. The problem, therefore, was how best to turn
the existing state of things to the king's advantage. So
regarded, Edward I's policy toward the middle class may
advantageously be compared to his great-grandfather's
manipulation of scutage. Henry II had not encouraged
the holders of knight's fees to beat their swords into
plough-shares nor the tenants in chief to provide for
their relatives and dependents by creating new fees[1].
He accepted the new conditions and the *agrarii milites*[2],
but he saw that the composition which could lawfully
be exacted from them constituted what we might style an
unearned increment and took steps to attract it to the
treasury. He could scarcely have foreseen the consequences that were to follow, and the same is perhaps
true of Edward I's dealing with the middle class.

[1] See *Red Book of the Exchequer*, ed. Hall, Rolls S. 1, p. 413.
[2] The phrase is from the chronicle of Robert de Monte s.a. 1159.
The passage is given in Stubbs, *Select Charters*, p. 152.

It must be kept in mind however that the question of
origin is one thing and the question of the nature of a
developed institution is another. Here, although it
draws us for a moment out of Dr Pasquet's field, a word
of caution may be useful. The emphasis that has been
laid on the judicial aspect of the medieval parliament,
on its unity in the sense of its being the king's court at
which representatives attended as juries might at an
inferior tribunal, has been invaluable in helping us to
revise our views of the origin and growth of the institution. We must not allow it, however, to obscure
what might be called the political side of that growth[1].
We may remind ourselves of a few conspicuous examples.
If the king had accepted the *confirmatio* of 1296 in its
original form he would have committed himself to the
necessity of obtaining the consent of the knights and
burgesses to certain forms of taxation[2]. This he avoided,
but it is significant that the opposition, or an important
section of it, considered it desirable that he should so
commit himself. The statute of York, however you
interpret it[3], still leaves the impression that it was
thought in 1322 that on certain occasions and for certain
purposes the co-operation of the commons in parliament
was a thing of such importance that it should be made
indispensable. The part played by the commons in the
transactions that resulted in the great statutes of 1340
and 1341 is well known. They succeeded in securing

[1] We must keep in mind also that the early parliaments were
"acting in a manner which to us seems half judicial and half
administrative." Maitland, *Collected Papers*, II, p. 486.

[2] See App. III, note A.

[3] See *English Hist. Review*, XXVIII, p. 118 ff.: cf. Davis in Stubbs,
Select Charters, 9th ed. p. 56 n.; Tout, *Edward II*, p. 151; Holds-
worth, *English Law*, I, 2nd ed. p. 360, II, 2nd ed. p. 410 n.; Hatschek,
Englische Verfassungsgeschichte, p. 222.

the recognition of the necessity of obtaining their consent to taxation, and their petitions were incorporated in the statute that was extorted from the king in the spring of 1341. Then by the end of the century it is pretty clear that they were acting upon some theory[1] of the character and authority of parliament which treated it as something more than the court of the king and something greater than an assembly of estates, though, of course, it was both of these also. It is hard to avoid this inference from the official account of the proceedings leading to the accession of Henry IV[2]. We must be on our guard, therefore, against over emphasizing the judicial aspect of the medieval parliament at the expense of what we have learned from earlier writers of its representative and political character. What is definitely gained seems to be after all a shift in emphasis. It is coming to be seen that the great struggle of the fourteenth and fifteenth centuries was really the last phase of the secular opposition between the crown and the magnates. From the middle of Edward II's reign, when the attempt to control the king through his own administrative machinery was begun, the struggle takes on a constitutional character. But parliament is only gradually involved in it and is never the sole factor. Stubbs, following Hallam, taught that "the victory of the constitution was won by the knights of the shire[3]." This no doubt is true in the sense that

---

[1] That this and most other theories were supplied by the lawyers whom Professor Holdsworth regards as the leading element in the fourteenth and fifteenth century parliaments can scarcely be doubted. See Holdsworth, *History of English Law*, II, 2nd ed. p. 430 ff.

[2] *Rot. Parl.* III, p. 415 ff.

[3] *Const. Hist.* II, 3rd ed. p. 450.

the precedents accumulated in the middle ages effectively equipped the parliament in its later struggle against the crown. But if we keep to the middle ages we shall find that the parliament was only one, and possibly not the most important, of the forces that tended to limit the crown. A great constitutional lawyer as long ago as 1909 observed that "if we look for an habitual check on the prerogative we shall find it in the council rather than the parliament[1]." It is hard to derive any other impression from Fortescue's tract on the Governance of England[2]. Of course by the end of the middle ages the principles that taxes could not be raised nor legislation accomplished without the consent of parliament had long been accepted. What we need to remember however is that neither of these processes was as frequent or as important then as it was in the seventeenth century—to say nothing of the nineteenth.

[1] Anson, *Law and Custom of the Constitution*, I, 4th ed. 1909, p. 33.
[2] Ed. Plummer, Oxford, 1885.

G. L.

TRINITY COLLEGE, CAMBRIDGE

August, 1925

TRANSLATOR'S NOTE

THE French edition of Dr Pasquet's essay was published in 1914 and has long been out of print. As it is recommended for the Historical Tripos at Cambridge, it seems highly desirable that English students should be able to procure it. Dr Pasquet has kindly revised the text and incorporated a large amount of fresh material. I desire to thank him for his generous assistance and advice; also Mr Lapsley for his preface and additional notes; and my wife for helping to make the index.

The references given below to Stubbs, *Select Charters*, are to the 9th edition, 1913, unless otherwise stated. Those to Stubbs, *Constitutional History*, are to the 5th edition of vol. I and to the 3rd edition of vols. II and III.

R. G. D. L.

CONTENTS

INTRODUCTION

IN this essay we propose to study the origins of the
house of commons. That is to say, to show how
during the thirteenth century there arose the practice
of summoning to parliament not only the bishops,
abbots, earls and barons, but also those representatives
of the communities of the shires and of the communities of the towns, whose meetings in the fourteenth century formed the house of commons.

This summons was indeed no more than the extension to new classes of society—the bourgeoisie of the
towns and the freeholders of the countryside—of that
suit of court which the king had hitherto only demanded of his barons. The delegates of the communities, therefore, came to take their place in a
pre-existing organization. And to understand the true
bearing of the innovations made in the reigns of Henry
III and Edward I we must recall the essential characteristics of that organization.

Along with military service, suit of court was, in
England as in France, one of the principal obligations
of a vassal. The Norman and the early Angevin kings
usually assembled their court at the great festivals
(Christmas, Easter, Whitsunday), and oftener, if circumstances demanded it. The oldest writ of summons
that we possess dates only from the reign of John[1].

[1] This writ, which belongs to the sixth year of King John
(27th May 1204—27th May 1205), is undated and is addressed to
the bishop of Salisbury, who is ordered to present himself in

But the custom of summoning by special writ the bishops, earls and principal barons, or at least those whose presence seemed indispensable, probably goes back well beyond the first years of the thirteenth century. Perhaps the whole body of immediate vassals (*tenentes in capite*) of the king was sometimes summoned at the same time by general writs addressed to the sheriffs of the counties¹. That was the method of procedure with regard to military service, the summons to which in so many other respects resembled that to suit of court.

These gatherings were described as courts (*curiae*), councils (*concilia*) or great councils (*magna concilia*)², the latter terms becoming the more usual. The word *colloquium* was at first used to describe the meeting of the great council. The word *parliamentum*, which

London on the Sunday before Ascension Day to deliberate, together with the other magnates whom the king has summoned, "on important and difficult business of ours and on the common interest of our kingdom," and especially on the news sent by the king of France. He is further ordered to see that the abbots and priors of his diocese are summoned to be present at this council (*Reports on the Dignity of a Peer*, App. I, p. 1). Stubbs, *Select Charters*, 9th ed. (1913), p. 277.

¹ The well-known passage, in which Gilbert Foliot (see *Sanctus Thomas Cantuariensis*, ed. J. A. Giles, vol. v, p. 98), speaking of those who had sworn fealty to the Empress Matilda, says: *eorum...qui statuto consilio patris, ut dicitur, consueverant appellari nominibus, nemo plane relictus est, qui non ei consilium de obtinendo et tuendo post regis obitum regno...promitteret*, seems to prove that personal summons to the king's court already existed, and on the other hand that certain persons were not so summoned. But the passage is not as conclusive as it appeared to Stubbs, who wrote *propriis* in mistake for *patris* (*Const. Hist.* vol. I, 5th ed. (1891), p. 608, n. 4).

² The expression *commune consilium*, or *commune consilium regni*, which has long been regarded as one of the names for the great council, seems in most cases to have been used in the sense of advice or counsel rather than council. When it is used to indicate an assembly, that assembly is the king's ordinary council rather than the great council. Cf. A. B. White, in *American Historical Review*, XXV, p. 1–17.

was doubtless in use in common speech long before[1], makes its appearance in 1237 in the *Historia Anglorum* of Matthew Paris, in 1239 in his *Chronica majora*[2], in 1242 in official documents[3]; that is to say, at the time when it began to be applied in France to gatherings which were not then unlike the English parliaments.

The courts, councils or great councils of the twelfth century and of the beginning of the thirteenth century do not seem to have been very. large assemblies. A general council, held by Stephen in 1136, was composed, according to a document quoted by Madox[4], of the two archbishops; eleven English bishops; the arch-

[1] In a passage in his *Chronique de la guerre entre les Anglois et les Ecossois*, which was completed in 1183, Fantosme speaks of a *plenier parlement* held by the king of Scotland in 1173 (*Chronicles of the reigns of Stephen, Henry II and Richard I*, ed. Howlett, Rolls S. III, p. 226).

[2] *Hist. Anglorum*, ed. Madden (Rolls S.), II, p. 393; *Chronica majora*, ed. Luard (Rolls S.), III, p. 526. The passage in the *Historia Anglorum* was certainly written after that in the *Chronica majora*, since the composition of the *Historia* does not appear to have been begun before 1250. In an article on the early use of the word *parliamentum* (*Modern Language Review*, IX, p. 92–93), Professor A. B. White mentions a passage in the Annals of Worcester referring to 1223 (*Ann. Wigorn.* p. 415), as the earliest example that he has been able to find in the work of any historian. But, as he observes, there is no proof that the passage was written in 1223.

[3] The oldest official document in which the word *parliamentum* occurs is dated the 30th June 1242 (*Close Rolls, 1237–1242*, p. 447) and runs: *Mandatum est G. de Segrave, justiciario foreste, quod permittat J. de Nevill' habere balliam suam de Sothour' et Stawd' usque ad parliamentum regis quod erit Lond' a die Sancti Johannis Baptiste in unum mensem, quo tunc venire nullatenus omittat.* But *colloquium* long continued to be used. A letter of Henry III, dated the 25th March 1258 (*Reports on the Dignity of a Peer*, App. I, p. 18) calls the Parliament of Scotland *parleamentum* and that of England *colloquium*. The word *parlement* does not appear in statutes till 1275 (*Statutes of the Realm*, I, p. 26).

[4] Madox, *History and antiquities of the Exchequer* (1711), p. 10, note *s*. The charter in question was granted at Westminster *in generalis concilii celebratione et Paschalis festi solennitate*.

bishop of Rouen and four Norman bishops; Henry, the king's nephew; Henry, the son of the king of Scotland; the chancellor, two constables, two chamberlains, a seneschal (*dapifer*) and a cellarer; three earls and six barons. In 1218 the decision, taken *per commune consilium regni nostri Angliae*, to prohibit the use of the great seal for any charter or letter patent of alienation or cession in perpetuity until the king should come of age, is attested by the papal legate, Gualo, the archbishops of Canterbury and York, William the Marshal, earl of Pembroke, the justiciar, Hubert de Burgh, twelve bishops and the bishop elect of Carlisle, nine abbots, eight earls and fifteen barons. The list probably contains all the important names, but further on there is added: "witnesses the above-named and many others[1]." An ordinance of 1234, with regard to bastards, is given by the king in the presence of the archbishop of Canterbury, the bishop of Chichester, the chancellor, nine other bishops, eleven earls, twenty-one barons "and several others then present[2]."

These lists, unfortunately rare, seem to prove that all the barons of the kingdom did not necessarily come to the council. As later, in Edward I's reign, the king no doubt only summoned those whose presence was required for the business in hand; and no one would have thought of protesting at any omission, since suit of court was then considered a duty and not a right. If need arose, the king could summon "barons of the

---

[1] Rymer, *Fœdera* (Record ed.), I, p. 152. If we accept Professor A. B. White's interpretation, the expression *per commune consilium regni nostri* might refer to the king's ordinary council.

[2] *Bracton's Note Book*, ed. Maitland, no. 1117. This ordinance, which figures in the roll *coram rege* of 18–19 Hen. III, is erroneously placed in 1236 by the author of the *Note Book*. Cf. *ibid*. Introd. I, p. 106 sq.

second rank" (*barones secundae dignitatis*), as he did for the trial of Thomas Becket[1]. In the thirteenth century Matthew Paris several times mentions "general" or "very general" assemblies including "all the nobility of the kingdom," and these seem to have been of greater importance than the ordinary gatherings[2].

In these assemblies the king consulted his vassals on the questions which he saw fit to submit to them: governmental measures, legislative projects, judicial causes of exceptional importance. He was in no way bound by the opinion expressed by his council, although in practice it would be difficult for him to ignore it. The chroniclers only mention a few cases of resistance to the king's will, before the thirteenth century, and these cases are nearly always concerned with some violation of the rights and privileges of the church—such cases as the assembly of 1095, when William Rufus failed to obtain the deposition of St Anselm; the assembly of 1163, when a violent discussion broke out between Henry II and Thomas Becket on the subject of the sheriff's aid; the great council of 1198, when St Hugh, bishop of Lincoln, caused the help demanded by the justiciar for the war in Normandy to be refused[3]. The

---

[1] *Vita S. Thomae auctore Willelmo filio Stephani*, in *Materials for the history of Thomas Becket* (Rolls S.), III, p. 67. The bishops had obtained permission from the king not to sit with the earls and barons to try the archbishop; the king decided to add new members to the court: *evocantur quidam vicecomites et secundae dignitatis barones, antiqui dierum, ut addantur eis et assint judicio.* According to Grim (*Materials*, II, p. 390) all the *tenentes in capite* had been summoned. See also IV, p. 42. The importance of the assembly struck contemporaries forcibly.   [2] See below, p. 63.

[3] Eadmer, *Historia novorum*, ed. Rule (Rolls S.), p. 62–64; Grim, in *Materials for the history of Thomas Becket*, ed Robertson (Rolls S.), II, p. 373–374; *Magna vita Sancti Hugonis*, ed. Dimock (Rolls S.), p. 248 sq. (Stubbs, *Select Charters*, p. 248).

ecclesiastical order alone was at that time organized and able to offer some resistance to the arbitrary will of the king.

Assemblies such as those of which we have just spoken could take place only at fairly long intervals and could only last for a short time. But the king, as supreme judge and head of the nation, needed a permanent council to deal with current affairs. So we see from the beginning of the twelfth century a permanent *curia regis*, which it is often difficult to distinguish from the great *curia regis*, in which sat the vassals summoned by the king. This king's court was composed of those who were, by the nature of their functions, the normal counsellors of the sovereign: great officials and chiefs of the royal administration, judges and lawyers whose duty was to examine the pleas submitted to the king's judgement, officials of the royal household, etc. Between the powers of this little *curia* and those of the great one there was no difference. Both the one and the other were the king's council. But when some particularly difficult question arose—such as the trial of some great lord accused of treason or the modification of ancient custom on an important point—the king usually reinforced, so to speak, his ordinary council by summoning a more or less considerable number of barons, who could not be always with him.

Certain elements of the *curia regis* sooner or later acquired a marked individuality. Such were first the exchequer, charged with questions of finance; then the court of common pleas or of common bench, charged with hearing the pleas that were judged according to the common law and that did not need the personal presence of the king; later, the court of king's bench, which heard the cases brought *coram rege*. This tendency towards specialization of functions within the *curia regis* is apparent from the reign of Henry I. But the transformation of the primitive *curia* into a group of institutions, clearly separated from each other, went on extremely slowly and by obscure processes during more than two centuries. It was not yet finished under Edward I. The king's bench was not yet quite distinct from the council, and the council, which was to become the privy council, was hardly distinct from parliament[1].

The king's council, on the origins of which the researches of Professor Baldwin have thrown considerable light[2], at the beginning of the thirteenth century is hardly to be distinguished from the confused mass of the *curia regis*. The minority of Henry III perhaps helped to give it a certain consistency. In 1233[3] and in 1237[4] we begin to hear of a special oath taken by the king's councillors. In 1257 we get the actual formula of the oath, which, on the demand of the barons, had to be taken by the councillors, the judges and the barons of the Exchequer[5]. From this period the council became a most important institution, so important that the barons did not cease to complain of being systematically

---

[1] See Appendix III, note B.

[2] J. F. Baldwin, *The King's Council in England during the Middle Ages*, 1913.

[3] *Perjuri sunt de fideli consilio quod juraverunt domino regi praestituros*, says Richard the Marshal, speaking of the evil councillors, English and foreign (especially the latter), who surrounded the king (R. Wendover, *Flores historiarum*, ed. Hewlett (Rolls S.), III, p. 67).

[4] The twelve councillors imposed on the king by the barons in 1237 *super sacrosancta juraverunt quod fidele consilium praestarent, et ipse similiter juravit quod eorum consiliis obediret* (*Ann. Dunst.* p. 146. Cf. Matthew Paris, *Hist. Angl.* II, p. 394).

[5] *Ann. Burton*, p. 395 sq. (Rolls S.). Cf. Baldwin, *The King's Council*, p. 346.

excluded from it by the king, who preferred his officials and foreigners to his "natural councillors," *i.e.* the magnates of the realm. On several occasions (1237, 1244, 1257) they made efforts to replace the council chosen by the king by an elected council, which should contain at least a certain number of representatives of the baronage. The Provisions of Oxford and the constitution of 1264 aimed much less at establishing a permanent "parliamentary" control of the king's acts than at giving the baronage power over the council. But all these projects of reform disappeared along with Simon de Montfort; there only remained the formula of the oath of 1257 and perhaps the custom of calling to the council, along with the royal officials, a certain number of ecclesiastical and lay magnates. The king remained free to choose the members of his council as he pleased.

He had the same freedom with regard to the composition of his great council, and it is this which makes it so difficult to distinguish a parliament from a council, even in the time of Edward I. Council and parliament have the same origin. They both derive from the earlier *curia*. They both have the same unlimited competence and the same undefined powers. They are both the high court of justice of the king; they are both the supreme political council. In the middle of a roll that contains the record of matters tried "before the king and his council," suddenly there is mention of the presence of bishops and barons[1]. The abbot of Osney in 1237 gives a palfrey to the king in order that a matter, which was to be tried by the court of common pleas, should "come before the king and his council and that judgement

[1] Cf. Maitland, Introduction to *Bracton's Note Book* (I, p. 56–57); Baldwin, *The King's Council*, p. 60.

be made there." A little later, "before the lord king, at Worcester, on St James's day, in the presence of bishops, earls, barons and other magnates," the affair is considered and the abbot solemnly condemned[1]. A legislative measure, approved by bishops, barons, magnates and the king's council, like the ordinance of 1234 mentioned above, is inserted in the *coram rege* roll of the year, between two trials; and this is neither a clerical error nor exceptional[2]. Later, under Edward I, the so-called "rolls of parliament," which form the first part of Volume I of the *Rotuli Parliamentorum*, are really for the most part, as the titles themselves indicate, "pleas before the king and his council." Amongst them are inserted, according to custom, legislative measures, whether approved by the magnates or not. Indeed, throughout the thirteenth century, and even later, parliament is primarily the "high court of parliament"; and in modern times it has preserved a number of traces of its primitive functions[3].

In one point, however, the great council begins under Henry III to be distinguished from the ordinary council and from the *curia regis* in general; namely the right of granting or refusing to the king the aids which he is sometimes obliged to demand from his vassals. This right was originally of no great importance, because the king largely lived on the produce of his demesnes and his other ordinary revenues, and because, when he needed exceptional resources, he perhaps paid but slight attention to the wishes of his feudatories. But the demesne became impoverished. The wars and the maladministra-

[1] *Bracton's Note Book*, ed. Maitland, No. 1189.
[2] See above, p. 4, n. 2.
[3] See C. H. McIlwain, *The High Court of Parliament*, 1910; and A. F. Pollard, *The Evolution of Parliament*, 1920 (esp. ch. 11).

tion of Richard I and John forced these kings more and
more to count on extraordinary revenues, to multiply
aids and especially scutages. Under John scutage took
the form of a regular tax, levied almost annually, usually
at the rate of two marks on the knight's fee and in 1213–
1214 of three marks, an amount for which there was no
precedent[1]. The abuse of scutages and feudal rights and
the aggression of the king's court, which was gradually
ruining the baronial courts[2], provoked a violent reaction
and checked the evolution of the English monarchy
towards absolute power.

An article of the Great Charter (art. 12) forbade the
king to levy scutages and aids[3], "except by common
counsel of our kingdom." Common counsel was defined
in another article (art. 14). For a valid grant of an aid
or a scutage, the archbishops, bishops, abbots, earls and
principal barons (*majores barones*) were to be summoned
personally, and all the other tenants-in-chief through
the sheriff, and at least forty days in advance. Once
the assembly was correctly convoked, business was to
go forward as though all were present, no account being
taken of absentees.

These articles, which were later regarded as the
foundations of England's political liberty, had not for
John's contemporaries the same importance as has
been attributed to them in modern times. The barons
were chiefly concerned not to pay aids or scutages; or

[1] From 1198–1199 to 1213–1214 (inclusive) John levied eleven
scutages. Cf. *Red Book of the Exchequer*, ed. H. Hall (Rolls S.), 1,
p. 10–12, and Kate Norgate, *John Lackland*, p. 123.

[2] See particularly article 34 of Magna Carta and the observations
of G. B. Adams on the writ *praecipe* and the *breve de recto* (*The
origin of the English Constitution*, p. 77 sq.). Cf. W. S. McKechnie,
Magna Carta, 2nd ed. (1914), p. 346 sq.

[3] Except the three ordinary aids.

to pay them as seldom as possible. Everything else was secondary in their view, and it is impossible to say with certainty whether article 14 (concerning common counsel), which does not figure in the Petition of the Barons, was inserted in the charter on their demand or on that of the king. Anyhow that article disappeared from the Great Charter after the death of John, along with article 12 of which it was the complement. Articles 12 and 14 were placed among the "weighty and questionable" matters, which demanded further consideration[1]. Such consideration was bound to be unfavourable. If the principle of consent for aids was admitted by all in the world of feudalism, it was otherwise as regards consent for scutages, which were, at any rate in theory, money payments in place of the service owed by vassals to the king's army. The later confirmations of the Great Charter, therefore, only declared that scutage should be levied as in the time of Henry II[2]. As for aids, there is no further mention of them in the text of the charter. In fact, however, Henry III does not seem ever to have tried to levy an aid, without having first obtained the consent of parliament. In 1237 he even offered to leave the control of expenditure to a commission nominated by his barons; but Matthew Paris tells us that the barons contented themselves with grumbling[3]. Indeed, since the king was supposed to "live of his own," the barons considered an aid as a quite exceptional gift and set more store by its abolition than by the right to consent to it. Several times they absolutely refused to grant the subsidies demanded[4].

[1] Stubbs, *Select Charters*, p. 339.   [2] *Ibid.* p. 343.
[3] *Chronica majora*, ed. Luard (Rolls S.), III, p. 380 sq.
[4] See Appendix III, note C.

The Great Charter seems to have had little influence on the composition of the great council. After 1215, as before, those parliaments, whose composition is known to us, contained only great magnates. We cannot take seriously the formulae in which the king declares that an aid has been granted to him by "the archbishops, bishops, abbots, priors, earls, barons, knights, freeholders and others of our kingdom" (1225), by the clergy, "earls, barons, knights, freemen *and villeins* of our kingdom" (1232), or by the clergy, "earls, barons, knights and freemen, for themselves and their villeins" (1237)[1]. But Roger of Wendover, under the date 1229, speaks of a great assembly held at Westminster, at which were present the archbishops, bishops, abbots, priors, Templars, Hospitallers, earls, barons, rectors of churches and tenants-in-chief of the king[2]. In this assembly the earls, barons "and all the laymen" refused to grant a tenth to the pope to enable him to continue the war against Frederick II. This gathering, if indeed the text of Wendover gives its true composition, would furnish an example, perhaps rare, of a great council summoned according to the form prescribed in the Great Charter of 1215.

Such assemblies could only have been brought together at long intervals. The large numbers present would have made them mere ceremonial gatherings, incapable of serious work, had not the lesser nobility habitually neglected to attend and left the conduct of affairs to

[1] *Statutes of the Realm*, I, p. 25 (*Charters*); Bémont, *Chartes des libertés anglaises*, p. 58; *Close Rolls, Henry III*, 1231–1234, p. 155; *Close Rolls, Henry III*, 1234–1237, p. 543. Stubbs, *Select Charters*, pp. 350, 356, 358. See, however, for 1237, the references given below, p. 63, n. 1.

[2] *Flores historiarum*, ed. Hewlett (Rolls S.), II, p. 375–376. Cf. Stubbs, *Select Charters*, p. 323.

the great magnates. These assemblies suffered also from being of strictly feudal composition, so that sub-tenants were only represented by their suzerains, an arrangement which no longer corresponded with the true state of society in the England of the thirteenth century; for there were highly important persons amongst the sub-tenants, while not all the tenants-in-chief were among the great men of the kingdom.

When, towards the end of the thirteenth century, the composition of the great council became enlarged, it was for reasons quite different from those which guided the authors of the Great Charter. It was the government itself that initiated the transformation. Henry III and his councillors when summoning the knights of the shires, Simon de Montfort when summoning the knights of the shires and the delegates of the towns, Edward I in the various experiments which resulted in the "model" parliament of 1295, by no means proposed to hamper the authority of the central power, but, on the contrary, intended to strengthen that power, whose depositories they were. To that end they ignored the former feudal distinction between tenants and sub-tenants; and, since it was impossible to summon all the king's subjects personally, they made all the communities of the realm appear, by means of their representatives, before the king.

CHAPTER II

THE ASSEMBLIES OF DEPUTIES OF THE COMMONS TILL 1265

THE entry of the knights of the shires and the representatives of the towns into the great council of the kingdom passed quite unnoticed by contemporaries. Under Edward I, as under Henry III, the chroniclers continue to mention only the presence of the magnates (*magnates, nobiles*) in parliaments, at which, as we know from official documents, there were also representatives of the "community of the land." The peculiar composition of the celebrated parliament of January 1265, on which so much has been written in modern times, is described in only one chronicle, the "Chronicle of the mayors and sheriffs of London"; and its author, a citizen of London, does not mention the knights and is mistaken in saying that each town sent four deputies, whereas they sent two[1].

The silence of contemporaries is partly explained by the insignificance in parliament of the representatives of the counties and towns at first. They were only occasionally summoned and their part in the assembly was but small. This explanation, however, is inadequate.

[1] *Hoc anno in octabis Sancti Hilarii venerunt Londoniis per summonitionem Domini Regis omnes episcopi, abbates, priores, comites, barones totius regni et de Quinque Portubus, de qualibet civitate et burgo IIII homines, ut essent ad Parlamentum* (*Liber de antiquis legibus; chronica majorum et vicecomitum Londoniarum*, ed. Stapleton, p. 71). Perhaps, instead of two delegates, London elected four, as often occurred later. That would explain the chronicler's mistake.

An innovation of this kind could only pass totally un-observed if the idea of representative institutions was already familiar in the middle of the thirteenth century and if the new service demanded by the king from the counties and towns appeared much less as a novelty than as an adaptation of ancient customs to new con-ditions.

All the historians of the English constitution have observed that the practice of representation had already long been in use in the county court, which was later to elect the county's representatives in parliament. By the terms of the royal writs ordering the sheriff to summon the county court for the visit of the itinerant justices, each *villa* had on that occasion to be represented by the reeve and four lawful men, each borough by twelve lawful burgesses[1].

The procedure by *inquisitio* or *recognitio*, which de-veloped so greatly at the end of the twelfth and the beginning of the thirteenth centuries, also necessitated a form of representation of the people, either with or without election. In the procedure for the grand assize the voice of the twelve knights, who came to "recognize" the facts of the case before the king's court or the itinerant justices, was regarded as the voice of the district. It was the same with the procedure for the petty assizes, and an article of the Great Charter of 1215 (art. 18) expressly stipulated that the assizes *novel disseisin*, *darrein presentment* and *mort d'ancestor* should be held in the county courts by two royal judges and four knights elected by the county (*electis per comi-*

---

[1] The oldest writ that we possess is one of 1217 (*Rotuli litt. clausarum*, ed. Hardy, I, p. 380), but the custom was not new at that date.

tatum)[1]. In the grand jury or jury of presentment the *villa* was represented by four lawful men and the hundred by twelve knights or lawful men obtained by a rather complicated method of nomination. The knights who had to "keep the pleas of the crown" (coroners) and the verderers were elected "in full county court," "by the county," "with the assent of the county."

For the collection of the royal taxes an assessment of everyone's wealth was made by a sworn jury of neighbours. The need of such recourse to the people themselves became more and more marked in the thirteenth century, as the older taxes on land gave place to taxes on movable goods.

In 1225, the fifteenth of movable goods, granted in a general assembly held in London (*generali colloquio Lundoniis celebrato*)[2] in exchange for the confirmation of the charters, was levied in the following way. To meet the justices charged with collecting the money the sheriff summoned all the knights of the county, who then elected four lawful knights for each hundred, or some other number suited to the size of the hundred. The four knights visited not their own hundred, but a neighbouring one, and assessed the amount due from each person in accordance with the declarations of that person and the sworn evidence of two neighbours. In case of dispute they could appeal to a jury of twelve

---

[1] The four knights thus elected no doubt had the duty of choosing a jury of twelve knights, after the method employed for the grand assize. Cf. McKechnie, *Magna Carta* (2nd ed.), p. 273. In the charter of 1217 and the later confirmations, there is no mention of election, but it is difficult to say if the omission has any significance. The king merely provides that the judges shall hold the assizes "with the knights of the shires" (Bémont, *Chartes des libertés anglaises*, p. 51. Stubbs, *Select Charters*, p. 342).

[2] *Ann. Dunstapl.* p. 93. Stubbs, *Select Charters*, p. 322.

honest men of the neighbourhood. In each *villa* the reeve and four lawful men collected the amount of the tax thus assessed and handed the money to the knights, who in turn handed it over to the justices sent by the king. The knights had to take an oath, before the justices, to discharge their duty faithfully, diligently and impartially. The justices for their part took a similar oath before the sheriff and the knights[1]. For the fortieth of 1232 the method of collection was somewhat simplified. Royal letters named a certain number of knights (two at least) in each county, who were ordered to collect the aid throughout the county. The tax was assessed in each *villa* by the reeve and four lawful men, who had taken an oath before the nominated knights[2].

The idea of representation appears again in other connections. For example, in accordance with the Great Charter, John ordered the election in each county of twelve knights to make an enquiry into abuses[3].

All these facts are well known, and, if Stubbs and the historians who have followed him are to be blamed, it is perhaps for having exaggerated the importance of them. The county court, it has been said, was already, in miniature, a parliament similar to those which were later to be summoned by Simon de Montfort and Edward I. At it there were members of all classes of society. The lesser gentry associated there with the townsfolk, as they did later in parliament. The use of representation became common. The representative

[1] Rymer, *Fœdera* (Record ed.), I, p. 177.
[2] *Close Rolls, Henry III*, 1231–1234, p. 155 sq. Cf. Stubbs, *Select Charters*, p. 356.
[3] *Rotuli litt. patentium*, ed. Hardy, I, p. 180; *Fœdera*, Rec. ed. I, p. 134. Cf. Bémont, *Chartes des libertés anglaises*, p. xxiv, n. 2.

L   2

system was constantly employed for local affairs. Soon it was to be employed for national affairs. All that was needed was to summon to parliament the representatives of the lesser gentry and of the townsfolk in the same way that they were summoned to the county assemblies.

This explanation neglects several nice points of the problem and does not solve all its difficulties. It is a far cry from the four lawful men and the twelve burgesses to a national representation, especially as the four men and the twelve burgesses only came to the county court for the visits of the royal judges, that is, occasionally. The constant use of the jury, the custom of nominating committees and of electing certain officials, such as the coroners, may have prepared the county court for its electoral functions. When it was asked to elect deputies, it did so according to methods already employed for other elections. There was no need to define the electoral body nor to prescribe the formalities necessary for the election. Everything took place quite naturally, according to traditional usage. But that in no way helps us to understand *why* the representatives of the counties and towns were summoned to parliament, and how it happened that their convocation passed so completely unobserved, especially as regards the knights of the shires. The four men from the *villa* and the twelve men from the borough, the jury, the election of committees or of coroners might have remained indefinitely merely local customs of the county court. Whence came the idea of applying to parliament this representative system used in local institutions? And why was this extension of the local representative system to a national institution not noticed by contemporaries?

Dr E. Barker has brought forward a theory[1], according to which the application of the representative system to parliament would be primarily an imitation of the methods used in ecclesiastical assemblies for the representation of the chapters and parochial clergy. In 1226 Stephen Langton, the same archbishop of Canterbury who, eleven years earlier, had helped to extort the Great Charter from John Lackland, twice assembled synods containing representatives or proctors of the chapters and monasteries, along with the bishops, abbots and priors who had till then constituted these assemblies. In 1255 (and perhaps in 1254) appeared representatives of the parochial clergy, at the very moment when the royal government was summoning representatives of the knights to make them grant an aid. In 1280 (for the province of York) and in 1283 (for the province of Canterbury), that is to say, at the time when Edward I was preparing to give to parliament its definitive form, the clerical convocations assumed their definitive form, with regular representation of the chapters and of the inferior clergy[2]. The king in fact so closely imitated the action of the church that in 1283, instead of a parliament, he summoned two assemblies containing clerks and laymen, one at Northampton for the province of Canterbury and the other at York for the province of York. Some years later, at the time of the assembly of 1294 and of the great parliament of 1295, he summoned the clergy in the manner in which they were summoned by the archbishop to the convocation of the province of Canterbury.

---

[1] In *The Dominican Order and Convocation, a study of the growth of representation in the Church during the XIIIth century*, 1913.

[2] Barker, *The Dominican Order, etc.*, p. 42 sq., 51 sq., 55–57, 66 sq.

The practice of representation in ecclesiastical assemblies would derive, according to Dr Barker, from the procedure of the Dominicans in assembling the general chapters of their order, the brethren of each house being represented at these chapters by delegates. We cannot follow Dr Barker over this ground, for we should be drawn far away from our subject. We will confine ourselves to remarking that the thread, which, according to Dr Barker, connects the Dominican institutions with the innovations of the church of England in the thirteenth century, seems to us to be extremely thin. The direct influence of Dominican institutions on Simon de Montfort and on the parliament of 1265 is still more disputable. To prove the existence of this influence, it is surely not enough to show that Simon's father had been in touch with Saint Dominic, that a Dominican treatise formed part of Simon de Montfort's library, and that the *Franciscan* author of the Song of Lewes should speak in vague terms of the necessity for consulting "the community of the realm[1]." Further, Dr Barker himself points out that the great parliament of Simon de Montfort, so complete in other respects, did not contain proctors of the chapters or delegates of the parochial clergy.

However, we believe that Dr Barker has rightly drawn attention to the relations that existed throughout the thirteenth century between the ecclesiastical assemblies and the parliaments. It is by no means proved that the use of representation is older in ecclesiastical assemblies than in parliaments, and Dr Barker passes too lightly over the writs of November 1213, by which John summoned four knights from each county "to

---

[1] Cf. *ibid.* p. 60.

discuss the affairs of the kingdom," thirteen years before Stephen Langton summoned the proctors of the chapters[1]. But the issue is not merely one of dates. Ecclesiastical assemblies probably influenced parliamentary assemblies and helped to give a permanent character to practices which might perhaps have disappeared but for that influence[2]. Long before the laity, the clergy understood the fundamental principle which was later to become the basis of parliamentary law; namely, that every undertaking, especially every pecuniary undertaking, in order to be valid, should be freely accepted by those concerned or by their representatives. The clergy defended this principle at once against the pope and against the king. Already under John the higher clergy refused to enter into undertakings in the name of the parochial clergy, to whom the king had to refer directly[3]. It was because the business in hand specially concerned the chapters that Langton asked them to send their representatives in 1226. The curious instructions given on that occasion by the canons of Salisbury cathedral to their deputies show how the representative system was then understood[4].

In 1255 "the proctors of the beneficed clergy of the archdeaconry of Lincoln, in the name of the whole community, declare that they are injured in that a tenth of

[1] One of the reasons for which Dr Barker attaches little importance to the summons of November 1213 is that, according to him (p. 51 and 55), John summoned "men" (*homines*) and not "knights" (*milites*). But, as Miss Levett has shown (*English Historical Review*, xxxi, p. 85), the roll says *milites*, as does the text of the *Reports on the Dignity of a Peer* (App. I, p. 2). Dr Barker's misapprehension arises from a slip on the part of Stubbs, who printed *homines* in place of *milites* in his *Select Charters*, p. 282.

[2] See Appendix III, note D.

[3] *Ann. Waverley*, in *Ann. monast.* I, p. 258; *Rot. litt. pat.* ed. Hardy, I, p. 72.

[4] Cf. Barker, *Dominican Order and Convocation*, p. 48–50.

their benefices has been granted to the lord king, though they had not been assembled." They added "especially when it is proposed to lay an obligation on anyone, it is necessary to have his express consent[1]."

In 1283 the absence of the representatives of the parochial clergy, who had not been summoned to the assemblies at York and Northampton, prevented the clergy present from making a decision and necessitated the holding of new assemblies[2]. The firmness with which on all these occasions the clergy in defence of their interests insisted on the necessity of a complete representation could not fail in the end to have some influence on the laity.

But this influence must not be exaggerated. To make parliament a mere imitation of the ecclesiastical assemblies is to forget that the lesser gentry of the counties and the townsfolk do not seem to have ever asked to send representatives to parliament, that the prelates and barons do not seem to have ever demanded it on their behalf, and that consequently the summoning of the deputies of the counties and boroughs took place under conditions quite different from those of the summoning of the ecclesiastical proctors. Further, if the central government's summons of the knights and burgesses to parliament was an imitation of the methods employed by the ecclesiastical authorities, if this summons was in lay affairs a real innovation, how was it that this innovation struck nobody and was mentioned by none of the contemporary chroniclers?

No more than the theory which derives the repre-

---

[1] *Ann. Burton*, p. 360. Stubbs, *Select Charters*, p. 329. The tenth had been granted, on the demand of the Pope, by the parliament at Easter 1253.

[2] See below, p. 85.

sentation of the commons from the practice of the county court, does Dr Barker's theory enable us to understand why the summoning of the deputies of the counties and towns made so little impression on contemporaries; nor why, although the summoning of the burgesses is at any rate mentioned by one chronicler, that of the knights, so long the essential element in the representation of the commons, is passed over in complete silence. To explain such facts we must admit that what seems to us an innovation appeared to contemporaries, at least as concerns the knights, to be merely the natural development of functions that had long been familiar.

***

The summoning of the representatives of the commons to parliament is essentially, as we shall see when studying the parliaments of Edward I, the summoning *before the king and his council* of a certain number of persons who are considered to represent the communities of the realm. In 1254 this is expressly stated in the writs ordering the election of two knights from each shire. The delegates, who have to appear in the name of the county to reply to the regents' demand for an aid, have to appear "before our council at Westminster." The formula later disappears from the writs of summons[1], but we shall find it again in other official documents, and in 1306 the account of the assembly shows us the estates of the realm—the clergy, the nobility and the knights first, then the deputies of the towns—appearing before the council, who explain the king's demands to them and register their assent[2].

[1] It is found in 1265 in the writ given to the knights for payment of their expenses (*Reports on the Dignity of a Peer*, App. I, p. 35).

[2] See below, p. 153.

Now, to summon before the council a certain number of knights charged to represent their county and to speak in its name was far from being a novelty in the middle of the thirteenth century. When a judgement of the county court was carried on appeal of false judgement before the court of the king, a custom, whose importance did not escape Maitland[1], demanded that the king's court should order the sheriff to have a record made in full county court of what happened at the time of the judgement and to have this record brought to the court by four lawful knights[2]. The *Note Book* attributed to Bracton contains numerous passages of the beginning of Henry III's reign, which show us how things happened. In 1219, for example, the sheriff of the county of Surrey received an order to send four knights with the record of a judgement given by the county court on a question of delivery of possession (*seisin*). On the appointed day the four knights sent by the county present themselves with the record which they communicate to the court. The plaintiff disputes the accuracy of the record; and the aforesaid knights, in the name of the county (*pro comitatu*), say that the record exactly corresponds with what they recorded before. They offer to prove it by judicial duel and present a champion. The plaintiff similarly offers to prove his words by judicial duel and presents a champion. The court then pronounces its judgement: Whereas the plaintiff was

---

[1] *Bracton's Note Book*, Introd. 1, p. 130.

[2] See an order given by the king to this effect (30th October 1234) in *Close Rolls, Henry III*, 1234–1237, p. 2. It seems that the county courts did not keep a regular "record" of their sessions. At least no document of that kind has yet been found. See Appendix III, note E.

unable to present himself to the county court to be placed in possession, because he was absent; and the county court has been held twice in the space of three weeks, which is contrary to the customs of the kingdom and did not enable the plaintiff to present himself in time; the county is "at the mercy" (*in misericordia*) of the king; so is the sheriff, since the second session, which he held after three weeks, was illegal; the plaintiff is placed in possession[1].

This case may be taken as typical, although there are a great many others in Bracton's notes[2]. The notes for the year 1222 alone contain three. The knights are sometimes bidden to present themselves "before the king[3]" or "by order of the king before the justices of the bench[4]." The number of knights summoned is generally four; but it sometimes falls to three or even to two, and can rise to as many as six.

This practice goes back to a time long before the beginning of Henry III's reign. On the first page for the sixth year of Richard Cœur-de-Lion in the *Rotuli curiae regis*, published by Palgrave, we read that, after the sheriff had been ordered to hold an inquest, four knights appeared "on behalf of the county of Oxford" to declare that it was untrue that Adam de Bedigefeld had ever been outlawed in the county.

[1] *Bracton's Note Book*, ed. Maitland, No. 40.
[2] *Ibid.* Nos. 185, 191, 212, 243, 445, 554, 955, 1019, 1077, 1130, 1383, 1406, 1412, 1436, 1672, 1730. A case of record sent to the king by the county of Essex appears on the *Rotuli litt. claus.* of the fifteenth year of John (ed. Hardy, I, p. 165). See also *Placitorum abbreviatio*, p. 136, 141, 181. In the last case a judgement of a seigneurial court is in question. The sheriff receives an order to have an inquest made on the spot by four discreet and lawful knights and to send the result by four knights.
[3] *Ibid.* No. 1730.
[4] *Ibid.* No. 243.

This reference is dated the 13th October 1194. On the 13th November of the same year in the course of one sitting the court orders the sheriff of Wiltshire to have an inquest made with regard to land, the tenure of which is contested, and to send the result to Westminster by four knights; and the sheriff of Yorkshire to send up a record similarly by four knights[1]. In this early period, then, the custom seems to us to be perfectly established. When the king's court needs information, the county sends it by four knights. When a judgement of the county has to be defended against the attack of a dissatisfied litigant, four knights come in the county's name to bring the record and to defend the judgement.

Probably such summons were quite frequent; and the knights seem sometimes to have regarded the action of the king's court as an abuse. They do not always appear on the day fixed; they do not always bring the record demanded; the group of four knights, who are to speak in the name of the county, is not always complete. But in that case the king's court can inflict a penalty on the county and does not hesitate to do so.

The knights are also bidden to appear before the king's court in other circumstances. For example, when a case is brought, either in the first instance or on appeal, before the king's court and the court considers it necessary to have the facts recognized by an assize of twelve knights. The rolls of the king's court for the first year of John, which have been published by Palgrave[2], show us numerous summons of this kind. The abuse to which they gave rise explains article 18 of the Great Charter, which forbids the holding of the

---

[1] *Rotuli curiae regis*, ed. Palgrave (1835), I, p. 44.
[2] In the *Rotuli curiae regis*, latter part of vol. I and vol. II.

three petty assizes of *mort d'ancestor*, *novel disseisin* and *darrein presentment* outside the county and provides that the king shall send two justices four times a year to hold these assizes with the help of four knights elected by the county[1]. Had this article been retained, the journeys of the knights to Westminster would have become very much rarer. But from 1217 the assize *darrein presentment* was again reserved for the justices of the bench. For the other two assizes the annual circuits of the justices were reduced to one. Cases which presented special difficulties were to be sent to the justices of the bench[2]. It is therefore probable that the knights continued to be fairly frequently summoned, when matters concerning their county were in question. These summons did not become rare till the end of the thirteenth century, after the statute of Westminster the second (1285) had provided for the new commissions of *nisi prius*[3]. From that time the sheriff was ordered to instruct the members of juries to repair to Westminster unless in the meanwhile (*nisi prius*) justices of assize should have arrived in the county. The new formula was applied to nearly all civil cases and juries of knights were less frequently summoned to Westminster. But by that time the knights had long been accustomed to present themselves in the name of their county before one or other of the subdivisions of the king's court.

Summons of this kind may seem at first sight to have but remote connections with parliamentary summons. However, the four knights, who come to defend a judge-

[1] Bémont, *Chartes des libertés anglaises*, p. 30. Stubbs, *Select Charters*, p. 295.
[2] Bémont, *Chartes*, p. 51. Stubbs, *Select Charters*, p. 342.
[3] *Statutes of the Realm*, I, p. 85–86.

ment of the county court before the king's council, represent the county and speak in its name. If their explanations seem unsatisfactory, it is the county that is sentenced. We do not know how they were appointed, but the method of nomination perhaps did not differ much from that of a parliamentary election under Edward I. They appear before the king's court or the king's council, exactly as they will appear in 1254 and after. The function which they perform is judicial. But is not parliament itself, above all, the king's high court of justice?

Thus between the citation of the knights of the shire before the council or the king's court to bring and defend the record of a judgement, and their citation to parliament there was a striking similarity, which must have early accustomed them to the summons that bade them appear before the king. The functions which the knights performed in parliament were not indeed so different from those which they had so often discharged at Westminster as might be supposed. They no longer had to defend judgements or make recognitions but the *Rotuli Parliamentorum* show us that the greater part of their time would be employed in "ensuing" the petitions which their constituents had instructed them to present to the king and his council and which had as object the remedy of wrongs "that cannot be remedied by the common law[1]." In this way they still defended their county.

₊

There is, it is true, a difference, which may seem all-important, between the summons of which we have

[1] Article 6 of the petition of 1309 (*Rot. Parl.* I, p. 444).

just spoken and parliamentary summons. For judicial business before the council only the county in question is summoned; whereas in the case of parliament summons are issued for a general assembly, in which the representatives of all the counties of the kingdom are to appear. It would be absurd to deny this difference; but in reality it is less serious than might appear.

We shall see that in these early parliaments each county is held to be acting individually. The representatives of a county are not the representatives of England, but the attorneys of their county, empowered to speak and enter into engagements only in the name of that county and capable of accepting liabilities different from those of other counties. The simultaneous presence of all the deputies is not necessary. In 1265 two counties fail to send deputies to parliament. After the session they receive orders to see that their deputies appear before the king and his council, no doubt in order that they too shall be able to enter into the engagements undertaken by the other delegates of counties[1].

But even before the celebrated parliament of Simon de Montfort the counties were not always summoned individually. We find numerous cases of collective summons, often applying to the whole of England; and, although we may hesitate to give the name of parliaments to these gatherings, whose composition is in some cases uncertain, it must not be forgotten that the word had not at that time the precise meaning that it later acquired. It is also true that the services demanded of the knights were often of a humble nature and by no means correspond with the functions of parlia-

---

[1] *Reports on the Dignity of a Peer*, App. I, p. 35. See also below, p. 60.

mentary assemblies in modern times. But we shall see that even under Edward I the position of the representatives of the commons in parliament was still decidedly subordinate and their functions not very different from those discharged in the previous reign. These gatherings, assembled for various purposes, enable us to understand how the representation of the counties insinuated itself into parliament, without any importance being attached to the process.

The delegates of the counties were summoned for inquests into the administration of government, particularly in pursuance of complaints brought against the sheriffs. Thus in 1226 the sheriffs of Gloucestershire, Dorsetshire and Somersetshire, Bedfordshire and Buckinghamshire, Westmoreland, Northamptonshire and Lincolnshire received orders to provide that at the next county court the knights and honest men of the county should elect four of the more lawful and discreet knights. These four were to come, in the name of the county (*pro toto comitatu*), to Lincoln, where their grievances against their sheriff, touching certain articles of the charter of liberties granted to them, would be heard, as well as the sheriff's counter-claims[1]. The summons had been issued on the demand of the barons (*magnates*), whom the king had assembled at Winchester.

The summons were cancelled by a writ of the 2nd September, as the king was unable to be at Lincoln on the appointed date; but the next year similar summons were sent to the sheriffs of thirty-five counties. The four knights elected by each county were to present

---

[1] *Rot. litt. claus.* ed. Hardy, II, p. 153; *Reports on the Dignity of a Peer*, App. I, p. 4. The writ is dated the 22nd June at Winchester, and the meeting is fixed for the 22nd September. Stubbs, *Select Charters*, p. 353. See Appendix III, note F.

themselves before the king at Westminster three weeks after Michaelmas. In nineteen counties a special clause ordered the sheriff also to send the knights who had made the inspection (*perambulatio*) of the forests, and other persons concerned in that matter[1].

Possibly the presence of knights, at least for certain counties, at the parliament of Easter 1258 was due to similar causes; but, as will soon appear, various considerations lead us to believe that these deputies were called together rather for financial purposes. As to the parliament of October 1258, there cannot be any doubt. The knights came to make known the results of an inquest on the sheriffs' administration and on abuses in general. It had been decided in an article of the Provisions of Oxford that in each county four discreet and lawful knights should be elected, who should meet together, every time the county court was held, to hear complaints with regard to injuries and injustices done to any persons whether by sheriffs, bailiffs or others[2]. The knights do not seem to have been really elected, but nominated by the party which was then in power, that is to say, by Simon de Montfort and the confederate barons[3]. They were without doubt summoned to the parliament of October 1258 to give an account of their activities, for, by a writ of the 4th November, witnessed at Westminster, the king orders the sheriff of the county of Huntingdon to see that the community of the

[1] *Rot. litt. claus.* ed. Hardy, II, p. 212–213. Dated the 12th August at Northampton.
[2] *Ann. Burton*, p. 446, in *Annales Monastici* (Rolls S.), vol. I. Stubbs, *Select Charters*, p. 378.
[3] Cf. *Ann. Burton*, p. 453, 456; *Calendar of patent rolls*, 1247–1258, p. 645–649, 655–656. Three of the knights originally nominated for Shropshire were changed on the advice of Peter de Montfort (*Calendar*, p. 647).

shire pays to the four knights, who have been occupied with "certain inquests to the common profit of the said shire and thereafter have for the aforesaid matters waited on our council at Westminster at the parliament after last Michaelmas, their reasonable expenses for coming and returning and for the stay that they have made at the parliament on account of the aforesaid matters[1]."

Another motive which sometimes caused the king to assemble the deputies of the counties was the need of money. Perhaps knights were present at those parliaments of 1225, 1232 and 1237, of which we have spoken above and in which, if we may believe the writs for collection, aids were granted by the knights. But the fact that villeins figure beside the knights on one of these writs makes us rather suppose that the inclusion of the knights among the grantors is a mere form of words. In any case the necessity for the services of the knights in collecting aids would sooner or later lead the king to demand their consent to aids, in addition to the consent of the barons. It is even possible that at a time when the knights were not yet regularly summoned to parliament their consent was demanded in the county court. A considerable number of historians have accepted this hypothesis as undoubtedly true[2]; but we have no conclusive proof of it.

[1] In R. Brady, *Introduction to the old English history* (1684), p. 141, quoting Rot. Claus. 42 Hen. III, m. 1 d. But see App. p. 231.
[2] See especially Stubbs, *Const. Hist.* II, 3rd ed. (1887), p. 225. The instance of the county court of Yorkshire in 1220, which is quoted by Stubbs and to which we shall revert later, does not prove that the aid was approved in the county court. Madox (*History and antiquities of the Exchequer*, p. 419–420, 504 sq.) quotes numerous cases in which the justices itinerant imposed aids and tallages on various localities, but they did not discuss the amount of such aids with the county court.

The first occasion on which we see the royal government concerned to obtain the consent of the lesser
gentry and freeholders is in 1254. Henry III was then
in Gascony, and had left his brother, Richard of Cornwall, and Queen Eleanor as regents of the kingdom.
At the end of the year 1253 the regents received from
the king a demand for supplies of men and money,
because, as he averred, he was about to be attacked by
the king of Castile. At the parliament which met a
fortnight after St Hilary's day (28th January 1254[1]) the
prelates replied that, if the king of Castile advanced
against the king, they would give the king a subsidy out
of their own property, but that they could make no
promise for their clergy without the latter's consent.
They added that they did not believe that the clergy
would be persuaded to give an aid, unless the king
abandoned the clerical tenth which had been granted
to him before for the crusade. The earls and barons, for
their part, promised to go to the assistance of the king, if
the king of Castile attacked him. "But," said the regents
in the letter in which they told the king of the result
of their efforts, "we do not believe that we can obtain
an aid from the rest of the laity who are not bound to
join you in Gascony, unless you write to your lieutenants
in England to see to the strict observance of your great
charters of liberties, and give emphatic orders to that
effect in letters addressed to all the sheriffs of your kingdom, and have it proclaimed in all the counties of the
kingdom. In this way perhaps they may be moved to
accord you an aid (*quia sic forte animarentur ad auxilium
vobis impendendum*)." The regents ended by informing

[1] Writ of summons addressed to the archbishop of Canterbury
and dated the 27th December, in *Reports on the Dignity of a Peer*,
App. I, p. 12.

the king that they were going to have a discussion (*habituri sumus tractatum*) at Westminster with the clerks and laymen in question on the subject of this aid[1].

On the 11th February 1254 the regents had indeed asked each of the bishops to assemble a diocesan synod and therein to do their best to persuade the clergy to give an aid, the nature and amount of which should then be stated before the council by trustworthy persons a fortnight after Easter[2]. By writs addressed to the sheriffs, on the same day and for the same date of meeting, they summoned before the council at Westminster two lawful and discreet knights of each county, specially elected by the county (*quos iidem comitatus ad hoc elegerint*) in the name of one and all (*vice omnium et singulorum*), "to consider, together with the knights of the other counties whom we have had summoned for the same day, what aid they will be willing to grant us in our great need" (*ad providendum una cum militibus aliorum comitatuum quos ad eum diem vocari fecimus quale auxilium nobis in tanta necessitate impendere voluerint*). The sheriff was bidden to explain the king's difficulties to the knights and other inhabitants of the county and to persuade them to grant a suitable aid "so that the said knights shall be able on the date fixed to answer exactly to our council in the name of the counties in the matter of this aid[3]." The attempt failed. Simon de Montfort, who

[1] *Royal Letters*, ed. Shirley (Rolls S.), II, p. 101. Cf. Matthew Paris, *Chronica majora*, V, p. 423, 445; VI (*Additamenta*), p. 282. The letter quoted in the *Additamenta* is reproduced in Rymer, I, p. 296.

[2] *Proviso quod aliqui viri discreti ex parte praedictorum certificent consilium nostrum apud Westm. in quindena Pasch. prox. fut. de modo et quantitate subsidii memorati.* The writ is in Hody, *A History of English Councils and Convocations* (1701), pt. III, p. 339.

[3] Writ witnessed at Windsor on the 11th February by Queen Eleanor and Richard, Earl of Cornwall. In *Reports on the Dignity of a Peer*, App. I, p. 13. The writ is addressed to the sheriff of

had returned from Gascony, informed parliament that there was nothing to fear from the Castilians, and the assembly dispersed having granted nothing[1].

As we have said above, the knights who appeared at the parliament of Easter 1258 were probably summoned for reasons similar to those that had caused the gathering of 1254. We know that at least certain counties sent representatives to this parliament, for writs of the 4th November 1258 order the sheriffs of these counties (Northumberland, Yorkshire, Lincolnshire, Huntingdonshire, Northamptonshire) to see that the four knights, who came before the king at Westminster by the king's orders a month after Easter, are paid their expenses, at the charges of the community of the county[2]. Other documents inform us that a parliament was opened at London in the second week after Easter (the 2nd April probably) and that it lasted till the 5th May[3]. Since Easter fell on the 24th March, the knights presumably arrived after the opening of parliament, but still in time to take part in the discussions. This is not the only occasion on which the deputies of the commons were thus summoned for a date subsequent to that fixed for the magnates.

The king wished to obtain from parliament an extraordinary aid. He was having great difficulties with the Welsh and Scots. Further, on behalf of his son Edmund

Bedfordshire and Buckinghamshire and ends with an order to see that all arrears of monies owed to the king are paid in without delay. Stubbs, *Select Charters*, p. 366.

[1] Matthew Paris, *Chr. majora*, v, p. 440.

[2] *Reports on the Dignity of a Peer*, I, p. 461; II, p. 7.

[3] Matthew Paris, *Chr. majora*, v, p. 676, 689. Cf. Stubbs, *Const. Hist.* II, p. 75, n. 1. A letter from the king dated the 2nd May (Rymer, *Fœdera*, Rec. ed. I, p. 370) says that parliament met *in quindena Paschae*.

he had accepted the crown of Sicily, of which the pope had deprived the heirs of Frederick II; and Alexander IV was demanding the payment of the monies that the papacy had advanced during the war against Manfred, as well as an English expeditionary force. The treasury was empty and the king hopelessly in debt. In these circumstances Henry III demanded an aid which, according to one chronicler, meant a tax of one-third of all the movable and immovable property in the kingdom[1]. Parliament refused him this aid about the 28th April[2], that is to say, after the arrival of the knights; and Henry III had to accept the proposal of reforms which was embodied later in the Provisions of Oxford.

It is impossible to say what part the knights took in these proceedings. The writs of the 4th November 1258, for the sheriff of Northumberland and the sheriffs of the other four counties, only say that the knights had come by the king's orders for certain affairs touching the community of the whole county (*pro quibusdam negociis communitatem tocius comitatus praedicti tangentibus*). From this formula it has been thought possible to conclude[3] that the knights of the counties mentioned in the writ of the 4th November had come to London for local matters affecting only their own county, and not in order to take part in the parliament. But this interpretation is not so "evident" as Stubbs has suggested. We have before us not a parliamentary summons, but a writ for the payment by the community of the county of the expenses of the four knights who, whatever the reason of the summons, had represented

---

[1] *Ann. Theokesb.* p. 163, in *Annales Monastici* (Rolls S.), vol. I.

[2] *Ibid.: circa festum Sancti Vitalis martyris.* The annalist seems to mention the presence of the knights: *comites, barones et milites*.

[3] *Reports on the Dignity of a Peer*, I, p. 462; Stubbs, *Const. Hist.* II, p. 232, n. 3.

the county before the king and his council. It is highly probable that writs of this kind were not an innovation at this time and that the knights, who for any purpose were called before the king "in the name of the county," usually received writs permitting them to charge their expenses "on the community of the county," since the matters concerning which they had been summoned affected "the community of the whole county[1]." In November 1258, even if the delegates had had to discuss questions of general interest, a customary formula, which moreover was not inapplicable to the circumstances, might very well have been retained.

In our opinion, therefore, the knights were summoned to the parliament of Easter 1258, as they had been in 1254, for a financial purpose; and, as in 1254, the experiment failed. Parliament demanded reforms before it would grant an aid. In a sort of proclamation addressed on the 2nd May to all his subjects, the king himself explained that he had assembled the magnates and the trustworthy men of the kingdom (*proceres et fideles regni*) in the fortnight after Easter and that they had informed him that, if he would reform the state of the realm according to their advice and obtain a morè satisfactory arrangement from the pope with regard to Sicily, then "they would bring their best efforts to bear on the community of the realm so that a common aid should be granted for this purpose" (*ipsi diligentiam fide-*

[1] It is certain that the knights were repaid their expenses by the county. A writ of the 5th June 1222, addressed by the king to the sheriff of Wiltshire (*Rot. litt. claus.* ed. Hardy, I, p. 498), orders him to exempt Faukes de Bréauté *de demanda quam ei facis de necessariis inveniendis duobus militibus de comitatu tuo ad eundum ad curiam nostram ad libertates foreste ponendas... Si quid autem ab eo ceperis occasione predicta id ei sine dilacione reddi facias.* See also *Bracton's Note Book*, ed. Maitland, No. 1412 (1220 A.D.) where the king's court fixes the date on which the knights representing a county are to reappear before it, *ut comitatus minus gravaretur et vexaretur.*

liter apponent erga communitatem regni nostri quod nobis commune auxilium ad hoc praestetur)[1]. The knights had probably refused to commit themselves, declaring that they had to consult their constituents.

Other gatherings of deputies of the commons are to be explained by reasons of general policy. In a moment of political crisis the king might find it to his advantage to rely on the support of the lesser gentry against the magnates. It might be to his advantage to neglect that distinction between tenants-in-chief and sub-tenants, which had been upheld by article 14 of the Great Charter but which, as we shall see when we study Edward I's policy, was most objectionable from the point of view of royal power. Also it might be to his advantage to ensure the co-operation of the towns, which by their commerce were becoming a power in the state. And what the king could do the English nobility could likewise do, if thereby it could gain an advantage in its struggles against the king. In fact the king and his opponents rivalled each other in zeal for the destruction of the old feudal conception according to which the great council of the king was an assembly of royal tenants-in-chief.

In 1213, during his struggle against the church, John summoned representatives of the commons. Few historical documents have given rise to more diverse interpretations than these summons.

We know of the first summons not from an official document, but only from the text of a chronicler. According to Roger of Wendover[2], John, the day after he had been reconciled to the church by the archbishop

[1] Rymer, *Fœdera* (Record ed.), I, p. 370.
[2] *Flores historiarum*, ed. Hewlett (Rolls S.), II, p. 82: *Misit rex litteras ad omnes vicecomites regni Angliae, praecipiens ut de singulis*

of Canterbury, that is, on the 21st July 1213, sent writs
to all the sheriffs of England ordering them to send to
St Albans on the eve of the nones of August (4th
August) "four lawful men and the reeve from each of
the *villae* of his demesnes," in order that from them and
his other officials he might learn the facts with regard
to the damages and losses sustained by the bishops and
the amount that he owed to each of the latter. Five
years before, the king had laid hands on the bishops'
property and, naturally, as a condition of his reconcilia-
tion with the church, he had to pay them an indemnity.

Stubbs attributes a great importance in constitutional
development to this summons[1]. Mr McKechnie, who
at first accepted Stubbs's view, has modified his earlier
opinion on this point (in the second edition of his
commentary on the Great Charter)[2], and contents
himself with referring the reader to Professor A. B.
White's article in the *American Historical Review*[3].

A great council did in fact take place at St Albans
probably at the beginning of August. The king was not
present. He was at that moment starting on an expedition to France, though the expedition never got
further than Jersey. The assembly included the justiciar, Geoffrey FitzPeter, the bishop of Winchester,
Peter des Roches, the archbishop of Canterbury,
Stephen Langton, and the bishops and magnates of the
kingdom. Various measures were adopted to repress

*dominicorum suorum villis quatuor legales homines cum praeposito
apud Sanctum Albanum pridie nonas Augusti facerent convenire, ut
per illos et alios ministros suos de damnis singulorum episcoporum et
ablatis certitudinem inquireret et quid singulis deberetur.* Cf. Stubbs,
Select Charters, p. 271.

[1] *Const. Hist.* I, p. 566–567.
[2] McKechnie, *Magna Carta* (2nd edition), p. 28. Cf. A. B.
White, *Am. Hist. Rev.* XVII, p. 12–16.
[3] See below, p. 41.

the abuses committed by the sheriffs and the officers of the forests and to ensure the observance of the laws of Henry I. But Roger of Wendover never mentions the presence of the four lawful men and the reeve, who should, by the terms of the letter that he has just quoted, have represented each of the *villae* of the demesne. It seems that the assembly did not think it worth while to discuss the question of indemnities in the absence of the king. After his return, discussions were opened on this subject, and during the last months of 1213 numerous meetings took place, in which attempts were made to reconcile the interests of the king, of the church of England and of the pope, whose vassal John had just acknowledged himself. In none of these assemblies do the four men and reeve of each *villa* appear to have participated. Further, on the 31st August and during October, we see the king taking measures for the holding of inquests in the counties, in concert with the ecclesiastical authorities, into the damages and losses (*de ablatis et dampnis*) suffered by the church[1].

It may be doubted if John ever dreamed of convening an assembly, which would necessarily have been very large and very expensive for those concerned, when he could so easily obtain the information required by having inquests held on the spot and ordering the sheriffs to send him the results. Sir J. H. Ramsay[2] solves the

[1] The writ of the 31st August is in Rymer, *Fœdera*, Rec. ed. 1, p. 114. Cf. *Rot. litt. claus.* ed. Hardy, 1, p. 164. The king orders the sheriff of Somersetshire and Dorsetshire to send three persons named in the writ on the day and to the place of which the bishop of Bath will inform him, so that they may be present at the inquest, which is to be made before the clerks named by the archbishop of Canterbury. The sheriff must also send all those who have been in charge of ecclesiastical property. See also *Rot. litt. claus.* 1, p. 165.   [2] *Angevin Empire*, p. 442, n. 7.

difficulty by denying the authenticity of the writ para-
phrased by Roger of Wendover, who must have mis-
understood and inexactly quoted the writ of the 31st
August. But we cannot accept so radical a method.
The terms used by the chronicler show that he had, or
had had, before him an official document, from which
he retained certain formulae that are quite in the style
of the English chancery.

Other solutions have been proposed. Mr G. J.
Turner[1] thinks that the reeve and four men summoned
to St Albans were the representatives not of royal, but
of episcopal manors. This hypothesis still leaves us
confronted with a large assembly, the need of which is
not clear. Such an assembly, moreover, is open to the
objection that it formally contradicts the text of Roger
of Wendover on a point where a chronicler's error is
far from probable. How can we admit that he could
have written: *de singulis dominicorum suorum villis*,
instead of: *de singulis episcoporum villis*, or of: *de singulis
dominicorum episcoporum villis*?

Professor A. B. White[2] has compared Roger of Wendover's text with a passage in the *Annals of Waverley*
which says that in 1208 in each *villa* the care of the movable
and immovable property of ecclesiastics was confided
to persons of the neighbourhood, who were to provide
the clergy with what they needed. The comparison is
interesting and enables us to understand why the king
summons four men and the reeve from each of the *villae*
of the royal demesne on a matter that does not seem to

[1] *The St Albans council of* 1213 (*English Hist. Review*, April 1906,
p. 297 sq.).
[2] *The first concentration of juries* (*American Hist. Review*, October
1911, p. 12 sq.). The passage from the *Annals of Waverley* is in
Annales monastici, ed. Luard (Rolls S.), II, p. 260.

have concerned them. But we cannot conclude, as does Professor White, that the persons summoned in 1213 are those to whom the administration of ecclesiastical property was entrusted in 1208; and we do not perceive, any more than on Mr Turner's hypothesis, the reason for the "concentration of local juries" at St Albans.

Professor H. W. C. Davis[1] has suggested a third hypothesis which takes account of the principal difficulty. He denies that the four men and the reeve from each *villa* on demesne were summoned to St Albans. These humble folk were merely to be ordered to "recognize" the facts before the sheriff in the county court, according to custom; and the results of this inquest were to be brought to the king at St Albans by the sheriff. Unfortunately, in order to achieve this interpretation, Professor Davis is forced to torture the chronicler's text, to which he gives the following form:

> Praecipiens ut de singulis dominicorum suorum villis quatuor legales homines cum praeposito facerent convenire, ut per illos et alios ministros suos apud Sanctum Albanum pridie nonas Augusti de damnis singulorum episcoporum et ablatis certitudinem inquireret et quid singulis deberetur.

As Mr Turner and Professor White have observed, the royal chancery never expressed itself in such terms.

If a fourth hypothesis may be added to those mentioned, may we not suppose that the chronicler, who wrote in Hertfordshire, indeed at St Albans itself, had in his hands the king's writ ordering the sheriff of Hertfordshire to assemble four men and the reeve from each *villa* on demesne and indicating St Albans as the place

---

[1] *The St Albans council of* 1213 (*English Hist. Review*, April 1905, p. 289 sq.).

of meeting? Such a gathering can be explained in various ways. Possibly John wished to take advantage of the great council, which was to be held at St Albans, to have an inquest made with regard to Hertfordshire in the presence of himself and the prelates. Or it is possible that he merely wished to have an inquest made by the sheriff. The chronicler knew that a great council had met at St Albans, that four men and the reeve from each of the *villae* on demesne in Hertfordshire had been summoned to St Albans, and that the sheriffs of the various counties had received writs with regard to the inquest to be made into the losses suffered by the clergy. He connected these three facts with each other, presumed that the writs addressed to the other sheriffs were expressed in the same terms as in that for his own county—whereas in them other places of assembly might have been indicated—and naturally concluded that the representatives of all the *villae* on demesne had been summoned together to St Albans on the occasion of the great council.

Be that as it may, it is very difficult to make much of a passage that lends itself to such diverse interpretations. In any case it is certain that the summoning of the reeve and four lawful men from each royal *villa* to the great council at St Albans, even admitting that the gathering ever took place, has but a remote connection with a parliamentary summons. To see in it the origin of the representation of the towns in parliament, as some modern historians have done, is an error too evident to need refutation.

The second summons of 1213, on the contrary, is known to us through the actual text of the royal writ, dated at Witney, 7th November, and transcribed on the rolls of letters close of the fifteenth year of John[1]. This writ is addressed to the sheriff of Oxfordshire. The sheriff receives an order to see that all the knights, who had before been summoned to come to Oxford, appear with their arms before the king a fortnight after All Saints' Day. Similarly he is to see that the barons attend in person without arms on the same date, and also four discreet knights of the county "to speak with us of the affairs of our kingdom" (*ad loquendum nobiscum de negociis regni nostri*). The roll adds that similar writs were sent to all the sheriffs of England (*eodem modo scribitur omnibus vicecomitibus*).

The writ of the 7th November was therefore intended to supplement another writ which we do not possess. We do not know who were the knights who had been summoned before and had to appear with their arms. Do the words refer simply to a military gathering in connection with the projected expedition against France? Or, as happened later in 1297, did the king instruct his supporters to come armed, in order to protect himself from violence, while he only sent the usual summons to the barons? As for the four discreet knights, all that we know of them is that they had to come to speak with the king of the affairs of the kingdom. We do not know the precise object that John had in summoning them. Was he, like Simon de Montfort later on, seeking support among the lesser gentry against the magnates? Did he merely wish to obtain information on some

[1] *Rot. Claus.* 15 Joh. p. 2, m. 7 d. Published in *Reports on the Dignity of a Peer*, App. I, p. 2. This writ is also in Rymer, *Fœdera*, Rec. ed. I, p. 117; but the comment: *De summonitione ad parliamentum Oxon*, given in Rymer, does not appear on the roll (cf. *Reports on the Dignity of a Peer*, I, p. 61) and the writ is dated in error the 15th November. Cf. Stubbs, *Select Charters*, p. 282.

particular question; for instance, on the indemnities claimed by the clergy, the amount of which was discussed in several assemblies at this time? Probably we must be content never to know. Nor can we say whether the knights were to be elected by the county court or chosen by the sheriff. The writ is dated the 7th November; the assembly is fixed for the 15th November. The interval is extremely short, if the sheriffs of distant counties were to receive the writ, assemble the county court and make it proceed to an election. Finally, we do not know if the assembly provided for in this writ ever took place[1].

We must be careful, therefore, not to exaggerate the importance of this summons of November 1213. There is nothing to prove that John ever thought of treating

[1] According to the itinerary drawn up by Sir Thomas Duffus Hardy in the introduction to the *Rotuli litt. patentium*, John was at Oxford (coming from Woodstock and returning thither) on the 15th, 16th and 17th November 1213; but that does not prove that the assembly was held and that the knights were present. In an article in the *American Historical Review* (XXII, p. 87–90) Mr E. Jenks has gone so far as to argue that John had no intention of assembling a council at Oxford or of summoning thither four knights from each county. He points out that the sheriffs had no time to send the knights by the appointed date, and he interprets *eodem modo scribitur omnibus vicecomitibus* as merely meaning that the sheriffs were to summon the four knights to the county towns. But not only does this hypothesis contradict the text of the document, it makes nonsense of the words *ad loquendum nobiscum de negociis regni nostri*. It seems, therefore, to be untenable. Although the insufficient notice given to the sheriffs does raise a difficulty, the problem is perhaps not insoluble. This was not the only occasion in the history of parliament, on which the notice given to the sheriffs was too short to allow the deputies of distant counties to arrive in time. For example, in 1261 the king wrote to the sheriffs on the 11th September requiring the knights to be at Windsor, and not at St Albans, on the 21st (see below, p. 46; also for 1264, p. 48; and for 1297, p. 144, 145). Very probably in such cases those who arrived late were required to ratify the decisions taken in their absence.

the four knights from each county as a constituent part of the great council. The summons is of great interest because it is the first occasion, as far as we know, on which representatives of all the counties of England were thus summoned to discuss the affairs of the king-dom with the king. But it is improbable that either John or his subjects saw in this measure an important con-stitutional innovation.

The summons of September 1261 raises problems similar to those which we have just discussed Here again we have only a writ intended to modify the terms of a former summons, which we do not possess. The royal order is dated the 11th September, at Windsor, and addressed to the sheriff of Norfolk and Suffolk and to all the sheriffs of the counties south of the Trent. Henry III, who was then trying to recover power, re-minds the sheriffs that three knights from each county were summoned by the bishop of Worcester, the earls of Leicester and Gloucester and other magnates of the realm, to appear before them at St Albans on St Mat-thew's day (21st September), "to join them in a dis-cussion on the common affairs of the realm" (*secum tractaturi super communibus negociis regni nostri*). But, as the king and the magnates in question are to meet on that same day at Windsor, there to negotiate conditions of peace, the sheriff is to order the knights to betake themselves to Windsor, and not elsewhere, on the day fixed. The discussion (*colloquium*) which they will have with the king will make clear to them "that we propose to undertake nothing but what we shall be sure is for the honour and general interest of the kingdom[1]."

We do not know in what circumstances Simon de

[1] *Reports on the Dignity of a Peer*, App. I, p. 23. Stubbs, *Select Charters*, p. 394-395.

Montfort and the other members of the king's council had summoned the knights or what exactly were the "common affairs of the realm" which they wished to discuss. Nor do we know for what reason the king's writ is addressed only to the sheriffs of counties south of the Trent; nor whether the assembly anticipated in this writ was actually held either at Windsor or at St Albans[1]. The only certain facts are the desire of the barons to have a meeting with the knights and the desire of the king to prevent that meeting by making the knights come to Windsor.

Another gathering of knights representing the counties was ordered in 1264, after Simon de Montfort's victory at Lewes. The writ is issued in the name of the king; but Henry III was then the prisoner of the victorious barons, and the government was in fact in the hands of the earl of Leicester and his party.

It had been provided in the Mise of Lewes that the conditions of a durable peace should be further discussed at leisure[2]. For this purpose a parliament was necessary. To this parliament the barons decided to

---

[1] According to a letter from Henry III to the king of France, given in Rymer (*Fœdera*, Rec. ed. I, p. 409) with the date 2nd September 1261, but which probably should be dated 25th September (cf. E. Green, *Lives of the princesses of England*, II, p. 121, n. 5), Simon de Montfort was then in France. It is, however, possible that a meeting of the king and the barons took place in November, for in a letter of the 7th December (*Fœdera*, I, p. 441) the king declares that difficulties (*contenz e demandez*) have arisen between him and his barons concerning the measures adopted at Westminster and at Oxford in the forty-second year of his reign, but that these difficulties have been smoothed away by a mutual agreement. There follows a general pardon for the earl of Leicester and his chief partisans. Cf. *Fœdera*, I, p. 412.

[2] According to the chronicle of William of Rishanger (ed. Halliwell, p. 38) the seventh article of the mise was conceived thus: *Septimum, quod cum promissum istud in regno Angliae tractetur et infra festum Pascae proximum ad ultimum terminetur.*

call four knights from each county, no doubt in order to strengthen their party, which the great magnates had abandoned during the last few years. The writ which we have is addressed to Adam of Newmarket. That individual is informed that, in view of the king's decision, on the advice and with the consent of his barons, to nominate "guardians of his peace" (*custodes pacis nostrae*) in each of the counties of the kingdom, he has been chosen as "guardian" for the county of Lincoln. The king "must necessarily discuss his affairs and those of the kingdom with the prelates, the magnates and his other faithful subjects" at the approaching parliament. Therefore the new "guardian" receives an order to provide for the election for this purpose, by the assent of the county, of four of the more lawful and discreet knights of the county (*quatuor de legalioribus et discretioribus militibus dicti comitatus per assensum dicti comitatus ad hoc electos*) and to send them before the king on behalf of the whole county (*pro toto comitatu illo*), so that they shall be in London on the octave of Trinity Sunday (22nd June) at the latest, "to discuss the aforesaid affairs with us" (*nobiscum tractaturi de negotiis praedictis*)[1].

The writ is dated the 4th June at St Paul's in London. The interval between the summons and the meeting is therefore much shorter than the forty days demanded by article 14 of the Great Charter of John. It is not quite certain that all the counties were summoned. Apart from the counties of Chester and Durham, which never sent representatives to parliament during the thirteenth century, Middlesex, Surrey, Sussex, Rutlandshire, Her-

---

[1] Rymer, *Fœdera*, Rec. ed. I, p. 442. Stubbs, *Select Charters*, p. 399–400.

fordshire and Lancashire are missing from the list of counties to which were sent writs similar to that addressed to Lincolnshire.

The parliament was held in London "about the feast of the Nativity of St John Baptist" (24th June) and gave its approval to a "form of government of the lord king and the kingdom" (*forma regiminis domini regis et regni*). Three electors chosen by the barons, namely the bishop of Chichester and the earls of Leicester and Gloucester, were to nominate a council of nine members, of whom three were to be always present with the king. Without the council's consent the king could make no decision. The king could change the members of the council with the consent of the three electors[1].

The knights of the shires were not called upon to take part in the nomination of the electors, nor in that of the councillors. One of the articles of the new constitution indeed expressly states that, if it seems desirable "to the community of the prelates and barons " to change one or more of those originally chosen as electors, the king shall make the alteration "on the advice of the community of prelates and barons." But, at the beginning of the document, the "form of peace " is approved by "the lord king, the lord Edward his son, the prelates and all the barons, and all the community of the realm of England"; and at the end is the declaration that the ordinance is made "by the consent, will and order of the lord king, the prelates, the barons and also of the community there present at the time " (*de consensu, voluntate et praecepto domini Regis necnon praelatorum, baronum ac etiam communitatis tunc ibidem*

[1] Rymer, *Fœdera*, Rec. ed. 1, p. 443. Stubbs, *Select Charters*, p. 401–403.

L

4

praesentis). The knights of the shires probably constituted this "community," whose function was to approve
the measures adopted by the magnates. Perhaps a more
popular element, drawn from the inhabitants of London,
was admitted within the body of the assembly, to make
the manifesto more impressive. It is to be noticed that
the mayor of London was required to place his seal at
the bottom of the charter, beside those of a number of
bishops and barons[1].

.

Events, even more than principles, urged Simon de
Montfort more and more to rely on the support of the
lesser gentry and the townsfolk. Yet the constitution
which his party had elaborated in 1258 was purely
aristocratic. It made over the government of England
to a small number of great lords—the Twenty-four to
whom reforms were entrusted, the Fifteen of the king's
council, the Twelve elected by the "*commun*" (that is
to say, by the community of the barons) to represent
it in parliament. The constitution of 1264, with its three
all-powerful electors and its council of the Nine, is not,
whatever Stubbs may say, much more democratic.
Further, it must not be forgotten that no one then
dreamed of making parliament a permanent means of
control of the king's government. It is certain that only
with considerable difficulty could some of the great
lords be persuaded to be regular attendants at the king's
council. What would have happened had it been suggested that parliaments should be held more frequently,

---

[1] Rymer, *Fœdera*, Rec. ed. 1, p. 443. The term "barons," it is
true, might be taken to comprehend not only the *barones majores*
but also the *barones minores*, represented by the knights of the shires.
This interpretation is most unlikely to be correct. The deputies
were often sub-tenants who had no right to the title of "baron."

that their duration should be prolonged beyond the usual few days, and that representatives of the counties should be regularly summoned to attend?

The mass of the English people do not appear to have shown any wish to take part in the government of the state, which was the business of the king and the magnates. But they were very ill-content with the king and his favourites. In 1258 Matthew Paris tells us that the Poitevins were not safe in their castles; for, even if the barons did not attack them, the whole people (*universitas regni popularis*) might besiege them and destroy their strongholds[1]. In 1264, according to the chronicler of London, Fitzthedmar, almost the whole community of the people (*fere omnis communa mediocris populi regni Angliae*) had refused to accept the arbitral decision of St Louis and had taken the side of Simon de Montfort[2]. The city of London, in particular, remained faithful to him to the end. The clergy on the whole also supported him[3]. But nearly all the magnates abandoned him either before or after Lewes.

It was in these circumstances that Simon de Montfort made Henry III assemble the great parliament of January 1265. Already a declaration had been circulated through the country, according to which the bishops, abbots, priors, earls and barons, and the clergy and people of the kingdom of England approved the nomination of the three electors[4]. But the very fact that

[1] *Chronica majora*, ed. Luard (Rolls S.), v, p. 698.

[2] *Liber de antiquis legibus*, p. 61: *Londonienses autem et barones de Quinque Portubus et fere omnis communa mediocris populi regni Angliae, qui vero non posuerunt se super Regem Franciae, penitus arbitrium suum contradixerunt.*

[3] On the attitude of the clergy, see the *Annals of Tewkesbury* (*Annales monastici*, Rolls S. 1, p. 175), where those who abandoned Simon de Montfort's party are called "satellites of Satan."

[4] This declaration has been published by Mr Gilson in the

he felt obliged to have recourse to this expedient proves that Simon de Montfort was no longer very sure of his authority and that he was disturbed by the attacks directed against him and his supporters. In 1258 the acceptance of the Provisions of Oxford by the "barons" of London in a ceremony at the Guildhall had been considered to meet the case[1]. This time Simon de Montfort resolved to have the new constitution approved by a solemn assembly containing not only the barons, the higher clergy and the knights of the shires, but also representatives of the towns of the kingdom.

The first summons are dated at Worcester, the 14th December [1264]. They are addressed to the archbishop of York, to twelve bishops (Durham, Carlisle, London, Winchester, Exeter, Worcester, Lincoln, Ely, Salisbury, Coventry and Lichfield, Chichester, Bath and Wells), ten abbots, nine priors and five deans. The writ addressed to the bishop of Durham, which was transcribed on the rolls of letters close, reminds him that after the troubles in the kingdom the king's eldest son, Edward, was given as a hostage "to assure and confirm the peace." Now that the troubles are over, the king desires to confer with the prelates and

English Historical Review, July 1901, p. 500, after a transcript made at Ramsey Abbey. It is dated the day after the Nativity of St John Baptist (25th June 1264), in London, and witnessed, *de voluntate et expresso omnium consensu*, by the bishops of Exeter and Salisbury, Roger, earl of Norfolk, and John Fitzjohn. Mr Gilson attaches considerable importance to the expression *clerus et populus regni Angliae*, and thinks that this expression, as well as the use of the word *communitas* in the *Forma regiminis* quoted above, proves an active participation of the representatives of the "commons" in the discussion of the new *régime*. But the words *clerus et populus* are vague terms, indicating the clergy and laity in general.

[1] Matthew Paris, *Chronica majora*, v, p. 704; *Liber de antiquis legibus* , p. 39.

magnates concerning the liberation of his son and the restoration and complete establishment of peace, and also "on certain other affairs of our kingdom that we do not wish to decide without your counsel and the counsel of our other prelates and magnates." The bishop of Durham is accordingly required, *in fide et dilectione quibus nobis tenemini*, to present himself in London before the king on the octave of the coming St Hilary's day (20th January 1265) "there to discuss these affairs with us and our aforesaid prelates and magnates, whom we have caused to be summoned thither, and to give us your counsel[1]."

On the 24th December similar writs, dated at Woodstock, were addressed to fifty-five abbots, twenty-five priors, the grandmaster of the Temple, the prior of the Hospitallers and the prior of the order of Sempringham. According to the Close Rolls the same writs, *in forma predicta*, were sent to five earls and eighteen barons[2]. In these the formula *in fide et dilectione* was no doubt replaced by the usual *in fide et homagio*.

The close rolls add:

Similarly in the above form all the sheriffs of England[3] have been ordered to provide for the appearance (*venire faciant*) of two knights from among the more lawful, trust-

[1] *Super premissis tractaturi et consilium vestrum impensuri* (*Reports on the Dignity of a Peer*, App. I, p. 33). Stubbs, *Select Charters*, p. 403.

[2] *Reports on the Dignity of a Peer*, App. I, p. 34.

[3] The committee of the house of lords, which drew up the *Reports on the Dignity of a Peer*, wondered (I, p. 146) whether recourse was had, as in June 1264, to the "guardians of the king's peace," to whom reference is made in June 1265 (cf. a royal letter of the 7th June 1265 in *Fœdera*, Rec. ed. I, p. 456). But there is mention here only of the sheriffs, and it is to the sheriff of Shropshire and Staffordshire that the writ is addressed, in which the king demands the dispatch of the knights who were to come on the octave of St Hilary.

worthy and discreet knights (*de legalioribus, probioribus et discrecioribus militibus*) of each county, before the king on the aforesaid octave.

Similarly letters have been written in the above form to the citizens of York, the citizens of Lincoln and to other boroughs of England ordering them to send (*mittant*), in the above form, two of their more discreet, lawful and trustworthy citizens or burgesses.

Similarly in the above form orders have been sent to the barons and honest men of the Cinq Ports, as contained in the writ enrolled below[1].

In reality the writ addressed to the barons and bailiffs of the port of Sandwich, in accordance with a custom still in force in Edward I's time for writs addressed to laymen, is shorter and conceived in simpler terms than that destined for the clergy. In it the king points out the purpose for which he has summoned "the prelates, magnates and nobles of the realm" to London for the octave of St Hilary, namely the liberation of his son and "other affairs concerning the community of our realm." As he is much in need of their presence, as of that of his other faithful subjects, he orders the barons of Sandwich, *in fide et dilectione quibus nobis tenemini*, to send (*mittatis*) him four of the more lawful and discreet men of their port "to treat with us and the aforesaid magnates and to give us your counsel on the subject of the said affairs[2]."

It is probable that the summons addressed to the towns were expressed in similar terms. The formula, *in fide et dilectione*, was perhaps omitted, and the number of delegates was reduced to two.

As to the writs addressed to the sheriffs, we can reconstruct their sense well enough from that of the

---

[1] *Reports on the Dignity of a Peer*, App. I, p. 34.   [2] *Ibid.* p. 35.

writ addressed on the 23rd February 1265 to the sheriff of Shropshire and Staffordshire, who had not sent knights to the parliament. The first part of the new writ seems in fact to be copied from its predecessor. First the king explains, almost in the same terms as in the summons addressed to the "barons" of Sandwich, the reasons for which he had assembled the prelates, magnates and nobles of the kingdom. Then he orders the sheriff to see that two of the more discreet and lawful knights of the counties come before him (*ad nos venire faceres*) "to treat of these affairs with us and with the said magnates in the name of the communities of the counties (*ex parte communitatum comitatuum*) and to give us their counsel[1]."

It has often been remarked that the direct summons of the towns, without the intervention of the sheriff, was contrary to the practice that obtained under Edward I. Simon de Montfort and his friends no doubt made a point of carefully choosing the towns that were to be summoned. The change made by Edward I had important consequences, for it helped to assimilate to each other the two classes of deputies, so different at first. The presence of the deputies of the Cinq Ports is also a fact that should be emphasized, because under Edward I they were only summoned to parliament on one occasion and then rather as litigants than as deputies.

Another peculiarity that distinguishes the parliament of 1265 from the "model" parliaments of the following reign is that the closing formula in the summons of the knights, of the deputies of the Cinq Ports, and probably of those of the towns (*nobiscum et cum predictis magnatibus tractaturi et consilium impensuri*) is the same

[1] *Reports on the Dignity of a Peer*, App. I, p. 35.

as for the prelates and barons. Later, although the authority of the commons in no way diminished, distinctions were carefully maintained and the privileges of each class clearly indicated.

Finally, one cannot but be struck by the absence of all allusion to an election of the deputies. It is true that we possess no text of the writs, except for the Cinq Ports. But the barons of Sandwich were ordered "to send" four of their number. The same was true of the towns, according to the abstract of the writ—*quod mittant duos de discrecioribus*, etc. In the case of the counties, the abstract and the supplementary writ to the sheriff of Shropshire and Staffordshire have *venire faciant*, that is to say, the formula always employed when knights were summoned to represent the county before the council or the king's court. Possibly this omission has little meaning. It has been observed that the writ of the 4th June 1264 clearly ordered the election of the knights by the assent of the county, and that it is highly unlikely that Simon de Montfort changed his views in the meanwhile. But it is also not impossible that he wished to leave something to the discretion of the sheriffs, in order to allow them to exclude opponents of the government.

Simon de Montfort's parliament was indeed from many points of view a revolutionary assembly, although the writs of summons were held to emanate from the king. The government's opponents had not been summoned, and the assembly appeared to be rather a general convention of a party than a true parliament. It had not been thought necessary to bid the inferior clergy to send representatives, but the higher clergy were more numerous than they had ever been in a parliamentary gathering. They included an archbishop, thirteen bishops—the bishop of Norwich, who had not been summoned along with the twelve other bishops on the 14th December, received his summons by a writ dated at Woodstock the 26th December[1]—sixty-five abbots, thirty-four priors, five deans and the grandmasters of the three orders. Many of these ecclesiastical dignitaries were never summoned again, or were only summoned by way of the clause *Praemunientes*, added to writs from 1295. The abbot of Leicester was later at great pains to obtain exemption from suit of court, to which he had on this occasion been summoned for the first time[2]. Nevertheless, despite the numerical importance of the clergy, some conspicuous persons were not present at the parliament, in particular the first dignitary of the church of England, the archbishop of Canterbury.

Beside the 121 representatives of the ecclesiastical order, the five earls and eighteen barons, who represented the lay nobility, made a poor show. Great historic names, Bigod, Bohun, Warenne, Arundel, Mortimer, Percy, Grey, Neville, with many others, are absent from the list, which only contains the partisans of Simon de Montfort and the earl of Gloucester. Peter of Savoy, John de Warenne, Hugh le Bigod and William de Valence were later summoned to appear before the king and his council at the parliament of the 1st June, in London, but only to stand their trial[3].

---

[1] *Reports on the Dignity of a Peer*, App. I, p. 35. The bishop of Norwich had probably been omitted because he refused to execute in his diocese the government's demand for a tax of one-tenth of the revenues of ecclesiastical benefices (cf. *ibid.* p. 32).

[2] Cf. Bémont, *Simon de Montfort*, p. 227, n. 1.

[3] Writs of the 19th March (*Fœdera*, Rec. ed. I, p. 449). The parliament of the 1st June was in fact summoned to Winchester.

It was no doubt because he realized the inadequacy of a baronial assembly, from which the majority of the great lords of England were absent, that Simon de Montfort convoked the representatives of the counties and towns. Circumstances, perhaps more than his own will, forced him to a policy whose almost demagogic character did not entirely escape the notice of contemporaries. The chronicle of Thomas Wykes attributes to him the deliberate desire "to put down the mighty and ruin their power, to break the horns of the proud, that he might the more freely and easily subdue the people, after having destroyed the strength of the magnates[1]." To resist the great lords, he was forced to rely on the townsfolk and on the knights and freeholders of the countryside.

But, as M. Bémont has shown, there is no doubt that such summons as those of December 1264 were intended by Simon de Montfort to be exceptional. It is improbable that he demanded the presence of the knights and burgesses a second time at the parliament which was summoned for the 1st June 1265 at Winchester and to which the cathedral chapters had to send delegates[2]. Frequent assemblies, moreover, would have been resented both by electors and elected. In this connection we may notice the conditions attached by the writ of the 15th February 1265 to the order for the payment of the expenses incurred by the knights of the shires during their journey and their presence at the parlia-

[1] *Chr. Th. Wykes*, p. 160, in *Ann. monastici*, IV.

[2] Writ of the 15th May, at Gloucester, addressed to the dean and chapter of York (*Reports on the Dignity of a Peer*, App. I, p. 36; Stubbs, *Select Charters*, p. 406, 407). The assembly may have been caused, as Stubbs thinks (*Const. Hist.* II, p. 98, n. 3), by the differences that had arisen between Simon de Montfort and the earl of Gloucester.

ment: *proviso quod ipsa communitas occasione presta-
cionis istius ultra modum non gravetur*[1].

Simon de Montfort's parliament resembles rather one
of those large assemblies, which were sometimes held
at the accession of a king—that of 1273 was much like it
in composition—than an ordinary parliament. Indeed,
even if there was no question in 1265 of taking an oath
of fealty to a new sovereign, Simon de Montfort and
his associates did wish to obtain from the country a
solemn recognition of the new constitution. It was much
more for that purpose than for discussions on the
liberation of Prince Edward that the knights and burgesses had been assembled. We do not know what
exactly were the activities of the parliament during the
last days of January and the beginning of February;
but probably it was mainly occupied with expressing
approval of the new institutions.

The declaration made by the king in the solemn
session held in the chapter-house of Westminster Abbey
on the 14th February 1265 is a kind of summary of
results achieved up to that date[2]. The king announced
that he and his son had promised to take no hostile
action against the earls of Leicester and Gloucester, or
the citizens of London, or any of their adherents, and
ordered the strictest observance of the charters of
liberties and of the forest, as well as of the other articles
drawn up in June of the preceding year.

With this sitting no doubt parliament ended as
far as the knights and burgesses were concerned.
Amongst the letters close for the next day, the 15th

---

[1] *Reports on the Dignity of a Peer*, App. I, p. 35. The whole writ
is characteristic.
[2] *Liber de antiquis legibus*, ed. Stapleton, p. 71.

February, appears the writ that we quoted above. It commands the sheriff of Yorkshire to provide that the community of the county shall pay the expenses of the knights who have come, "in the name of the community of the county," to deliberate with the king and his council. However, in accordance with a practice which we shall meet again at the end of Edward I's reign, the parliamentary session did not end with the departure of the delegates of the commons. Indeed it was after their departure that the important question of the liberation of the hostages was taken in hand and the discussion was only brought to an end on the 8th March[1]. Meanwhile, on the 23rd February, the sheriff of Shropshire and Staffordshire was ordered to provide that the knights, who ought to have come on the octave of St Hilary, should appear before the king and "the lords who are of his council" on the 8th March, at whatever place in England the king might be[2]. The object in view was clearly to make these knights enter into the engagements accepted by the representatives of the other counties.

The parliament of January 1265 was the first in which representatives of the counties and of the towns took part, if not side by side, at least simultaneously. In this sense Simon de Montfort was the creator of the house of

[1] The *Fœdera* (Rec. ed. 1, p. 450) contain, under the date 16th February, a letter from the king to the earls of Gloucester and Leicester, ordering them to attend on the day after Ash Wednesday for the final discussion (*finalem tractatum*) on the liberation of his son. But the conditions of the peace between the king and the barons were not definitely approved till the 8th March (*Fœdera*, 1, p. 451–452). On the 10th the king acknowledged that he had received the hostages and Prince Edward promised to observe the charters of liberties (*ibid.* 1, p. 452). On the 14th the king confirmed the Great Charters (*ibid.* 1, p. 453). Probably not till then did the parliament finally disperse.

[2] *Reports on the Dignity of a Peer*, App. I, 1, p. 35.

commons. But there is no proof that he intended the institution which he had thus founded to survive the exceptional circumstances which had called it into being. At a moment of danger he had convened an extraordinary assembly. With the return of peace came also a return to the old ways, and care was taken not to be continually summoning to London knights and burgesses, who not only did not ask to come, but saw in suit of court merely an intolerable nuisance. Nor must it be forgotten that the idea of assembling the knights of the shires and the burgesses of the towns in a single "house" was quite alien from Simon de Montfort's political theories and even from those of Edward I.

With these reservations it must be admitted that the precedent set by Simon de Montfort was of extreme importance for the future. Until 1910 it was possible to dispute this importance on the ground that the "model" parliament of Edward I was not held till 1295 and that, after thirty years of constitutional experiments of all kinds, the precedent of 1265 would have been completely forgotten. But the discovery of the writs summoning four knights from each county and four or six burgesses from each town to the first parliament of Edward I in 1275 has shown us that Edward I was not slow in following the example of the great earl, who had long been one of his friends. Simon de Montfort had wished by means of the new institution to consolidate the quasi-royal power, which he had held after Lewes, against the attacks of the English nobility. Might not that institution in the same way serve to strengthen the power of the king?

In the preceding pages we have tried to show what were the precedents that might explain the assembly of 1265 and at the same time to explain why the form of that assembly was scarcely noticed by contemporaries. The practice of ordering the attendance of knights, in the name of their county, before the king's court or council was not new; since, from the time of Richard Cœur-de-Lion, we see four knights attending in order to bring the results of an inquest or to defend a verdict of their county court. Official documents provide us with a fair number of instances of collective summons, simultaneously addressed to several counties or even to all the counties of England. We have found summons of this kind, due to various causes, in 1213, 1226, 1227, 1254, 1258 (twice in the one year), 1261 and 1264. It is quite possible that there are others of which we do not know. We are entitled to make this assumption by what we know of the uncertain fate of the records and the discovery of the writs for the first parliament of Edward I in the dust of a little subterranean chapel of Westminster Abbey.

An assembly similar to those which have just been enumerated perhaps took place in 1222. But we do not possess the writ of summons and we only know of the incident through a letter from the king addressed to the sheriff of Wiltshire ordering him to exempt Faukes de Bréauté from all payment on account of the two knights who had been summoned before the king's court (*ad curiam nostram*) in order to define the liberties of the forest (*ad libertates foreste ponendas*)[1]. Consequently we cannot say whether the summons applied only to Wiltshire or was more general. Roger of Wendover and Matthew Paris also mention numerous parliaments, which appear to have been of more than usual importance—in 1229, 1237, 1246, 1248, 1253, 1255,

[1] *Rot. litt. claus.* ed. Hardy, I, p. 498.

1257—but the language of the chroniclers is not precise
enough to enable us to draw any definite conclusions[1].
The cities and boroughs do not seem to have been col-
lectively summoned before 1265, but before that date
they too, like the counties, were sometimes required
to send delegates before one or other of the departments
of the king's court[2].

The importance of these precedents has been dis-
puted. In his work on the origin of the English constitution Professor G. B. Adams has been at pains to
prove that before 1264, at any rate, the delegates of the
counties did not enjoy a representative capacity and
that not till the parliament of 1264 can we "see unmis-
takeably the beginning of the new institution[3]."
In the writ of 1213, in which John orders the sheriffs
of Oxfordshire and of the other counties to provide for

[1] 1229: *fecit rex convenire apud Westmonasterium...archi-
episcopos, episcopos, abbates, priores, Templarios, comites, barones,
ecclesiarum rectores et qui de se tenebant in capite* (Roger of Wendover, in Matthew Paris, III, p. 186). 1237: *convocato magno colloquio
archiepiscoporum, episcoporum, abbatum et priorum, comitum et
baronum, civium et burgensium et aliorum multorum* (*Ann. Theokesb.*
p. 102); *venit igitur Londonias infinita multitudo nobilium, scilicet
regni totalis universitas* (Matthew Paris,*Chr.majora*,III,p.380). 1246:
totius regni tam cleri quam militiae generalis universitas (*ibid.* IV,
p. 557). 1248: *advenerunt igitur illuc, excepta baronum et militum,
nobilium necnon et abbatum,priorum et clericorum multitudine copiosa,
novem episcopi cum totidem comitibus* (*ibid.* V, p. 5). 1253: *tota edicto
regio convocata Angliae nobilitas* (*ibid.* V, p. 373). 1255: *tenuit rex
parliamentum suum apud Westmonasterium, convocatis ibidem episcopis, abbatibus et prioribus, comitibus et baronibus et totius regni
majoribus* (*Ann. Burton*, p. 360). 1257: *parliamento generalissimo*
(Matthew Paris, V, p. 625); *populoso valde* (*ibid.* V, p. 624); *clero et
populo in magna multitudine congregatis* (*Ann. Burton*, p. 386).
[2] See Pike, *Constitutional history of the House of Lords*, p. 337,
who refers to *Rotuli chartarum*, p. 57, 65. See also *American Hist.
Review*, XIX, pp. 742 sq., where Professor A. B. White has collected
the earliest instances of summons of burgesses.
[3] *The Origin of the English Constitution*, p. 327.

the presence at Oxford of the barons, unarmed, and of four discreet knights of the shire "to discuss the affairs of our realm with us," as also of the knights previously summoned, who are to present themselves armed, Professor Adams merely finds a proof that "the idea occurred to somebody in 1213 that discreet men from the counties could be asked to be present at the same time and place as a meeting of the great council[1]." Over the events of 1226 and 1227 Professor Adams passes in silence. But he discusses a fairly similar case, that of the parliament of October 1258, in which four knights from each county are ordered to bring to the king's council the results of an inquest that they had had to make into the conduct of the sheriffs and into abuses in general. He concludes that there is here no trace of representation, and further that the knights in question in 1258 were nominated by the government[2].

The precedent of 1254 is more difficult to explain on this hypothesis; and Professor Adams admits that certain phrases in the writ (*ad providendum...quale auxilium nobis in tanta necessitate impendere voluerint*) would at first sight lend weight to the supposition "that the knights were chosen to act in a representative capacity and that they were to consult together and decide about the aid after they had met at Westminster[3]."

But, according to him, the end of the document proves that it is not so. The sheriff is there ordered to explain to the knights and other persons of the county how critical the situation is and to persuade them to give an adequate aid, so that the two knights sent to Westminster shall be able to answer precisely to the

---

[1] *The Origin of the English Constitution*, p. 340–341.
[2] *Ibid.* p. 323.　　　　　　　　　　[3] *Ibid.* p. 319.

council on the subject of this aid, in the name of the county. This, says Professor Adams, is the proof that the decision was to be made in the county court and that the function of the delegates was to be confined to the official report of that decision at Westminster. "The modern idea of representation is not to be found here in spite of the language in the writs to the sheriffs, except so far as it may be involved in mere delegation, the knights speaking for the county in making known officially its decision[1]."

This interpretation seems to Professor Adams all the more probable since the inferior clergy also received orders to report to the council, through discreet persons, the nature and amount of the subsidy, which they were asked to vote in their assembly[2]. The function of the delegates would thus be the same in the two cases.

As for the summons of 1261, Professor Adams points out that we do not know whether the three knights, who were summoned by the barons to St Albans and by the king to Windsor, were nominated by the barons or elected by the counties; nor do we know whether the assembly in which the knights were to take part was a great council; nor what was to be the business of the proposed assembly. "In any case it would seem that their share in the business was not to be a very active one, for it is implied that the chief object of their attendance is that they may see and understand that the king proposes nothing against the honour and common utility of the kingdom." Here again we cannot speak of representation "in anything like the modern sense." However, "we do get here for the first time evidence

[1] *The Origin of the English Constitution*, p. 320.
[2] See above, p. 34.

of an intention, on the part of the barons at least, to have selected knights, we know not how, take part in a discussion to be held in some central body. Even if we reduce the case to these lowest dimensions, we may fairly count it a step towards the future parliament[1]."

For our part, we believe that it is impossible to give so precise a date for the origin of the representation of the commons in parliament, and that Professor Adams has drawn from facts, the statement of which is on the whole sound, conclusions which are questionable. He seems to us to have been, like so many others, a victim of that illusion, which consists in projecting the modern house of commons into the past and assimilating the deputies of the thirteenth century to those of the fifteenth or even the twentieth. It is useless to look for the modern idea of representation in the times of Simon de Montfort.

We do not know whether the four discreet knights from each county demanded by John in 1213 were or were not elected. Probably they were not. But contemporaries did not attach to this point the importance that we are tempted to attribute to it. The main thing is that in 1213 the king thought that it would serve his interests to summon not only his barons but also knights, whom he evidently considered to be, as far as he was concerned, representative of their county and with whom he wished "to speak of the affairs of the kingdom." In this small fact lay the germ of a policy that was to be developed by John's successors.

Similarly in 1226, in 1227, in October 1258, there is no question of "parliamentary" summons, in the later sense of the word. But contemporaries probably made

[1] *The Origin of the English Constitution*, p. 325–326.

no sharp distinction between the function of the knights, who came in 1227 to lay before the council the complaints of the counties against their sheriffs with reference to the charters, and the function of those, who came in 1265 to treat with the king and his council (*nobiscum et cum consilio nostro*)[1] of the liberation of Prince Edward and of the other affairs of the kingdom.

The events of 1254 are particularly interesting, because they show clearly the way in which the representative system then arose. The modern idea of representation is absent. No one dreamed, either then or for a long time to come, of nominating a deputy for a long period with unlimited powers of making agreements in the name of those whom he represented. The regents were trying to get an aid out of the lesser gentry and the mass of the freemen. The delegates were to be elected for that particular purpose, *ad hoc*[2], *i.e.* to make an undertaking on that point before the council. The sheriff was ordered to explain the situation in the county court, not in order that the county court should make a final decision, but that it should discuss the matter and choose delegates who were prepared to give the necessary time and trouble. The delegates were to be elected " on behalf of one and all " (*vice omnium et singulorum*), a regulation that would have been quite pointless if, as Professor Adams would have it, they had only to transmit to the council a decision already made in the county court. The regents wrote to the king that they were going

[1] Writ addressed to the sheriff of Yorkshire, for the payment of the knights' expenses (*Reports on the Dignity of a Peer*, App. I, p. 35). The knights of the shires of Shropshire and Staffordshire who did not attend were similarly summoned *nobiscum et cum magnatibus qui sunt de consilio nostro... locuturi* (*ibid.* p. 36).

[2] The same expression is found in the writ of summons for the parliament of June 1264.

to have a discussion (*tractatum*) with the delegates; which would have been equally pointless if the council had only to ratify a *fait accompli*. In reality the regents hoped that, thanks to the efforts of the sheriffs, the delegates would be empowered to give generous assistance to the king. When the delegates were assembled, the council would once more explain the treasury's needs to them and get them to make a hard and fast agreement. The delegates were to have powers to speak definitely (*praecise*) and not to be able to avoid the issue—as did the commons as late as 1339[1]—by declaring that they must refer to their electors.

This system might be called one of procuration rather than of representation properly speaking, and it reminds us of the methods employed in 1226 in the assembly of the clergy. In both cases it was a question of entering into a pecuniary engagement. In 1226 the king, through the agency of the pope, demanded an aid from the church of England. Thereupon the chapter of Salisbury informed the archbishop of Canterbury, through their bishop, of their desire to be represented by proctors. The archbishop agreed that one proctor should come on behalf of the chapter. The chapter nominated not one, but two delegates. The instructions given to the delegates by the chapter are extant. The chapter considers that it would be well to give the king an aid, provided that the delegates of the other chapters are of the same opinion. It thinks that a twentieth would suffice (the archbishop had spoken of a twelfth or a fourteenth). According to the canons, the aid should be collected by a trustworthy man, selected by the chapter. Finally, the delegates are instructed to discover what should be

---

[1] Cf. *Rotuli Parliamentorum*, II, p. 104.

done if one of the canons refused to agree to the decision of the majority of the chapter[1].

The assembly of clergy granted a sixteenth.

Here we see nearly all the characteristics of the representative system in its first stage. The number of delegates is immaterial. Their powers are given for a specified purpose. These powers are vague in character and do not absolutely bind the proctors, since the latter grant a sixteenth instead of a twentieth. The rights of the majority are still undefined. Still, it is undeniable that the delegates of the chapter of Salisbury were real representatives of the chapter; and that the knights elected in 1254 by the county court were also real representatives of the county. And very possibly the knights of 1254 received oral or written instructions similar to those of the proctors of 1226.

We believe that Professor Adams has been preoccupied with trying to find a " clear intention " and the " beginning of a new institution " in the assemblies held before 1265. The facts all show that the first gatherings of representatives of the commons were not the result of a deliberate plan on the part of the crown. There was no idea of creating alongside of or within the great council, another assembly which should be inferior, but similar, to that of the prelates and barons. Slowly and almost unobserved arose the custom of summoning before the king and his council first knights as representatives of the counties and then burgesses as representatives of the towns. This was done for many different purposes; to obtain information about the forests, to hear complaints about the sheriffs' admini-

[1] Wilkins, *Concilia*, I, p. 605. The canons had fixed a tax of one-sixth as the maximum for the tallage.

stration, to demand an aid, to discuss the affairs of the kingdom, to submit a new constitution for approval. The appearance of these new elements in an assembly, which the Great Charter would have made strictly feudal, does not seem to have caused any surprise or provoked any protest on the part of the baronage. This was possible not only because the king had the right to ask counsel of whom he would, whether they were his vassals or not; but also because the knights and burgesses were not at first considered to be an integral part of the great council. They were delegates of the commons, whom the king consulted upon occasion, who were dismissed as soon as possible, and who would not appear at the next parliament. They were not, strictly speaking, councillors of the king.

For the purposes for which the king summoned these delegates; it was usually a matter of indifference whether they were nominated by him or by the sheriff or elected by the county court. The important point was that they should be "discreet" enough to give the council the information required. Sometimes, as in 1254, when it was a question of entering into a formal and serious engagement on behalf of all the county, their election was ordered. But, elected or not, they were ordinarily held to be the representatives of the county. They appeared before the council *pro comitatu*, as had been their custom. We shall see that there was no competition for this honour and that neither electors nor elected were much concerned about regular electoral procedure.

CHAPTER III

THE PARLIAMENTS OF EDWARD I

IT is uncertain whether parliaments like that of 1265 were convened during the last years of Henry III's reign, *i.e.* from 1265 to 1272. Possibly the king's councillors and especially his son, Prince Edward, early perceived the advantage that the crown could derive from such assemblies, and some of the "great" parliaments, mentioned by the chroniclers[1], may have included representatives of the commons amongst their members. The most probable instance of such an assembly is the parliament on the octave of St Martin's day (18th November) 1267, in which Henry III promulgated the important statute of Marlborough. The king promulgated this statute "after convening the more discreet persons of the realm, both great and small" (*tam de majoribus quam de minoribus*)[2]. The same expression is found in the preamble to the statute of Gloucester in 1278[3]. It is highly probable that at least knights attended these two parliaments. The wording of the writ of the 26th December 1274, in which Edward I orders the dispatch of four knights "amongst the more learned in the law" from each county, proves that the king sometimes consulted the knights on questions of law, in which he could profit by their experience gained in the county court.

[1] Cf. *Ann. Waverley*, p. 371; *Ann. Winton.* p. 108; *Chr. Th. Wykes*, p. 221.
[2] *Statutes*, I, p. 19; Stubbs, *Select Charters*, p. 333.
[3] See below, p. 82.

Another parliament, that of October 1269, perhaps included representatives of the towns. The chronicle of Thomas Wykes[1] tells us that the king summoned for the 13th October "all the prelates and magnates of England, as also the most important persons of all the cities and of all the boroughs of his kingdom," and that they attended the solemn translation of the relics of St Edward. The chronicler adds that after the ceremony the nobles (*nobiles*), as usual, began to discuss the affairs of the king and kingdom in parliament[2]. The assembly promised the king a twentieth of the movable goods of the laity. Now, were the prominent townsmen (*civitatum pariter et burgorum potentiores*) summoned only for the ceremony? And did they return home without taking part in the parliament? We do not think so. In the events of 1282 and of 1294 we shall see to what long and troublesome negotiations the king was sometimes reduced when he wished to obtain money from the towns of the kingdom. It is most unlikely that no one thought of profiting by the presence of the "more powerful" burgesses to make them participate officially in the grant of the twentieth[3]. As to the knights of the shires, terms like *nobiles*, *majores* and even *magnates* are vague enough to include them, especially in what is not an official document.

Again, it is not impossible that representatives of the commons attended the parliament at Easter 1270 or that of July in the same year. In a letter dated at

[1] *Chr. Th. Wykes* (in *Ann. Monastici*, IV), p. 226.

[2] *Coeperunt nobiles, ut assolent, parliamentationis genere de regis et regni negotiis pertractare* (*Ibid*. p. 227).

[3] According to Bartholomew Cotton, *Historia Anglicana* (Rolls S.), p. 144–145, the twentieth was discussed, but not granted till the next year.

Windsor on the 4th August the king declares that he ought to have gone on crusade with his son, Edward; but that he has had to renounce the fulfilment of his vow, because "the prelates, the magnates *and the community of the realm*" did not approve of the simultaneous absence of the king and his son[1]. While the Annals of Winchester speak of the parliament assembled a fortnight after Easter "to discuss the twentieth," as being a "parliament of all the magnates of England," a phrase that seems to imply an exceptionally large gathering[2]. However, as we unfortunately do not possess the writs of summons, we cannot interpret such vague expressions with certainty.

The reign of Edward I opens with a great assembly, which met on St Hilary's day (13th January) 1273. The king himself was absent. Not only "the archbishops and bishops, earls and barons, abbots and priors" had been summoned, but also "four knights from each county and four persons from each city[3]." The necessary arrangements were made for the regency pending Edward's return and the assembly took the oath of fealty to the new king. No doubt it was rather for this ceremony than for a discussion of affairs of state that the delegates of the counties and towns had been summoned. Nevertheless, this unusual parliament deserves notice for several reasons and in particular because it clearly shows that the tradition inaugurated by Simon de Montfort was not set aside during the ten years which separate the parliament of January 1265 from that of April 1275.

---

[1] *Fœdera*, I, p. 485.
[2] *Ann. Winton.* p. 108; Stubbs, *Select Charters*, p. 333.
[3] *Ann. Winton.* p. 113; Stubbs, *Select Charters*, p. 421.

Edward I's parliamentary assemblies begin, properly speaking, with the great parliament of April 1275. Between this parliament and that of Carlisle in January 1307, a few months before the king's death, he summoned a very large number of parliaments of the most various compositions. Yet the constitutional history of his reign, as described by Stubbs, seems to present a perfect unity. It is sharply divided into two periods. Before 1295 is the period of experiments, when the king hesitates between the old conception of parliament and the new. After 1295 is the period of great parliaments, when, in accordance with the "model" of 1295, he summons the representatives of the commons and of the inferior clergy, at least for matters of importance. Thus Edward I's policy developed steadily from the beginning of his reign to the end, with the single interruption of the crisis of 1297.

This theory, with its charming simplicity, has been upset by the discovery of the writs summoning knights and burgesses to the parliament of April 1275. This discovery has shown that Edward I's innovations were much more closely connected with preceding events than had been supposed. But it has made a satisfactory explanation of Edward's policy more difficult. The parliament of 1295 can no longer be considered as the outcome of twenty years of a policy of constitutional experiments, since its composition only differs from that of the first parliament of the reign in one particular, namely the presence of delegates from the inferior clergy. On the other hand, why did Edward summon a parliament similar to the later "model" parliaments; then for twenty years cease to summon assemblies of that kind; and finally revert to them again at the end of his reign?

Before trying to discover the principles that guided Edward's policy throughout its apparently incomprehensible vacillations, we must first study these vacillations themselves. We will therefore devote this chapter to a detailed examination of the various parliaments of Edward I, and particularly of those which were either certainly or probably attended by deputies of the commons. *_*

Before 1910 there was much discussion over the composition of the "famous and solemn[1]" parliament of April 1275, in which the statute of Westminster the first, almost a code in itself, was promulgated. The text of the statute says that these "establisemenz" were made in the first parliament of Edward I "by his council and by the consent of the archbishops, bishops, abbots, priors, earls, barons and the community of the land thither summoned[2]." The last words might have indicated that representatives of the "community of the land" were actually present. Other evidence also led to the same conclusion. On the other hand, a writ addressed by the king to the judges of Cheshire spoke of the statute of Westminster as having been made "by the common counsel of the prelates and magnates of the kingdom[3]," without mentioning the consent of the "community." Thus the question was unsolved, for the only known writ of summons was that addressed to the archbishop of Canterbury[4].

[1] *Chr. Th. Wykes*, p. 263.
[2] *Statutes of the Realm*, 1, p. 26; Stubbs, *Select Charters*, p. 442.
[3] *Statutes of the Realm*, 1, p. 39.
[4] *Reports on the Dignity of a Peer*, App. I, p. 36. Writ dated at Woodstock on the 27th December [1274], proroguing the parliament, first fixed for a fortnight after the Purification, till the 22nd April 1275.

Two discoveries put an end to this uncertainty. The writ addressed to the sheriff of Middlesex was found in the Tower of London; while in the chapel of the Pyx in Westminster Abbey were found fragments, of various sizes, of writs addressed to three other sheriffs (Bedfordshire and Buckinghamshire, Surrey and Sussex, Wiltshire), as well as lists of knights and burgesses for several counties (the six mentioned above, Somersetshire and Dorsetshire, Warwickshire and Leicestershire). The text of these documents was published by Mr Jenkinson in the *English Historical Review* for April 1910[1]. They are the earliest parliamentary summons of which we possess the originals.

The only complete writ is the one addressed to the sheriff of Middlesex. It is dated at Woodstock on the 26th December [1274]. Its opening phrases are the same as those of the writ addressed the next day to the archbishop of Canterbury. The king announces that for certain reasons he has prorogued the "general parliament," which he had intended to hold in London a fortnight after the Purification (*i.e.* 16th February), to the day after the octave of Easter (*i.e.* 22nd April). Then follows the order to the sheriff to "send to this place" (*venire facias ibidem*) four of those knights of his county who were more discreet in the law (*de discrecioribus in lege militibus*) and also "six or four citizens, burgesses or other honest men" from each of the cities, boroughs and market towns" of his bailliage on the day after the octave of Easter "to discuss with the magnates of our realm the affairs of the said realm." Like several other summons of this early period (those of

---

[1] *Eng. Hist. Review*, xxv, April 1910, p. 231 sq. (*The first Parliament of Edward I*). Stubbs, *Select Charters*, p. 441.

1254 and 1264, for example) the writ is used for several purposes. After the summons itself there follows an order to the sheriff to see that various persons in the county receive the letters addressed to them without delay. Apparently these letters had reference to the payment of certain sums due to the king[1]. Finally, at the end of the writ, the sheriff is bidden not to forget the orders which he has received, and on the appointed date to inform the king of the manner in which he has discharged the duty placed upon him.

The lists relating to the ten counties mentioned above and published by Mr Jenkinson are in a poor state of preservation. They are the lists that the sheriffs sent to Westminster in accordance with the king's final order. They display certain peculiarities which are not found in connection with the parliaments at the end of the reign. Although by the terms of the writ the number of knights should have been four from each county, Bedfordshire and Buckinghamshire, which had only one sheriff between them, sent only four knights for the two counties[2]. It was the same with Warwickshire and Leicestershire; while, on the other hand, the sheriff of Surrey and Sussex returned the names of four knights for each of his counties. The towns summoned by the sheriffs were exceptionally numerous; and it is clear that a generous interpretation was given to the words *villae mercatoriae*[3]. In Warwickshire, five of the towns

---

[1] *Eng. Hist. Review*, loc. cit. p. 235 and 240.

[2] In the case of these two counties, the names of the four knights as written on the back of the writ are, with one exception, not the same as those on the list (cf. *loc. cit.* p. 236–237). Possibly the first candidates were not elected or those first elected had refused to serve.

[3] Perhaps these words were taken to mean not "market-towns," but "towns of merchants." Mr Jenkinson is not sure that the word

summoned (Alcester, Birmingham, Colehill, Eaton and Stratford) never again sent deputies till modern times; while a sixth (Tamworth) did not begin once more to send them till 1584. All the towns, whose lists of deputies we possess, were content with four representatives; while for one of them (Cricklade, in Wiltshire) the bailiff of the liberty in which it lies only sent three names to the sheriff, who noted the fact[1]. In certain counties (Bedfordshire and Buckinghamshire, Surrey and Sussex, Wiltshire) the name of each deputy, whether knight or burgess, is accompanied by the names of two sureties (*manucaptores*) who guarantee his appearance in parliament. There seem to have been no sureties in the other five counties.

The actual wording of the writ differs in important particulars from those of earlier and later dates. The towns are not summoned by direct citation, as they were to the great parliament of 1265. A general summons is addressed to the sheriff, who apparently himself decides which towns to summon, in accordance with the terms of the writ. This is the method that was henceforth employed for all the great parliaments of Edward I, except that of Michaelmas 1283.

The knights and burgesses are summoned "to discuss the affairs of the kingdom with the magnates" (*ad tractandum una cum magnatibus regni nostri de negociis ejusdem regni*). The formula is almost the same as that at the end of the writ addressed to the archbishop of Canterbury (*ad tractandum et ordinandum una cum pre-*

mercatorum is not indicated on some of the returns. We may notice that the "new custom" on wool and leather was granted at the request of the "communities of merchants" (*Parl. Writs*, I, p. I). See Appendix III, note G.

[1] Jenkinson, *Eng. Hist. Review*, xxv, April 1910, p. 242.

latis et magnatibus regni nostri de negociis ejusdem regni).
In this the writs of 1275 resemble those of 1265. The
terms in use at a later period (*ad faciendum quod tunc de
communi consilio ordinabitur*), seem greatly to diminish
the dignity of the duties assigned to the representatives
of the commons. But probably we ought to be on our
guard against making too much of this difference.

Further, it is noticeable that the writs for the great
parliament of 1275, like those for the great parliament
of 1265, do not order the election of the delegates, but
only their dispatch. The sheriff of Middlesex repeats
the formula—*venire feci coram vobis*. The knights, however, probably were elected, as they were a few months
later for the parliament of October 1275. As to the
burgesses, they were undoubtedly selected by the
"communities" of the towns; but in what manner we
cannot say with certainty.

The king had a double purpose in summoning this
parliament. Without doubt there was to be a discussion
on the ordinances which the council had prepared and
which formed the statute of Westminster the first. It was
probably on this account that the knights of the shires
were required to be learned in the law (*de discrecioribus in lege*). The burgesses were summoned for a
wholly different purpose. Edward I was convinced that
one of the chief sources of weakness on the part of the
royal government of England was the inadequacy of
the regular revenue. This placed the king at the mercy
of the prelates and barons. He had, therefore, resolved
to make an agreement with the merchants for the establishment of a permanent tax on the wool and leather
exported from the kingdom. This tax, the "new custom,"
was now accorded "by all the magnates of the realm

and at the request of the communities of merchants of all England[1]."

The representatives of the towns were not called to the parliament of October 1275. But the knights of the shires attended, although the chroniclers only mention the magnates[2]. Just when the list of the members of the house of commons, which appeared as a parliamentary paper in 1878, was being prepared, a writ addressed to the sheriff of Kent was discovered. "Whereas we have required the prelates and magnates of our realm to be present at our parliament, which with God's leave we will hold at Westminster fifteen days after Michaelmas next [13th October] there to discuss with us both of the state of our realm and of certain of our affairs which we will then make known to them, and whereas it is expedient that two knights of the said county, from among the more discreet and lawful knights of the same county, should be present at this parliament; for these reasons we bid you to have the two aforesaid knights elected in your full county court with the assent of the same county (*in pleno comitatu tuo de assensu ejusdem comitatus eligi facias*) and to make them come to us at Westminster, in the name of the community of the said county (*pro communitate dicti*

---

[1] *Parl. Writs*, ed. Palgrave, I, p. 1 (rule for the collection of the custom). A letter addressed to the sheriff of Gloucestershire similarly mentions "the assent of the magnates and the desire of the merchants" (*Ibid*. p. 2). Another letter from the king says that "the custom has been granted" by the prelates, the magnates and all the community of the merchants of the kingdom (*ibid*. p. 3). Cf. also the earl of Pembroke's letter, *ibid*. p. 3. Stubbs, *Select Charters*, p. 443. It was not the last time that Edward I was to approach the merchants in such circumstances. See Appendix III, note H.

[2] Cf. *Chron. Th. Wykes*, p. 265; *Ann. Winton*. p. 119. Stubbs, *Select Charters*, p. 422.

comitatus), there to treat (*ad tractandum*) with us and
the aforesaid prelates and magnates on the aforesaid
affairs. And fail not to do this....[1]"

The "certain matters" that the king wished to dis-
close had reference to a demand for money. Those
present at the parliament granted a fifteenth of movable
property, "voluntarily or against their will," says the
chronicle of Thomas Wykes. A few days later we see
the king ordering two persons to make an estimate,
under the dean of Salisbury's direction, of the movable
property in Devonshire and Cornwall, for the assessment of the fifteenth granted "by the prelates, earls
and all others of the kingdom[2]."

In the years that followed, parliament seems only to
have been composed of the king's ordinary councillors,
perhaps reinforced on important occasions by a certain
number of prelates and great lords specially summoned.
The statute *De bigamis* was made "at Westminster, in
the parliament after Michaelmas in the fourth year of
King Edward" (1276). This parliament, according to
another passage in the statute, was no more than the
king's council, for we read that "these constitutions"
were prepared by a certain number of persons "and then
heard and published before the king and his council[3]."

[1] The text of the writ is in Stubbs, *Const. Hist.* II, p. 234, n. 5.
It is dated at Chester, 1st September. On the back of the writ are
the names of the two knights elected, without *manucaptores*.

[2] *Parl. Writs*, I, p. 3 (24th October). On the 3rd November 1275
(*Parl. Writs*, I, p. 4) the king asks the archbishops, bishops, abbots,
priors, earls, barons, knights, freemen and all other his faithful
subjects of the county of Cheshire also to grant him a fifteenth.
The king had also tried to obtain an aid on spiritual benefices
from the clergy. But the bishops made no promise and only
undertook to assemble their clergy at Easter (*Chr. Th. Wykes*,
p. 265–266).

[3] *Statutes of the Realm*, I, p. 42–43.

The statute *De justiciis assignandis*, or statute of
Rageman, promulgated in the same parliament, was
"granted by our lord the king and by his council[1]."
The statute of Gloucester, promulgated in the parliament of St John Baptist's day 1278, begins by declaring
that the king had summoned "the more discreet of his
realm, as well greater as lesser[2]," which may be an
allusion to the presence of knights of the shires. But
several years later, when the king, in the preamble to
the statute of Westminster the second (1285), recalls
the promulgation of the statute of Gloucester, he only
mentions the presence on that occasion of the prelates,
earls, barons and the council[3]. Again, the important
statute *De viris religiosis*, promulgated in the parliament
of Michaelmas 1279, is made "on the advice of the
prelates, earls and other faithful subjects of our realm,
who are of our council[4]." A parliament, at which knights
of the shires were probably present, is that of St John
Baptist's day 1281, which was held at Worcester and in
which the great expedition against the Welsh was undertaken. In the next year, in the writ with which he summoned the assemblies at York and Northampton, the
king declares that the pacification of Wales had been
decided on "by the counsel of the leaders (*proceres*) and
magnates of the realm and also of the whole community
of the said realm[5]." But the phrase is far from precise.
Not till the year 1282 can we be sure of the summoning
of representatives of the *commun* to a new kind of parlia-

---

[1] *Statutes of the Realm*, I, p. 44.
[2] *Ibid.* I, p. 45. Stubbs, *Select Charters*, p. 449.
[3] *Statutes of the Realm*, I, p. 71. (*Convocatis prelatis, comitibus,
baronibus et consilio suo.*)
[4] *Statutes of the Realm*, I, p. 51. Stubbs, *Select Charters*, p. 451.
[5] *Parl. Writs*, I, p. 10.

ment, or rather to assemblies which, in exceptional circumstances, took the place of parliament.

The king was then engaged in the conquest of Wales and in great need of money. In 1279 he had imposed a scutage of forty shillings from each knight's fee on all those who had not joined the army[1]. The promulgation of the statute of Gloucester in 1278 had been partly due to financial considerations. The holders of franchises were required to produce their title-deeds, and the inquests *Quo warranto* were followed up by fines. In the same year, 1278, contrary to all feudal custom, the king decided that all who had land of an annual value of twenty pounds or more or a knight's fee worth twenty pounds or more *per annum*, without distinction of their tenures, should assume the military obligations of knighthood before Christmas. From this measure, confirmed in 1279, the treasury obtained further profits in consequence of the fines imposed[2]. Later the king put the finishing touch to these provisions by ordering all who had an income of thirty pounds or more to obtain a war-horse and armour. This again was a source of further fines[3]. The clergy, too, were forced to contribute. In 1279 the king obtained a tenth for two years from the clergy of the northern province; and in 1280, after a lively resistance, the province of Canterbury granted him a fifteenth for three years[4].

But these resources were insufficient; and in June

---

[1] *Chr. Th. Wykes*, p. 274, 291; Madox, *Exchequer*, p. 449, gives the writ for its collection (16th February, 7. Edw. I).

[2] *Parl. Writs*, I, p. 214, 219 (26th June 1278 and 12th March 1279).

[3] *Ibid.* I, p. 226 (26th May and 22nd June 1282).

[4] Wilkins, *Concilia*, II, p. 37, 41, 42. The *Annals of Osney* (p. 286) erroneously attribute the tenth to the province of Canterbury and the fifteenth to the province of York.

1282 Edward I sent John de Kirkby, who later became his treasurer, to negotiate an aid in the provinces. John de Kirkby carried letters recommending him to the sheriffs of the counties, the mayors, bailiffs and burgesses of the towns, the abbots and priors of religious houses, the deans and chapters, etc. The letters declared that he was ordered to report without delay on "the response and will" of those concerned with regard to the aid demanded. A similar letter, but not containing this last phrase, recommended John de Kirkby to the two archbishops and the bishop of Norwich[1].

Certain towns were no doubt won over, for we have a letter of the 28th October, in which the king warmly thanks the inhabitants of Hereford for their promise of a "courteous subsidy[2]." Another letter, of the 20th December, is addressed to the sheriffs of the counties and the magistrates of the towns, requests them to provide for the collection of the aid negotiated by John de Kirkby and recommends to them the clerk sent down for that purpose[3]. It is, however, probable that John de Kirkby was coldly received in most places, for the king found it necessary to change his method of procedure. He sent writs, dated at Rhuddlan in Wales on the 24th November 1282, to the two archbishops, in which he ordered them to summon their suffragan bishops, the abbots and the proctors of the deans, chapters and collegiate churches to York, in the case

---

[1] *Parl. Writs*, I, p. 384 (19th June 1282). Cf. Stubbs, *Select Charters*, p. 456.

[2] *Parl. Writs*, I, p. 387. Stubbs, *Select Charters*, p. 457.

[3] *Parl. Writs*, I, p. 387. According to J. E. Morris (*Welsh wars of Edward I*, p. 186), London granted 6000 marks, Newcastle 1750, York 1040, Lincoln 1016, Yarmouth 1000. The sums seem to have been paid as loans, but they were deducted from the thirtieth of 1283, as we shall see below.

of the northern province, and to Northampton, in that of the southern province, "to hear and to do that which we in the public interest shall cause to be declared to you and them on these matters, and to give us counsel and assistance." Writs, dated at the same place and on the same day, were sent to the sheriffs, ordering them to summon to Northampton or York, as the case might be, all those who had lands of more than twenty pounds' annual value, who were capable of bearing arms and who were not with the king in Wales. Further, the sheriffs were to send four knights from each county and two men from each city, borough or market-town, with full powers "to hear and to do that which we for our part shall see is disclosed to them" (*ad audiendum et faciendum ea que sibi ex parte nostra faciemus ostendi*)[1]. The date of the assemblies was fixed for the octave of St Hilary (20th January 1283). The barons were not summoned; for most of the great lords were accompanying the king on his expedition.

The purpose of these two assemblies was a demand for money. The writs are described, by a note in the margin of the roll, as *de subsidio petendo*. On various pretexts[2] the clergy in both assemblies refused to commit themselves to any definite undertaking. But the laity at Northampton promised a thirtieth of their

---

[1] *Parl. Writs*, I, p. 10. Stubbs, *Select Charters*, p. 457–459.

[2] One of the reasons was that the inferior clergy were not represented and that the summons had been irregular. Cf. *Parl. Writs*, I, p. 11: the archbishop of Canterbury writes to the bishop of London that it had been impossible at Northampton to give a reply to the king's agents, *tum propter absenciam maxime partis cleri tunc temporis modo debito non vocati, tum propter alia diversa*. The king then ordered the seizure of the funds for crusade, but restored them later, after the clergy in October had granted a twentieth for three years.

movable goods, on condition that the barons also gave a thirtieth. Writs of the 28th February 1283 named two persons in each county to assess the tax, seeing that "through the four knights sent to Northampton on behalf of the community of the aforesaid county you have courteously granted to us a subsidy on account of our present expedition in Wales, according as our magnates should provide....And whereas the said magnates, knowing that the knights of the other counties of our realm, who were sent on behalf of the community of the said counties to the same place, had granted...a subsidy of a thirtieth, have agreed to make a similar subsidy." In the writs addressed to the sheriffs of Essex and twenty-one other counties the king adds that, at the request of the four knights, he has decided that those who have land worth more than twenty pounds a year should contribute "in common" to the thirtieth[1].

As to the assembly at York, a writ of the 1st February 1283 names two persons "to order and arrange, in our name and on our behalf, the *services* which the knights, freemen, communities and all others of each of the counties beyond the Trent have granted to us at York, upon our demand[2]." These "services" no doubt included the grant of the thirtieth, for the thirtieth was levied north as well as south of the Trent. Commissions were issued on the 18th March 1283 for the assessment and collection of the tax in Cumberland, Lancashire, Northumberland, Westmoreland and Yorkshire[3]. No goods were exempt from payment of the thirtieth, which the "good men" of the realm had "freely agreed to give the king by reason of his war in Wales," except the personal property of certain great lords, who were with

[1] *Parl. Writs*, I, p. 13. Stubbs, *Select Charters*, p. 462.
[2] *Parl. Writs*, I, p. 11.   [3] *Ibid*. I, p. 14.

the king, and that of their villeins. But from the amounts to be paid by the citizens, burgesses, religious and others, who had responded to the king's appeal through John de Kirkby, their previous contributions were deducted.

These assemblies were not unlike that of 1254, of which we have spoken above. As in 1254, we see that the king was led to assemble the representatives of the counties and towns by his desire to avoid long discussions and considerable loss of time. We may also observe that the assimilation of the burgesses to the knights of the shires was more pronounced in the assemblies of 1283 than in the parliaments at the end of the thirteenth and the beginning of the fourteenth century. The towns, like the counties, promised a thirtieth; whereas, later on, the aid granted by the towns was nearly always at a higher rate than that accorded by the knights and the barons.

In the same year, 1283, the king held a parliament at Shrewsbury, on the Welsh frontier, to try the Welsh prince, David, for high treason. The clergy were not summoned, doubtless because the assembly was to be concerned with a criminal action. Writs of summons were sent to eleven earls, ninety-nine barons and nineteen judges or officials. The sheriffs received orders to provide for the election of two knights from each county; and twenty-one of the principal towns each received a direct writ of summons for the election of two burgesses[1]. These writs, which are conceived in

---

[1] The towns summoned were London, Winchester, Newcastle, York, Bristol, Exeter, Lincoln, Canterbury, Carlisle, Norwich, Northampton, Nottingham, Scarborough, Grimsby, Lynn, Colchester, Yarmouth, Hereford, Chester, Shrewsbury, Worcester. Neither the town of Chester nor the county of Cheshire was summoned to Edward I's other parliaments.

almost identical terms, enumerate at length the misdeeds of the Welsh and dwell on the ingratitude of David. The king ends by ordering the persons summoned to meet him at Shrewsbury the day after Michaelmas "to speak with us of this and other matters" (*nobiscum super hoc et aliis locuturi*)[1].

The presence of the knights is clearly to be attributed to the rank of the accused, who was to be tried "in full parliament," and who was in fact so tried by a commission of judges nominated for the purpose. The judgement was to be as solemn as possible. The summoning of delegates from certain towns is much more surprising. It is true that, after David had been hung and quartered, the four quarters of his body were made over to the representatives of four towns at the four corners of England, to be exposed on the town-walls—the citizens of London being given his head[2]. But it is hard to believe that that was the cause of the summons; and we are therefore led to suppose that the summons had reference to the preparation of the statute of merchants, promulgated by the king at this time, not at Shrewsbury, but at Acton Burnell[3]. The text of the statute only says

[1] *Parl. Writs*, I, p. 15–16 (28th June 1283).

[2] *Ann. Osney*, p. 294.

[3] It is doubtful whether this statute was made at Acton Burnell or at Shrewsbury. According to the text of the statute, it was "donee a Actone Burnel le duzim jor de octobre en l'an de nostre regne unzime" (*Statutes*, I, p. 54). A statute of 1285 (*Statutes*, I, p. 98) speaks of the statute of merchants as having been made by the king and his council "a sun parlement qe il tint a Actone Burnell apres la Seint Michel le an de sun regne unzime." On the other hand, the *Statutes* (I p. 53), according to the *Lib. Scac. Westm.* x, fol. xl, give the following title "Les estatuz de Slopbury ke sunt appele Actone Burnel. Ces sunt les estatuz fez at Salopsebur, al parlement prochein apres la fete Seint Michel, l'an del regne le rey Edward fiz le rey Henry unzime."

that "le Rei par luy et par sun conseil ad ordine, e establi[1]," but the omission of the delegates of the towns in such circumstances need not be considered extraordinary. According to the close rolls, the text of the statute was given to the mayors of York, Bristol, Lincoln, Winchester and Shrewsbury[2].

From 1283 to 1290 the parliaments seem to have been composed only of the council, sometimes perhaps reinforced by the presence of barons and prelates, according to traditional practice. The statute of Westminster the second (1285) is promulgated "by the king at Westminster, in his parliament, after Easter[3]." It is clear that the representatives of the counties and towns were not summoned to this parliament, for there is no mention of their presence in connection with the confirmation of the charters. We are merely told that the king confirmed the Great Charter and the Charter of the Forest, after having conferred with his council and "at the request of divers persons of his realm, as well prelates, religious and other ecclesiastics as earls, barons and other secular or lay persons[4]." The statute of Winchester, which was also promulgated in 1285, probably in the parliament of October, is made entirely in the name of the king, who "commands" and makes no allusion to the presence of any magnates or even to the co-operation of the council[5]. The king then hastened to leave England for Gascony, where he remained for

[1] Statutes of the Realm, I, p. 53. Stubbs, Select Charters, p. 462.
[2] Statutes of the Realm, I, p. 54; Calendar of close rolls, 1279–1288, p. 244.
[3] Dominus Rex in parleamento suo post Pascha anno regni sui tercio decimo apud Westmonasterium... statuta edidit (Statutes, I, p. 71).
[4] Rot. Parl. I, p. 225; Statutes, I, p. 104.
[5] Statutes of the Realm, I, p. 96. Stubbs, Select Charters, p. 463–469.

three years, from May 1286 till August 1289. In his absence the council perhaps continued to meet on the usual dates, to receive petitions and to dispatch the judicial business reserved to it; but we have no official documents for this period. We only know that in the parliament of Candlemas 1289, the king, through John de Kirkby, his treasurer, demanded an aid "of the earls and barons and indeed of all the inhabitants of the realm in general"; and that the earl of Gloucester replied, on behalf of the assembly, that they would give nothing so long as they did not see the king in England. The treasurer thereupon proceeded to tallage very heavily "the cities and boroughs and royal domains throughout the realm[1]."

From 1290 the documents published in *Rotuli Parliamentorum* and *Parliamentary Writs*—parliamentary summons, replies of sheriffs, petitions to the king in his parliament, records of matters tried in parliament, *coram rege*, writs appointing collectors of aids granted by parliament, regulations for the collection of such aids, *memoranda* of all kinds—enable us to follow in greater detail the development of parliamentary activity and the modifications made by the king in the composition of his parliaments.

The first parliament of 1290, which the king held, as usual, on the octave of St Hilary (20th January), seems to have been concerned with judicial matters only and included only the council and perhaps a few barons and prelates who were not of the council[2]. The parliament held after Easter was of the same character. In it the king promulgated two statutes, *De quo warranto*, which is given by the king "of his special favour

[1] *Chr. Th. Wykes*, p. 316.   [2] *Rot. Parl.* I, p. 15 sq.

and for the affection that he bears to his prelates, earls and barons and to the others of his realm," and *De consultatione*, which is a royal ordinance concerning the administration of justice and in which the king merely states that he "wills and commands[1]."

At this parliament "on the day after Trinity Sunday [29th May 1290][2], in full parliament of the lord king," six bishops, the king's brother, Edmund of Cornwall, five earls, eleven other persons individually named "and the other magnates and leaders (*proceres*) then present in parliament, on behalf of themselves and of the community of the whole realm, as far as in them lies," granted the king, "for the marriage of his eldest daughter[3]," an aid corresponding to that which his father had levied in similar circumstances. The aid could even be levied at the rate of forty shillings on the knight's fee, whereas Henry III had only received two marks or a little more, but on condition that this concession should not be used as a precedent to the prejudice of the grantors[4].

For the moment the king did not collect this aid, which was not levied till 1302. On the 14th June 1290 he informed his sheriffs that, since he had received "special requests on certain matters from the earls, barons and certain other magnates of our realm[5]," he

[1] *Statutes of the Realm*, I, p. 107, 108.

[2] In the writ of the 7th November 1302, ordering the collection of the aid (*Rot. Parl.* I, p. 266; *Parl. Writs*, I, p. 132–133), the king erroneously gives the 1st June 1290 as the date.

[3] She was not the king's eldest daughter, but was the first daughter to marry.

[4] *Rot. Parl.* I, p. 25; *Parl. Writs*, I, p. 20. Stubbs, *Select Charters*, p. 472.

[5] *Cum per comites, barones et quosdam alios de proceribus regni nostri nuper fuissemus super quibusdam requisiti....* Stubbs, *Select Charters*, p. 472–473.

wished to confer and discuss with the magnates and other persons of the counties of his kingdom. He therefore ordered the sheriffs to provide without delay for the election of two or three knights, who should appear before him at Westminster not more than three weeks after the feast of St John Baptist [*i.e.* 15th July]. These knights were to be from among the more discreet and diligent (*de discrecioribus et ad laborandum potenciori-bus*), furnished with full powers "to give counsel and to consent, in their own name and that of the community of the county, to what the earls, barons and magnates shall see fit to decide[1]." The clergy do not seem to have been summoned; and if writs of summons were sent to the baronage, they are not extant. On the 8th July, that is to say, a week before the date fixed for the arrival of the knights, the king, "in his parliament after Easter" and "at the instance of the magnates of his realm" (*ad instantiam magnatum regni sui*), promulgated the famous statute *Quia emptores*. This statute provided that, if a fief or part of a fief were alienated, the purchaser should become the vassal not of the vendor, but of the overlord from whom the vendor had held his fief[2]. *Quia emptores* does not seem to have been amongst the "certain matters," which had arisen between the king and the nobility and which the king wished to discuss with the knights of the shires, since it was thought unnecessary to postpone its promulgation till after their arrival. It was probably also in this

[1] *Ad consulendum et consenciendum pro se et communitate illa hiis que comites, barones et proceres predicti tunc duxerint concordanda* (*Parl. Writs*, I, p. 21).

[2] *Statutes of the Realm*, I, p. 106. Stubbs, *Select Charters*, p. 473–474.

parliament that the king induced the barons to approach the pope with one of those collective protests against the pretentions of the Roman curia, which occur from time to time during his reign[1]. Perhaps he wished to obtain an approval of this protest from the communities of the counties, both to give it more weight and to shelter himself behind the unanimous opinion of the laymen of England. The principal cause of the gathering seems, however, to have been the question of the banishment of the Jews, which the king wished to use as a means of obtaining a considerable subsidy from his subjects. The banishment of the Jews was probably decided in this parliament, although a chronicler describes the measure as an act of the king and the "secret council[2]." The safe-conduct granted to the Jews for leaving the country is dated the 27th July 1290, *i.e.* twelve days after the arrival of the knights at the parliament[3]. On the 22nd September[4], by a writ addressed "to the knights, freeholders and all the community" of each county, the king provides for the collection of a fifteenth granted to him "by the archbishops, bishops, abbots, priors, earls, barons and all others of

---

[1] *Fœdera*, I, p. 740; *Calendar of close rolls*, 1288–1296, p. 134 (without date).

[2] Hemingburgh, *Chronicon*, ed. Hamilton, II, p. 20, says that the magnates laid complaints before the king in the parliament held after Easter and that the expulsion was decided *per secretum consilium*. Stubbs, *Select Charters*, p. 426.

[3] *Fœdera*, Rec. ed. I, p. 736.

[4] This late date has worried historians and driven them to conclude that, despite the words of the writ, the fifteenth was not granted regularly (see below, p. 181, note 1). But, since the valuation was to be made on the movable goods in each person's possession between the 1st August and the 29th September, it was to the king's interest to postpone the valuation to the end of September, when his subjects would have got in the harvest.

the realm[1]." A few days later the clergy agreed to give
the king a tenth of their spiritual revenues[2]. The
Annals of Dunstable definitely represent the grant of
the tenth and the fifteenth as a consequence of the
expulsion of the Jews[3]. An official memorandum drawn
up in 1306 gives the same explanation[4].

No trace can be found of the presence of knights or
deputies of the towns in the parliament of Michaelmas
1290 or in the parliaments of 1291, 1292 and 1293. In
the parliament of January 1292 the statute *De vasto*
was promulgated "after serious discussion in full parliament." But this "full" parliament was no more than
an ordinary one, probably composed only of members
of the council. That is the conclusion to be drawn from
the text of the ordinance *De brevi de inquisitione con-
cedenda*, which was likewise promulgated "in full parliament," but "by the king and his council[5]." The
parliament of Easter 1293, at which the archbishop of
York was tried "in full parliament," was composed,
according to the actual text of the sentence, of "earls,
barons and judges and all the king's council[6]."

1294 was one of the critical years of Edward's reign.
He was at war with the king of France; and a parliament

---

[1] *Parl. Writs*, I, p. 24. The county of Cheshire granted the
fifteenth in 1292 (*Parl. Writs*, I, p. 391).

[2] On the 2nd October, in the assembly at Ely.

[3] *Et quia dicta expulsio Judaeorum multum placuit Anglicanae
ecclesiae et populo, clerus concessit regi decimam bonorum spiritu-
alium... Et barnagium et clerus concesserunt quintam decimam
bonorum temporalium taxandam et assidendam per legales homines...*
(*Ann. Dunst.* p. 362). Cf. Hemingburgh, II, p. 22. Stubbs, *Select
Charters*, p. 427.

[4] From the thirtieth of 1306 are exempted those goods which
were exempted *in taxatione quintae decimae a communitate regni
domino Regi anno regni sui decimo octavo concessae propter exilium
Judaeorum* (Brady, *An historical treatise of cities and burghs*, ed.
1777, App. p. 28. See Appendix II, p. 236).

[5] *Rot. Parl.* I, p. 78–79.   [6] *Ibid.* I, p. 104.

held on the 6th June at Westminster decided that an expedition should be equipped for the reconquest of Gascony[1]. To obtain money the king seized the wool and leather of the kingdom, which he only returned to the merchants in exchange for a more or less voluntary augmentation of the regular "custom[2]." He took possession of the treasures of churches and monasteries and terrified the clergy—the dean of St Paul's died of fright in his presence—into surrendering half of their revenues temporal and spiritual[3]. On the 14th June 1294 and the following days he had ordered his barons to be at Portsmouth on the 1st September ready to leave for

[1] Cotton, *Hist. Angl.* p. 233–234.

[2] The king claimed that the merchants had granted him this augmentation. The *Calendar of fine rolls*, I, p. 347, gives (according to Rot. Fin. 22 Edw. I, m. 2) the substance of an order, transmitted to the treasurer and barons of the exchequer at Dublin, to collect one mark, in place of half a mark, on each sack of wool or of woolfells and on each last of leather. The king adds that he is making a concession to the Irish merchants, since the English merchants had made him a grant for two or three years, if the war lasted so long, of 5 marks or 3 marks (according to quality of the wool) on each sack of wool exported and 5 marks on each last of leather. In an account of 28 Edw. I (1299–1300), quoted by Stubbs, (*Const. Hist.* II, p. 551), from Hale, *Customs*, p. 135, it is similarly affirmed that the augmentation of 1294 had been graciously (*gratanter*) accorded by the merchants. But Bartholomew Cotton has inserted in his chronicle (p. 245–247) a writ of the 22nd year of Edward I, attested by the treasurer, in which the king explains that it had first been decided, *per nos et magnates regni nostri, prelatos, comites et barones, et per consilium nostrum*, to sell the confiscated wool for the benefit of the treasury and for the defence of the country; but that the king has decided, in his council, *ad instantiam et requisitionem mercatorum de regno nostro*, to return the wool to the merchants, on condition that the custom should be augmented during the continuance of the war. There may have been an assembly of merchants as in 1303. But anyhow the nature of the "gracious" aid is obvious.

[3] The clergy had been summoned on the 10th and 19th August 1294, for the 21st September at Westminster. As in the parliament of 1295, the inferior clergy were represented by proctors (*Parl. Writs*, I, p. 25–26). Cf. Stubbs, *Select Charters*, p. 429.

Gascony[1]. But the barons soon showed themselves recalcitrant. The Welsh revolted[2]. Scotland was ready to rise. On the 8th October, in the midst of these difficulties, the king wrote to his sheriffs, using the customary formula, that he intended to hold a conference and discussion on the day after St Martin's day (12th November) with the earls, barons and other magnates of the realm, "with regard to certain difficult matters" touching himself and his kingdom. The sheriff therefore was to provide for the election of two from among the more discreet and diligent knights of the county, and to send them to Westminster with full powers. The king insisted on this last point, "in order that matters shall not be left undecided for lack of such powers[3]." The knights were summoned "to give counsel and to consent to what the aforesaid earls, barons and magnates shall by common accord have ordained touching the aforesaid matters[4]." The next day, the 9th October, the king issued another writ ordering the sheriff to have two more knights elected and to send them along with the first pair. There is no demand that these two knights shall have full powers like the others, and they are simply summoned to Westminster "to hear and do what we will then and there more fully command them[5]." One of the principal reasons for holding this

[1] *Parl. Writs*, I, p. 259 sq.

[2] On the 15th, 18th and 27th October the king issued military summons for an expedition into Wales (*ibid.* I, p. 265).

[3] *Et ita quod pro defectu potestatis hujusmodi idem negocium infectum non remaneat* (*Parl. Writs*, I, p. 26). Stubbs, *Select Charters*, p. 476–477.

[4] *Ad consulendum et consenciendum hiis que comites, barones et proceres predicti concorditer ordinaverint in premissis* (*Parl. Writs*, I, p. 26).

[5] *Ad audiendum et faciendum quod eis tunc ibidem plenius injungemus* (*Parl. Writs*, I, p. 26). Stubbs, *Select Charters*, p. 477.

parliament was clearly the need of money. On the 12th November, that is to say, on the very day fixed for the opening of the assembly, a writ was issued for the collection of a tenth granted "by the earls, barons, knights and all others of our realm as a subsidy for our war[1]." No clergy were present at this parliament, and, as in 1290, the towns were not represented[2]. In 1290 the latter had probably paid the fifteenth like the rest of the kingdom[3]. This time the king demanded a sixth from the towns on royal demesne, instead of the tenth granted by parliament. He first applied to London, which, through Walter de Langton[4], master of the wardrobe, "liberally and freely" undertook to pay the sixth. Commissioners were then sent into the provinces with instructions to quote the example of London to the other towns on desmesne and to obtain a similar aid from them[5]. As the towns on demesne were tallageable,

[1] *Parl. Writs*, I, p. 391. The instructions for collection are in Cotton, *Hist. Angl.* p. 254.

[2] Dugdale (*A perfect copy of all summons of the nobility*, p. 7), under the date the 8th October 1294, gives a writ ostensibly taken from the close roll 22 Edw. I, m. 6, d. and addressed to the sheriff of Northumberland, in which the king orders the election of two knights of the shire and two burgesses from each town. But the writ is not extant, and the text given by Dugdale is the result of confusing the writ of the 8th October 1294 with that of the 3rd October 1295. The latter is not in Dugdale's collection. Cf. *Reports on the Dignity of a Peer*, I, p. 209.

[3] This is certainly true of London, where the aid produced £2860. 13s. 8d., according to an account quoted in Brady, *An historical treatise of cities and burghs*, ed. 1777, p. 58.

[4] The king's letter, thanking the citizens of London for the aid which they had promised him through Walter de Langton, is analysed in the *Calendar of close rolls*, 1288–1296, p. 438 (23rd November 1294).

[5] The writs for the collection of the sixth in London and for the nomination of commissioners (21st November 1294) are not in *Parl. Writs*. They were published by R. Brady in *An historical treatise of cities and burghs*, p. 66–68 (ed. 1777). See below, Appendix I, p. 231 sq.

L   7

they could not refuse, and the king succeeded in extracting "the sixth penny from the merchants and townsmen living in walled towns and small market-towns[1]."

An important gathering took place in August 1295. On the 24th June[2] the king had issued summons for the 1st August to the archbishops and bishops, forty-two abbots, eleven priors, the grandmasters of the orders of Sempringham and the Temple, the prior of the Hospitallers, eleven earls, fifty-three barons, some of the judges, the barons of the exchequer and other members or clerks of the king's council. But the *commun* of the kingdom was not represented. According to the *placita* which we possess[3], the business consisted of replying to petitions and trying cases reserved to the jurisdiction of the king in his parliament. But we read elsewhere that one of the chief purposes of the assembly was to consider the papal legates' offer of mediation between Edward and Philip of France. The king also promulgated the measure known as the statute *De prisonibus prisonam frangentibus*[4].

The next parliament is the famous one of November 1295, which has been called "the model parliament" and is regarded as marking the definitive entry of the "communities of the kingdom" into parliament. Edward I was at war with the king of France, the Scots and the Welsh, and had exhausted all means, legal and otherwise, of obtaining money. On the 30th September

---

[1] *Flores historiarum*, III, p. 275. On the 15th November the king had reduced the custom, which had been augmented shortly before (cf. Stubbs, *Const. Hist.* II, p. 551, note).

[2] *Parl. Writs*, I, p. 28, 29. Stubbs, *Select Charters*, p. 479.

[3] *Rot. Parl.* I, p. 132 sq.

[4] *Statutes of the Realm*, I, p. 113.

1295, by writs dated from Wingham[1], he summoned the archbishops and bishops to a parliament at Westminster on the Sunday after St Martin's day (13th November). The king begins with a general declaration that "what touches all should be approved by all." He then explains the object of the assembly, namely the necessity for recovering Gascony from the king of France, who has seized it "by fraud and sharp practice" and who, if his plans succeed, intends to destroy the whole English race from off the face of the earth. After stating the date of the assembly, the king orders the archbishops and bishops to provide for the attendance from each diocese of the prior of the chapter and the archdeacons with one proctor for the cathedral chapter and two proctors for the rest of the diocesan clergy. The proctors are to be furnished with full powers. This formula, known as the *Praemunientes* clause[2], is henceforth used by the king whenever he wishes to summon the representatives of the clergy. The prelates and other clergy are to come to Westminster "to discuss, ordain and do, together with us and the other prelates, magnates and other inhabitants of our realm, what is needful to obviate these dangers and evil designs." Similar summons, but without the *Praemunientes* clause, were addressed to sixty-seven abbots, the grandmasters of the Temple and Sempringham and the prior of the order of St John.

On the 1st October eight earls and forty-one barons were summoned by writs dated at Canterbury[3]. These

---

[1] *Parl. Writs*, I, p. 30. Stubbs, *Select Charters*, p. 480.
[2] The clause begins: *Praemunientes priorem et capitulum ecclesie vestre, archidiaconos, totumque clerum*, etc.
[3] *Parl. Writs*, I, p. 31. Stubbs, *Select Charters*, p. 481.

summons are much shorter than those sent to the bishops. The preamble is omitted, and the explanation of royal intentions reduced to a minimum: "As we wish to confer and discuss with you and the other leaders (*proceres*) on the measures made necessary by the dangers now threatening our whole realm," etc. The earls and barons are summoned "to discuss, ordain and do, together with us and the prelates, the other leaders (*proceres*) and the other inhabitants of our realm, what is needful to obviate these dangers."

From Canterbury on the 3rd October similar writs were issued to the sheriffs[1]. As the king wishes to "confer and discuss with the earls, barons and other leaders (*proceres*)" on the dangers that threaten the realm, the sheriff is ordered to provide for the election of two knights from each county, two citizens from each city and two burgesses from each borough. All these are to be from among the more discreet and diligent of their class. They must appear furnished with full and ample powers, on behalf of themselves and their constituent communities, in order that matters shall not be left undecided for want of such powers. They are summoned "to do that which shall then be ordained by common counsel touching the aforesaid matters."

By writs dated at Udimore on the 2nd November parliament was prorogued to the Sunday before St Andrew's day (27th November)[2].

An almost complete list of the deputies elected by the counties and towns in 1295 is in Palgrave's *Parliamentary Writs*[3]. A copy of the original lists transmitted

[1] *Parl. Writs*, I, p. 29–30. Stubbs, *Select Charters*, p. 481–482.
[2] *Parl. Writs*, I, p. 33. The second list of barons only contains 38 names, instead of 41.
[3] *Ibid.* p. 34 sq.

by the sheriffs for thirty-five counties is extant. Only the counties of Norfolk and Suffolk are lacking; for the palatinates of Chester and Durham received no summons and were not represented till much later. In these thirty-five counties the number of towns represented is 109, without counting the city of London, which is not included in the lists, since it received its writ direct from the royal chancery. The most striking omission is that of the Cinq Ports, which had been summoned in 1265, but were not summoned again for a long time. Beside the name of each knight and burgess the sheriff, as in 1275 and 1290, carefully enters the names of the persons who stand surety (*manucaptores*) for the delegates, *i.e.* who guarantee that the latter will appear before the king on the appointed day[1].

According to a writ of the 4th December, nominating a knight as collector in each county, the cities and boroughs on demesne granted the king a seventh of movable goods, the barons and knights an eleventh[2], and the clergy a tenth[3].

All the various groups, which together formed the parliament of November 1295, had been summoned before by Edward I to parliaments or to assemblies which took the place of parliaments. The knights of the

---

[1] For instance, the sheriff of Oxfordshire writes: *Manucaptio eorundem de veniendo ad diem et locum contentos in brevi* (*Parl. Writs*, I, p. 40).

[2] *Cum comites, barones et alii de regno nostro in subsidium guerre nostre nunc, sicut alias nobis et progenitoribus nostris regibus Anglie liberaliter fecerunt, undecimam de omnibus bonis suis mobilibus, et cives, burgenses et alii probi homines de dominicis nostris civitatibus et burgis ejusdem regni septimam de omnibus bonis suis mobilibus...curialiter concesserint et gratanter...* (*Parl. Writs*, I, p. 45). Stubbs, *Select Charters*, p. 482.

[3] *Parl. Writs*, I, p. 46, 47.

shires had been summoned to the parliaments of April
and October 1275, to the assemblies of January 1283
at Northampton and York, to the parliament of Michaelmas 1283 at Shrewsbury, to that of July 1290 and that
of November 1294. The representatives of the towns
had appeared at the parliament of April 1275 and at the
two assemblies of 1283. In the latter year the larger
towns had sent delegates to the parliament at Shrewsbury, and possibly the king had consulted the representatives of the towns before augmenting the custom
in 1294. As for the inferior clergy, the king had just
summoned them, in 1294, to a special clerical assembly
in the same manner as he now summoned them to the
parliament of 1295. The innovation that characterized
the parliament of 1295 therefore consisted in the union
in the same parliament of various groups, which represented every element of any weight in the national life
and which had never before been all assembled at the
same time. Henceforth, when the king wished to summon a similar parliament, the writs of 1295 would serve
as models.

***

May we, then, say that the innovation of 1295 became henceforth the rule; and that from that date the
king regularly, or almost regularly, summoned to parliament the prelates and inferior clergy, the earls and
barons, the representatives of the communities of
the counties and of the communities of the towns?
To answer this question and to give the parliament of
1295 its true place in Edward I's policy, we must briefly
examine the parliaments of the last twelve years of his
reign.

A parliament in every way similar to that of 1295 was summoned to Bury St Edmund's for the day following All Saints' day 1296. The writs, dated the 26th August[1], are addressed to the archbishops and bishops, with the *Praemunientes* clause, to sixty-six abbots, six earls and thirty-seven barons, and to the sheriffs for the election of knights and burgesses. The prelates, earls and barons are not required, as in 1295, to meet "with the other inhabitants of our realm" for discussion. This is the only change from the formula of the preceding year.

A writ of the 16th December 1296, addressed "to the knights, the freeholders and all the community" of the counties, informs us that the "earls, barons, knights and others" had granted the king a twelfth of their movable goods and that the "citizens, burgesses and other good men of all the cities and boroughs of the realm, whether on the estates or liberties of others or on our demesne," had granted an eighth[2]. The clergy, on account of the bull *Clericis laicos* promulgated by Boniface VIII early in the year, had refused to make any grant[3].

There is no need to describe the crisis of 1297, of which the clergy's refusal was the beginning. But we must mention some points in the events of that year, for they are of considerable constitutional im-

---

[1] *Parl. Writs*, I, p. 48. On the 24th September, by writs addressed directly to London and twenty-two other important towns (*Parl. Writs*, I, p. 49) the king ordered these towns to send delegates to give their opinions on the new organization which he proposed to give to Berwick.

[2] *Et cives, burgenses et alii probi homines de singulis civitatibus et burgis regni nostri de quorumcumque tenuris aut libertatibus fuerint et de omnibus dominicis nostris octavam...* (*Parl. Writs*, I, p. 51).

[3] Bartholomew Cotton, *Historia Anglicana* (ed. Luard), p. 314–315.

portance and illustrate certain aspects of Edward I's policy.

The resistance of the clergy was soon followed by that of the barons. Believing that he had definitely subjugated Scotland in the previous year, the king now wished actively to resume the war with France, to send some of his barons to Gascony and himself to assume the command of another army in Flanders. In the hope of persuading his vassals, he assembled a small parliament at Salisbury on St Matthias's day (Sunday, the 24th February 1297). The summons[1] are addressed only to six earls, seventy-five barons, nine judges, described as "knights," and four other persons who also were judges. No clergy and no representatives of the communities were summoned.

The parliament of Salisbury ended in a scene. The marshal of England, Roger Bigod, earl of Norfolk, refused to join the expedition to Gascony without the king. Violent words were exchanged. A party of malcontents was organized, at the head of which stood Roger Bigod and Humphrey Bohun, earl of Hereford and constable of England[2].

The king none the less persisted in his intention of crossing to Flanders. He summoned his barons and ordered them to appear in London with horses and arms on the 7th July. Writs were sent to the sheriffs ordering them similarly to summon all, whether tenants-in-chief or mesne tenants, who had lands of more than £20 annual value[3]. Barons and knights were to be ready

---

[1] *Parl. Writs*, I, p. 51–52.

[2] Walter of Hemingburgh, *Chronicon* (ed. Hamilton), II, p. 121; Cotton, p. 320. Stubbs, *Select Charters*, p. 432.

[3] Summons dated the 4th May for the barons (*Parl. Writs*, I, p. 281); the 15th May for the knights (*ibid.* I, p. 285 sq.).

to cross the sea, but the king did not mention the goal of the expedition.

Some of the knights summoned by the sheriffs did not appear[1]. Bohun and Bigod, after conferring with their adherents and probably with the archbishop of Canterbury, refused to discharge their official duties, on the pretext that they had come to the assembly at the request "and not on the summons" of the king[2]. They left London and presented their case and that of their adherents in the form of a petition to the king on behalf of the community of the realm[3]. They complained of the inadequacy of the summons, which did not specify the country for which the host was destined. They declared that neither they nor their ancestors had ever been bound to serve the king in Flanders; and, further, that even had they wished to do so, the exactions of the king, who respected neither the Great Charter nor the Charter of the Forest, had so impoverished the whole community that it could not bear the cost of such an expedition.

The king declared later[4] that this petition was never

---

[1] As may be deduced from the *Statutum de tallagio*, art. 5 (Bémont, *Chartes des libertés anglaises*, p.89. Stubbs, *Select Charters*, p. 494).

[2] Letter of the two earls, in the royal proclamation of the 12th August, 1297 (Bémont, *Chartes*, p. 81). In the writ of the 4th May the king had indeed used the words *vos affectuose requirimus et rogamus* instead of the more usual formula *vobis mandamus in fide et dilectione* (or *in fide et homagio*) *quibus nobis tenemini firmiter injungentes*. The king had used the former phrase more than once on other occasions.

[3] This is the *Articuli quos comites petierunt nomine communitatis* (Bémont, *Chartes*, p. 76 sq.), which we find in several chroniclers in either Latin or French. Cf. Stubbs, *Select Charters*, p. 434.

[4] In the proclamation of the 12th August (Bémont, *Chartes*, p.82). W. of Hemingburgh (II, p. 126) and Trevet (*Annales sex regum Angliae*, ed. Hog, p. 360, 362), on the contrary, say that the earls

presented to him and that he only knew of it by hearsay. Anyhow, he hastened to reconcile himself with the clergy, and from the lords, who were in London and preparing to accompany him, he obtained the promise of an aid, in return for the confirmation of the two charters[1]. There does not seem to have been any parliament summoned in the regular manner[2].

sent the Articles to the king by messengers, to whom the king replied that he could make no decision without consulting his council, of which part was in London and part in Flanders. The two accounts, however, are not irreconcilable. From the text of the two chroniclers it appears that the Articles were presented to the king after his departure from London. Trevet (p. 362) distinctly says that they were presented to him at Udimore. Now the king, who was still at Robertsbridge on the 8th August, was at Udimore two days later and stayed there at least till the 17th August. It is quite possible that the earls' messengers did not arrive at Udimore till after the 12th August.

[1] Such is the king's own account of the facts in a passage in his proclamation of the 12th August (cf. Bémont, *Chartes*, p. 83, 84). According to the *Flores historiarum* (III, p. 102) the king ordered the observance of the charters and for this concession demanded an eighth penny from the people. This was at once granted him by those who stood about him in his chamber (*qui protinus concessus est ei a plebe in sua camera circumstante*).

[2] In the passage in the proclamation of the 12th August, mentioned above, the king makes no allusion to a parliament, which he would not have failed to do, in order to legalize the collection of the aid, had a parliament been assembled. He only says that the lords who were with him granted him a "common gift," and he "prays all the good men and all the people of his realm, who never fail him, not to resent this gift." The resistance which the collection of the aid encountered shows that it had not been granted in the regular way. As for the *Articuli quos comites petierunt nomine communitatis*, that document is drawn up in the form of a parliamentary petition. It does not, however, follow that it was presented in a parliament or by members of a parliament. The chroniclers' texts do not favour such an interpretation; not even that of Trevet, who, however, speaks of a parliament. According to Trevet, a parliament met in London on the 1st August; the king was reconciled with the archbishop, demanded that those present should swear fealty to his son, and excused the exactions that he had made on the ground of military necessity. But the continuators

On the 30th July 1297 a royal writ drawn up in the usual form orders the collection of an eighth granted, in return for the confirmation of the charters, by the earls, barons, knights and other laymen who are not of the cities, boroughs and demesne; and of a fifth granted by the citizens, burgesses and other honest men of the realm, both on all other estates and liberties and on royal demesne[1]. Three weeks later the king, who had left London for Winchelsea, took measures for taxing the property of the clergy[2]. He also ordered the seizure of a great quantity of wool.

Resistance soon followed. On the 22nd August the earls and their supporters came to protest at the bar of the exchequer against the tallage, which the king had imposed without their consent or that of the community[3]. The king gave orders that no notice should be taken of the protest, and himself embarked for Flanders. But it was impossible to collect the tax. The city of London seems to have shown opposition from the beginning[4]; and subsequently the county court of Worcestershire answered the king's agents by recalling the behaviour of Henry III, who had promised to confirm the charters in return for a fifteenth and, after collecting the fifteenth, had let the promised liberties fall into dis-

of the *Flores historiarum* (III, p. 102, 295), usually well informed about events in London, put this ceremony on the 14th July. The summons for the 1st August, mentioned by Trevet (p. 354), is, by his own account, a summons to the army; and probably this summons refers to the general meeting, which was in reality fixed for the 7th July. Finally, if a parliament did meet on the 1st August, how does the writ for the collection of the aid come to be dated the 30th July?

[1] *Rot. Parl.* I, p. 239; *Parl. Writs,* I, p. 53. Cf. Stubbs, *Select Charters,* p. 434.   [2] *Parl. Writs,* I, p. 396 (20th August).
[3] *Transactions of the R. Historical Society,* N.S. III (1886), p. 284.
[4] *Fœdera,* I, p. 872 (5th August).

use[1]. On the 28th August Prince Edward, the king's son, was obliged to declare by letters patent that, for the defence of the kingdom and in consideration of the confirmation of the charters, it had been "ordained and agreed that the eighth of all the goods of all laymen should be collected *on this occasion*[2]." Thus it appears that the idea of levying a fifth in the towns was abandoned[3].

The opposition doubtless continued, for it became necessary to summon a parliament. Writs of the 5th and 9th September summoned to London for the day after Michaelmas the following persons—the two archbishops, ten bishops, fourteen earls and barons (Bohun and Bigod amongst them), seventeen abbots, four priors, the grandmaster of the Temple and the prior of St John, six judges, ten other clerks and officials, with a Dominican and a Franciscan who were of the king's council[4]. Other persons, supposed to be supporters of the king, were invited to come armed on the Sunday before Michaelmas (25th September) or on the 30th September[5]. Finally, on the 15th September, the sheriffs were informed that, as the king had confirmed the charters in return for an eighth, they should provide for the election of two knights to attend on the octave of Michaelmas (the 6th October), to receive the king's letters "and then to do what they shall be ordered by our son and our council[6]."

---

[1] *Ann. Wigorn.* p. 534. The writer says that on the 27th September the king's agents demanded a sixth in the city and an eighth in the county. [2] *Rot. Parl.* I, p. 240.

[3] See, however, note 1, above, with regard to the refusal of the county court of Worcestershire.

[4] *Parl. Writs*, I, p. 55–56.

[5] *Reports on the Dignity of a Peer*, App. I, p. 86; *Parl. Writs*, I, p. 56. [6] *Parl. Writs*, I, p. 56.

To this curious parliament, so oddly summoned, the earls and their friends, like the king's supporters, came armed. They demanded the confirmation of the charters from Prince Edward and presented to him a petition, which was probably the *Statutum de tallagio non concedendo*[1]. In article 1 of this document, which is evidently inspired by memories of 1215, the king formally undertakes to levy no tallage[2] or aid without the consent of the archbishops, bishops and other prelates, earls, barons, knights, burgesses and other freemen of the kingdom. The text of the *Confirmatio Cartarum*, accepted by the prince on the 10th October 1297 and ratified by the king at Ghent on the 5th November, is less explicit. The king indeed promises (art. 6) that henceforth he will not levy such "aids, mises and prises" except with the common consent of all the kingdom and only for the common profit of the kingdom; but he does not mention what shall henceforth be understood by the common consent of all the kingdom. Also he reserves to himself the ancient, due and customary aids and prises[3].

A writ of the 14th October 1297[4] informed the "knights, freeholders and community" of each county that, in view of the confirmation of the Great Charter, the archbishops, bishops, abbots, priors, earls, barons, knights and others, being not of the cities, boroughs or

[1] See Bémont, *Chartes*, p. xliii and 87. Stubbs, *Select Charters*, p. 493–494.
[2] It is doubtful if the word tallage is here used in its technical sense. The demand made by the barons in 1305 (see below, p. 119) seems to prove that they were not opposed to tallages. See Appendix III, note I.
[3] Stubbs, *Select Charters*, pp. 490–493.
[4] *Rot. Parl.* I, p. 241; *Parl. Writs*, I, p. 63. Stubbs, *Select Charters*, p. 436.

demesne, had granted a ninth. No doubt it was hoped that the demesne and the towns could be made to pay at a higher rate. But the idea was soon dropped, and on the 23rd October the order to collect the ninth was extended to the whole country. According to an official note, "the citizens and all the community of London granted" this ninth to the king. Probably there was no time to consult the other towns; and indeed the provision made with regard to them is described as an order of the council[1]. The clergy of the province of Canterbury, in convocation, granted a tenth and the clergy of the province of York a fifth, as a subsidy for the Scottish war[2].

The *Confirmatio Cartarum* of 1297 did not end the struggle between the king and the great lords. The latter had cause to fear that Edward I would consider his engagement annulled by the fact that he had been abroad when he ratified the confirmation. They therefore insisted in parliament and outside parliament on a further confirmation. The king avoided the issue, making reservations and constantly inventing reasons for delay. He did not definitely agree till March 1300 at a parliament in London. Five years later he had himself dispensed from his promises by a bull of Pope Clement V (29th December 1305)[3].

The first two parliaments of 1298 were ordinary parliaments, with neither knights nor burgesses. The

[1] The note, which is at the end of the writ of the 14th October reads: *Posteaque cives et tota communitas Londonie concesserunt regi nonam partem bonorum suorum ut patet inferius. Ordinatum est per consilium quod taxatores in singulis comitatibus Anglie taxent et levari faciant nonam in singulis civitatibus, burgis et dominicis regiis...(Rot. Parl.* I, p. 241; *Parl. Writs,* I, p. 64).

[2] W. of Hemingburgh, II, p. 155; Stubbs, *Select Charters,* p. 436. Wilkins, *Concilia,* II, p. 229–230.

[3] Text in Bémont, *Chartes,* p. 110.

first was held at York, as the Scotch war had begun
again. The king had not yet returned from Flanders[1].
The second, at which the king promulgated some
ordinances, was held in London about Easter, after
Edward's return[2]. On the contrary, the Whitsuntide
parliament (25th May), which met at York, contained knights and burgesses summoned, according to
the usual formula, "to do what shall then be ordained by common counsel on the aforesaid matters,"
that is to say, on "the matters concerning the king
and the state of the realm." A certain number of
barons were also present, but the clergy do not seem
to have been summoned[3]. At York it was decided to
prosecute the war in Scotland.

Neither knights nor burgesses were summoned to the
four parliaments of 1299. The parliament in Lent, at
which the subject of the confirmation of the charters
provoked some lively scenes[4], contained the archbishops,
eighteen bishops, thirty-four abbots, five priors, eleven
earls, ninety-nine barons, some judges and officials, but
no representatives of the "communities[5]." It was the
same with the parliament at Easter, to which were

[1] W. of Hemingburgh, II, p. 156. Before they would march
to Scotland the barons demanded a public reading of the charters
and of the confirmation.
[2] *Rot. Parl.* I, p. 143.
[3] Writs of the 10th April 1298 (*Parl. Writs*, I, p. 65 sq.). Stubbs
says (*Const. Hist.* II, p. 154) that in this parliament the magnates
demanded a fresh confirmation, which was promised on behalf of
the king, if he should return victorious. But Trevet (p. 371) and
W. of Hemingburgh (II, p. 174) place this demand at a later date
when the army had assembled at Roxburgh, prepared to march
against the Scots.
[4] See Bémont, *Chartes*, p. xliv sq. Stubbs, *Select Charters*,
p. 437.
[5] Writs of the 6th February 1299 for the 8th March in London
(*Parl. Writs*, I, p. 78 sq.).

summoned only the archbishop and bishops of the province of Canterbury, twenty-six abbots, eleven earls, forty-six barons and several persons described as knights[1], and at which the statute *De falsa moneta* was promulgated by the king "with common consent of the prelates, earls and barons of the realm[2]." Another parliament met in London on St Luke's day (18th October), but to it only a very small number of prelates, earls and barons were summoned, "to discuss and give counsel with some others of our faithful subjects who shall be present[3]." Finally Hemingburgh mentions a fourth parliament held by the king at York on St Martin's day (11th November). This was doubtless only a parliament of barons[4].

On the other hand, the parliament of Lent 1300 was a "full" parliament, in the sense which we now give to that phrase. That is to say, it was composed in the same manner as the parliament of 1295. It was indeed the first parliament since that of All Saints' day 1296 at which representatives of the inferior clergy, of the counties and of the towns met together, as in 1295. The assembly, which was opened in London on the 6th March, was more numerous than those of 1295 and 1296, for it included a larger number of abbots (72) and of earls and barons (110). Thirty-eight officials, judges and other members of the council were also summoned[5]. The knights and burgesses attended till the 20th March,

[1] Writs of the 10th April 1299 for a fortnight after Easter at Westminster (*Parl. Writs*, I, p. 80–81).

[2] *Statutes*, I, p. 131 sq.

[3] Writs of the 21st September 1299 for the 18th October in London (*Parl. Writs*, I, p. 81).

[4] W. of Hemingburgh, II, p. 186. Scottish affairs were discussed.

[5] Writs of the 29th December 1299 for the second Sunday in Lent, 6th March 1300 (*Parl. Writs*, I, p. 82 sq.).

on which day they were given writs to enable them to claim their "reasonable expenses[1]."

The *placita* published in the *Rotuli Parliamentorum*[2] are only composed of ordinances and judicial decisions. But it was at this parliament that the king, "at the request of the prelates, earls and barons" promulgated the *Articuli super cartas*[3]. These articles confirmed the Great Charter and the Charter of the Forest[4] and ordered the community of each county to elect three honest men, knights or others, to sit in judgement on infractions of the charters[5]. We cannot say whether the knights and burgesses took any part in the discussion on the articles, which were only sent to the sheriffs on the 15th April, more than three weeks after the departure of the representatives of the counties and towns[6].

On the 26th September 1300 summons were issued for another parliament to be held at Lincoln on the octave of St Hilary (20th January 1301). As there was to be a discussion on the royal forests, which had already been a subject of debate in the preceding parliament

[1] *Parl. Writs*, I, p. 85 sq. The writs for the knights are addressed to the sheriffs, those for the burgesses to the mayors and bailiffs.

[2] *Rot. Parl.* I, p. 143 sq.

[3] Bémont, *Chartes*, p. 99 sq.

[4] An *Inspeximus*, identical with that of 1297, was sent to the sheriffs on the 28th March 1300 (*Statutes*, I, p. 38). The confirmation, awaited since 1297, was not even yet complete and unreserved. See the end of the *Articuli* (Bémont, *Chartes*, p. 108).

[5] An order to this effect was sent to the sheriffs on the 27th March. They were to see that the three persons elected appeared before the king and his council at York on the morrow of Ascension Day (*Reports on the Dignity of a Peer*, App. I, p. 120).

[6] Rymer, *Fœdera*, I, p. 920. We do not know what document is M. Bémont's authority for dating the *Articuli* (*Chartes*, p. 99) on the 6th March, which was the day of the opening of the parliament.

and had been under consideration since 1297, the king ordered the sheriffs to send to Lincoln the delegates who had attended the parliament of London. The knights and burgesses were to be present on the day fixed "with full powers to hear and to do what may be ordained in these matters for the common good of the realm[1]." The earls (9), the barons (80), the bishops, the abbots (80) and the grandmasters of the three orders were summoned; but the representatives of the inferior clergy were not called to this parliament. The king also summoned to Lincoln a certain number of judges and officials, and sent a demand to the chancellors of the universities of Oxford and Cambridge for the attendance of some experts in the written law[2].

The principal object of the assembly, according to the writs of summons, was to examine questions connected with the perambulation of the forests, which the king had promised several years before and which had at last been begun. The king said that, before making any definite decisions, he wished to hear the arguments and objections of all and to be guided by the counsel of his prelates, earls, barons and other magnates. He reminded them that they, like himself, were bound by their oath to maintain the rights of the crown. In reality his chief wish was to gain time; for the deforestations which would follow the perambulation were to him a hateful prospect[3].

[1] A special clause, inserted in the writs for the counties containing forests, provides that the knights' expenses shall be paid by the sheriff, and orders the latter publicly to proclaim that all who have objections to make in connection with the inspection of forests should attend at Lincoln (*Parl. Writs*, I, p. 90). Stubbs, *Select Charters*, p. 495.

[2] Writs in *Parl. Writs*, I, p. 88 sq.

[3] The question of the deforestations was one of the principal

When parliament met, the king sent a "bill" (*billa*) to the prelates and magnates, requiring that they should take the reponsibility for the measures which they demanded and should assure him that by consenting to them he would not violate his coronation oath. Parliament replied in a "bill from the prelates and leaders of the realm delivered to the lord king on behalf of all the community[1]." In this document of twelve articles the "men of the community of his land" informed the king that they could not undertake the responsibility of which he had spoken. They demanded the confirmation and observance of the charters, a phrase which was soon to become almost a matter of form. After enumerating the various reforms which seemed to them urgent, they added:

On condition that all the aforesaid things shall be done and be firmly established and accomplished the people of the realm grant him the fifteenth in place of the twentieth recently granted, so that all the aforesaid things be done between now and Michaelmas next; and that otherwise nothing be levied.

The aid thus conditionally granted was to be assessed and collected in each county by four knights, elected "by common consent of the counties."

This petition might almost be considered the first real parliamentary *bill*. On this occasion also we find one of the first manifestations of political activity by

reasons that moved Edward I to ask Pope Clement V to quash the charters (see M. Petit Dutaillis's study on the forests in vol. II of his *Studies supplementary to Stubbs*, esp. p. 219–226). The deforestations were revoked by the Ordinance of the Forests of 1306 (*Statutes*, I, p. 147–149).

[1] *Billa prelatorum et procerum regni liberata domino Regi ex parte tocius communitatis* (*Parl. Writs*, I, p. 104–105). The negotiations were carried on through the mediacy of the chief justice, Roger Brabazon.

the deputies of the commons in parliament. The prelates and magnates made use of a skilful manœuvre in having the bill presented by a knight, Henry de Keighley, knight of the shire for Lancashire. In this way it was made impossible for the king to regard parliament's list of grievances as a mere declaration of baronial ill-will. He was forced to accept it as the expression of the unanimous wish of the nation.

The incident seemed to Edward I an outrage on the royal authority. At the end of each of the articles, except the last in which the papal claims with regard to taxes imposed on the church were admitted, he had to place his *Placet expresse*. But he was extremely irritated. Several months later he had Henry de Keighley imprisoned in the Tower[1]; and he never forgave the archbishop of Canterbury, Robert Winchelsey, whom he regarded as leader of the opposition.

On the 30th January the delegates of the counties and towns received the necessary writs for the recovery of their expenses[2]. The barons no doubt continued their session, for on the 12th February we find them addressing a letter to the pope in energetic defence of the king's rights over the kingdom of Scotland, which Boniface VIII claimed as a papal fief[3]. But a royal ordinance, inserted amongst the *placita* of this parliament, mentions neither the consent of the magnates nor that of the knights and burgesses. It is made "by the king's council...in the presence of the lord king, and

[1] Cf. Madox, *History and antiquities of the Exchequer*, p. 615. Edward I's letter is reproduced in Stubbs, *Const. Hist.* II, p. 158, n. 2. The king pardoned Keighley after he had taken a solemn engagement never again to oppose the royal authority.

[2] *Parl. Writs*, I, p. 101.

[3] *Ibid.* I, p. 102–103.

with the king's consent[1]." On the 14th February the king once more confirmed the charters.

Edward was short of money, for he had to borrow from the cities of Lincoln and London[2]. But he was obliged to wait till the end of the year to levy the fifteenth. The writs authorizing the assessment and collection of the tax by the four persons elected in each county did not appear till the 24th October 1301[3].

What had happened at Lincoln did not encourage the king to summon other parliaments. There seems to have been no parliament between January 1301 and July 1302; for certain matters, which at Lincoln had been referred to the next parliament, were not discussed till the parliament held at Westminster on the octave of St John Baptist (1st July) 1302[4]. This parliament at Westminster contained neither knights, nor burgesses, nor representatives of the inferior clergy. The writs are addressed to the archbishop of Canterbury and sixteen bishops, forty-four abbots, the three grandmasters, ten earls, eighty-three barons and thirty-four judges or officials. The archbishop of York is invited to come in person or send a proctor[5]. In this parliament nothing seems to have been done beyond the ordinary parliamentary business, the examination of petitions and the delivery of judicial decisions. Official documents nevertheless call it a full parliament[6].

The parliament summoned to London first for Michaelmas 1302 and then for St Edward's day (14th

---

[1] *Rot. Parl.* I, p. 145.
[2] *Parl. Writs*, I, p. 105, 106.
[3] *Ibid.* I, p. 105.
[4] *Rot. Parl.* I, p. 146.
[5] Writs of the 2nd June 1302 (*Parl. Writs*, I, p. 112 sq.).
[6] *Rot. Parl.* I, p. 146.

October[1]) comprised all the elements of a full parliament except the inferior clergy. The archbishop of Canterbury and fifteen bishops were summoned, forty-four abbots, the three grandmasters, ten earls, eighty barons, and the delegates of the counties and towns. A special summons was sent to the Cinq Ports and to Yarmouth, for these towns were embroiled with each other over matters that were to be examined in parliament. The writs for the recovery of the knights' and burgesses' expenses are dated the 21st October[2]; so their stay in London lasted a week.

As to what happened in this parliament, it is only possible to put forward conjectures. The *placita*[3] "before the king and his council," as usual, contain only the records of suits determined before the king. Did Edward demand an aid, which parliament refused to grant or to which parliament attached conditions that the king did not feel justified in accepting? Anyhow, on the 7th November 1302[4] an order was issued to collect the aid "*pour fille marier*," which had been granted in 1290 and which the king, so he said, had hitherto refrained from demanding "in order to relieve the community." In this writ there was naturally no mention of the conditions laid down by the parliament of 1290[5].

It seems that no parliaments were assembled nor aids granted in 1303[6] and 1304. The king lived on his ordinary

[1] Writs of the 20th, 24th and 26th July (*Parl. Writs*, I, p. 114–115); prorogation on the 13th September (*Parl. Writs*, I, p. 116–117).

[2] *Parl. Writs*, I, p. 131.   [3] *Rot. Parl.* I, p. 150 sq.

[4] *Rot. Parl.* I, p. 266; *Parl. Writs*, I, p. 132.

[5] See above, p. 91.

[6] An assembly met at Odiham at the beginning of January 1303; and perhaps the council met at the usual times to deal "in parliament" with current affairs.

revenues, which he supplemented by all kinds of expe-
dients. To foreign merchants he granted a charter which
permitted him considerably to increase the duties that
he levied on their merchandise[1]. Then, on the ground
that a number of English merchants were demanding
the enjoyment of the same privileges on condition of
paying the same taxes, he assembled the representatives
of the principal towns (forty-two towns were summoned)
at York on the 25th June 1303, hoping to make them
agree to the *maltote* granted by the foreigners[2]. According to a document preserved among the archives
of London, they unanimously refused[3]. The king was
reduced to collecting a scutage[4], and then to tallaging
the demesne. On the 6th February 1304 three persons
were nominated "to assess our tallage in our cities,
boroughs and demesnes in the counties of Kent, Middlesex, London, Surrey and Sussex, separately by heads or
in common" as it should seem to them more profitable[5].
Similar nominations were made for the other counties.
The amount was a sixth. In the parliament of February
of the succeeding year the king authorized the magnates
similarly to tallage the portions of the ancient demesne
of the crown that were in their possession[6].

[1] The *Carta Mercatoria* is given in H. Hall, *History of the
Customs Revenue*, I, p. 202 sq. It was declared illegal in 1311 and
suppressed, but restored later. Cf. Stubbs, *Const. Hist.* II, p. 553.

[2] See Appendix III, note K.

[3] *Parl. Writs*, I, p. 134–135. Stubbs, *Select Charters*, p. 496.

[4] Madox, *Exchequer*, p. 449, n. *s*, gives an order of the 16th
April 1306 for the collection of the scutage of 1303; this collection
had not been completed in 1315 (*Parl. Writs*, II, ii, p. 434 sq.).

[5] *Rot. Parl.* I, p. 266. Stubbs, *Select Charters*, p. 497.

[6] *Rot. Parl.* p. 161; *Memoranda de Parliamento*, ed. Maitland,
p. 54. As Maitland observes, the authorization only affected the
ancient royal demesne, since the magnates needed no authorization
with regard to the rest of their estates.

This parliament of February 1305 was the first, since that of March 1300, to be formed on the model of 1295. It contained the archbishops and bishops, abbots (75), the grandmasters of the three orders, the proctors of the clergy, earls (9), barons (94), representatives of the counties and towns, and thirty-two judges or officials[1]. The date of assembly at Westminster, originally fixed for the 16th February, was postponed to the Sunday after St Matthias's day (28th February)[2]. The writs of summons declared that parliament would discuss "certain matters specially touching our realm of England and the settlement of our land of Scotland, and also divers other matters."

The rolls of this parliament are a little more complete than most. They have been published in the *Rotuli Parliamentorum* (I, p. 159 sq.) and Maitland has edited them more completely and critically in the Rolls Series. They provide sufficient detail for us to see the procedure for collecting and trying the petitions, the examination of which formed one of the chief activities of the king's council. But the conclusions to be drawn from this document with regard to the part played by the deputies of the commons are chiefly negative. They may have taken part in the discussion on the so-called statute of Carlisle, which was promulgated later in the parliament of January 1307; for the preamble of the statute informs us that it was drawn up in the parliament assembled on the Sunday after St Matthias's day in the thirty-third year of King Edward's reign, "on the advice of the earls, barons, magnates, leaders (*proceres*) and other

[1] Writs of the 12th November 1304 (*Parl. Writs*, I, p. 136 sq.).
[2] Writs of the 22nd January 1305 (*Parl. Writs*, I, p. 138 sq.).

nobles and the communities of the realm[1]." Anyhow, on the 21st March, before the discussion on Scottish affairs, a royal proclamation permitted the archbishops, bishops and other prelates, the earls and barons, the knights of the shires, the citizens and burgesses "*et autres gentz de la comune qe cy sont venuz al maundement nostre signeur le roy a cest parlement*[2]" to return to their districts, except for those bishops, earls, barons and judges who were of the king's council. They were to reassemble without delay when their presence was again demanded. The knights and burgesses could obtain writs for the payment of their expenses[3]. There is no reason to suppose that these orders were not carried out. Yet the parliament continued in session, and when the bishop of Byblos presented himself with a letter from the pope on the 5th April, he was received by the king in the archbishop of York's palace, "a general parliament being then assembled" (*generali parliamento tunc existente*)[4].

At the parliament of February 1305 it had been decided that a parliament should meet in London on the

[1] *Statutes of the Realm*, I, p. 151. As we shall see later (p. 205), the earls, the barons and the community of the realm did present two petitions in this parliament of 1305 with regard to the tallage of English religious by foreign superiors. The king replied that on the subject in question he had made a statute, *in forma quae sequitur*. But the promulgation of the statute was postponed to a later date (cf. *Memoranda*, No. 486).

[2] The meaning of the words "*et autres gentz de la comune*" is most obscure; but they seem to prove that the king had again summoned persons other than the knights and burgesses, and they show that the composition of parliament was not controlled by strict rules.

[3] *Parl. Writs*, I, p. 155; *Memoranda*, ed. Maitland, p. 4. The writs for the payment of expenses (*Parl. Writs*, I, p. 156) are dated the previous day, the 20th March.

[4] *Memoranda*, ed. Maitland, p. 297.

15th July (three weeks after St John Baptist's day), to which Scotland was to send ten representatives—two bishops, two abbots, two earls, two barons and two "for the community[1]." This parliament was first prorogued to the Assumption, and then to the octave of the Nativity of Our Lady (15th September). The writs of summons were addressed to only thirty-seven persons, all of whom, it appears, were of the king's council[2]: the archbishop of Canterbury, five bishops, two abbots, a Dominican, the prince of Wales, five earls, eight barons, and several judges and officials of England and Scotland. Of the ten delegates to be sent "on the part of the commonalty of the land of Scotland" only nine came; and the king chose the tenth. An important ordinance was made for the organization of Scotland, of which Edward had definitely taken possession[3]. Also at this parliament the ordinance *De conspiratoribus* was made "by the king and his council[4]."

In 1306 followed an assembly of so peculiar a character, that we might refuse it the title of a parliament, if we did not know that the word did not then carry the precise meaning which it later acquired and that gatherings of very varying composition were described as parliaments. On the 5th April 1306 the king informed the archbishop of York, fourteen bishops, fifteen abbots, four abbesses, seven earls and sixty-three barons that he had decided to proceed to the knighting of his son on Whitsunday, "wherefore, according to the rights of our crown, an aid should be given to us on such an occasion." He therefore summoned them to appear

[1] *Memoranda de Parliamento*, p. 15. See Appendix III, note L.
[2] *Parl. Writs*, I, p. 158 sq.
[3] *Rot. Parl.* I, p. 266–267; *Parl. Writs*, I, p. 160.
[4] *Statutes of the Realm*, I, p. 145.

before himself and his council on the morrow of Trinity
Sunday (30th May) in order to "discuss and ordain
with the prelates, magnates and leaders (*proceres*) of our
realm with regard to the aid which should be given us
on the aforesaid occasion and to consent to what shall
be ordained on this matter." The persons thus summoned might send proctors or *attornati*. The inferior
clergy were not summoned[1].

But Edward did not confine himself to summoning
his tenants-in-chief, as was usual on such occasions.
On the same day a writ conceived in similar terms
ordered the sheriffs to provide for the election of two
knights from each shire, two citizens from each city and
two burgesses from each borough, or one only if the
borough were small. At the same time the sheriffs were
bidden to remind the archbishops, bishops, abbots,
priors and other clerics that they were to appear in
person or send proctors[2].

The session was short. The writs for the recovery of
the knights' and burgesses' expenses are dated the 30th
May, the very day fixed for the opening of the assembly[3].
From a letter patent of the king of the same date we
learn that the prelates, barons and knights had granted
a thirtieth of their movable goods, the burgesses of all
the towns and the inhabitants of the demesne a twentieth
"on account of the aid that is due to us for the knighting
of Edward, our eldest son[4]." The collectors of the aid
were nominated by letters of the 22nd July 1306, to
which was added an instruction (*forma taxacionis*)

---

[1] *Parl. Writs*, I, p. 164–165.
[2] *Ibid.* I, p. 164.
[3] *Ibid.* I, p. 177–178.
[4] *Rot. Parl.* I, p. 270.

stating that the aid was to be levied on the goods of the clergy as on those of the laity[1].

The last great parliament of Edward's reign was summoned on the 3rd November 1306 to meet at Carlisle on the octave of St Hilary (20th January 1307). Like that of 1295, it contained representatives of the inferior clergy, knights and burgesses. Writs of summons were addressed to the prince of Wales, eleven earls and eighty-six barons, the archbishop of York, the bishops, forty-eight abbots, and fifteen judges and members of the council[2]. A large number of bishops, abbots and priors sent proctors to represent them. The abbot of Combe sent no proctor, but declared by letter patent that he accepted in advance all that the king in his parliament might decide[3].

The writs for the payment of the knights' and burgesses' expenses (twenty-six counties and nineteen towns) are dated the 20th January 1307, the day fixed for assembling. But a note adds that "the aforesaid knights, because of the long stay which they made at the said parliament by order of the king," received later other writs wherein the king ordained that regard should be had to the distance they had come and the length of their stay, which had been extended from the octave

---

[1] *Rot. Parl.* I, p. 269; *Parl. Writs*, I, p. 178–179. For reasons unknown to us, the writ for the collection of the aid in Staffordshire was not issued till the 10th November 1306 (*Rot. Parl.* I, p. 269).

[2] *Parl. Writs*, I, p. 182 sq. A writ of the 22nd February 1307 (*ibid.* p. 192), addressed to twenty-seven earls and barons, says that they had been summoned for the octave of St Hilary, but, since the cardinal sent from Rome had not arrived and could not be at Carlisle before the Sunday after mid-Lent (12th March), they were to present themselves on the latter date, under pain of forfeiture. According to the writs for the payment of expenses, the knights remained at Carlisle to be present at this assembly.

[3] *Ibid.* I, p. 185.

of St Hilary to Palm Sunday (19th March)[1]. In these second writs there is no reference to the deputies of the towns.

In the absence of the king, parliament was opened by the treasurer, Walter de Langton, bishop of Coventry, and Henry de Lacy, earl of Lincoln. The chief topic for discussion was the situation created in the church of England by the exactions of the pope and the foreign superiors of religious orders. The earls, barons and "all the community of the land" presented petitions on the subject[2]. Amongst the petitions is an unsigned letter, addressed to the pope, expressing the same complaints in the name of clergy and people[3]. The statute *De asportatis religiosorum* or statute of Carlisle, to which the "earls, barons, magnates, leaders and other nobles and the communities of the realm" had agreed in 1305, was promulgated "after full deliberation and discussion[4]." Its object was to forbid English religious to pay taxes imposed by foreign superiors of their orders and in general to prevent the payment of imposts intended for remittance out of the kingdom. The king temporarily suspended the operation of the statute, no doubt in order to avoid an open conflict with the papacy, and the question was again discussed in a small parliament held at Westminster on Trinity Sunday (21st May)[5].

No decision had been reached when, on the 7th July 1307, Edward died, just as he had assumed the command of another expedition against the Scots.

---

[1] *Parl. Writs*, I, p. 190–191. The second writ is dated in error the 10th March, instead of the 20th.
[2] *Rot. Parl.* I, p. 219.   [3] *Ibid.* p. 207.
[4] *Statutes of the Realm*, I, p. 152. Stubbs, *Select Charters*, p. 438.
[5] Cf. *Rot. Parl.* I, p. 222–223. The papal legate appeared before the king's council.

CHAPTER IV

THE COMPOSITION OF PARLIAMENT UNDER EDWARD I

THE chronological summary that we have given shows clearly that the composition of parliament under Edward I was by no means fixed. At the beginning of his reign, in April 1275, he summoned a parliament, which, but for the absence of representatives of the inferior clergy, was in every way similar to the "model" parliament of 1295. A few months later (October 1275) he summoned the representatives of the counties, but not those of the towns. In January 1283 both the knights and the burgesses were present; but parliament was divided into two assemblies, corresponding to the two ecclesiastical provinces. In October 1283 the knights were summoned; but only some of the greater towns were called upon to send delegates to parliament. In 1290 and 1294 the knights came to parliament, while the burgesses were not summoned. The documents do not enable us to say with certainty whether representatives of the commons were present at any other parliament of this first period of the reign. Indeed often parliament seems to have been composed only of those who were members of the king's ordinary council.

Nor was the parliament of 1295 the model for all the parliaments that succeeded it. Only in 1296, 1300, 1305 and 1307 was the composition of parliament, as summoned by the king, exactly the same as in 1295. The parliaments of 1298, 1301 and 1306 contained

representatives of the counties and towns, but those of
the inferior clergy did not attend. There were knights
at the parliament of 1297, but the towns and the inferior
clergy were not represented. All the other parliaments
towards the end of the reign were composed, in accordance with old custom, only of the king's council, sometimes enlarged by the presence of prelates, barons and
other persons whom the king saw fit to summon. We
have seen that the delegates of the communities did not
appear in any one of the four parliaments of 1299.
Thus, in the later part of his reign, as in the earlier,
Edward I modified the composition of his parliaments
according to his needs and the circumstances of the
moment.

The diversity of the assemblies which are described,
whether in official documents or in chronicles, as parliaments, is extraordinary. The assemblies of 1295 and 1305
were parliaments. Yet in the margin of the roll the
chancery clerks wrote the formula "to hold a parliament" (*de parliamento tenendo*) with reference to such
assemblies as that of February 1297, at which only
temporal lords were present, without either clergy or
commoners; or that of October 1297, attended only by
prelates, barons and knights; or that of March 1299,
at which there were only prelates and barons; or that
of a fortnight after Easter 1299, to which were summoned only barons and the higher clergy of the province
of Canterbury; or that of October 1299, to which only
a very small number of prelates and barons were summoned. The assembly of July 1302, which contained
only prelates and barons, is described in the *placita* of
the session as a "full parliament[1]."

[1] *Rot. Parl.* I, p. 146.

The number of persons summoned by the king varies enormously. The maximum is reached in the great assemblies, like that of 1305, at which, if no one failed to attend, the total membership of the parliament must have exceeded 600[1]. The minimum is supplied by the parliament of October 1299, when the archbishop of Canterbury and thirteen other persons were summoned to the New Temple, there to deliberate and give counsel on urgent matters with other faithful servants of the king[2]. The earls and barons numbered 49 in the first summons to the great parliament of 1295, 46 in the second. They were 43 at the great parliament of 1296, 81 at the parliament of barons held at Salisbury in 1297, 110 at the first parliament of 1299, 57 at the second, 9 at the third, 110 at the great parliament of 1300, 89 at the great parliament at Lincoln in 1301, 93 at the parliament of St John Baptist's day 1302, 90 at the great parliament of St Edward's day 1302, 103 at the great parliament of 1305, 13 at the parliament of September 1305, 70 at the parliament of 1306, 97 at the great parliament of 1307.

Counting only the parliaments at which delegates of the commons were present and omitting the exceptional parliament of 1306, the number of abbots varies between a maximum of 80 in 1301 and a minimum of 48 in 1307. The number of judges and royal officials summoned to parliament also varies considerably; and we shall see later that not all the towns summoned for one parliament were necessarily summoned for the next.

The two parliaments of 1305 are characteristic examples of this diversity. The first was a very large

[1] *Memoranda de Parliamento*, ed. Maitland (Rolls S.), p. xxxv.
[2] *Parl. Writs*, I, p. 81.

assembly containing representatives of the inferior clergy, the counties and the towns, as well as a considerable number of prelates and barons. To the second, at which the great ordinance on Scottish affairs was approved, only 37 persons were summoned. The name of parliament cannot be refused to this little assembly, for it is so described not only in the marginal note, but also in the writ of summons itself. The parliament was originally to have been held on St John Baptist's day; but the persons summoned were informed by two successive writs that the king had prorogued it, first to the Assumption, and then to the octave of the Nativity of Our Lady, and they were required to be present on the date fixed, to join the other members of the council in discussing those questions on account of which the holding of parliament had been ordered. The text of the second writ shows clearly that all who were thus summoned were of the king's council[1].

We have seen that the great parliament of 1305 only lasted, at full strength, from the 28th February till the 21st March, when a royal proclamation permitted all who were not members of the king's council to return to their localities. We have also seen that the parliament did not cease to exist from that date. Despite the departure of the knights and burgesses, of the inferior clergy and even of most of the prelates and barons, the parliament continued to sit at least till the 7th April, as a "full parliament." It was before a "full parliament" that Nicholas de Segrave was tried for having left the army in Scotland without the king's leave. He appeared

---

[1] *Nobiscum ac cum ceteris de consilio nostro tunc venturis ibidem super negociis pro quibus parliamentum nostrum ibidem in dicto festo Assumpcionis tenendum prius ordinavimus... tractaturi* (*Parl. Writs*, I, p. 159).

"in full parliament, in the presence of the lord king in person, the archbishop of Canterbury and several bishops, earls, barons and others of the king's council who were present[1]." When the bishop of Byblos was received by the king on the 5th April "in the presence of the bishops and other prelates, the earls, barons, judges and other nobles, clerks and laymen, councillors of the magnificent prince Edward I," the record of the session adds that "a general parliament was then assembled." On the 6th April the king in "full parliament" forbade the chancellor to issue royal letters of protection for Ireland. On the 7th certain persons came "before the king's council in this parliament" to provide surety for the new sheriff of Northumberland[2].

We are therefore forced to conclude that, even after 1295, the essential part of Edward I's parliaments consisted of the king and his council.

We need not enter into the very obscure question of the origins of the king's council and its various transformations. It will be enough to recall that in Edward I's time it generally contained several great spiritual and temporal tenants-in-chief, the principal judges, the chief officials, and in short whomever the king saw fit to summon. The total number of those who formed part

---

[1] *Memoranda de Parliamento*, ed. Maitland, p. 255. The lay members of the council (the clergy do not seem to have been consulted) declared that Segrave had incurred the death penalty. The king remitted the sentence on condition that Segrave should find seven persons willing to stand surety for him. On the 29th March seven persons declared by letters patent that they had undertaken this obligation, *coram ipso domino Rege et consilio suo* (*ibid.* pp. 258–260).

[2] *Ibid.* pp. 293, 296, 297. The meaning of the phrases, *in pleno parliamento*, *en plein parlement*, is by no means clear. Professor Pollard (*Evolution of Parliament*, p. 33) interprets it as "in open session."

of the council was probably considerable—about sixty perhaps—but the king did not necessarily assemble them all whenever he wished to consult his council. Most of the councillors were royal officials[1].

From time to time the council had plenary sessions, which often coincided with the four judicial terms of the year: St Hilary (January), Easter, Trinity and Michaelmas. Councils or parliaments—it is difficult to distinguish them from each other—were often summoned for the octave of St Hilary or for Candlemas, after Easter, for Trinity Sunday or St John Baptist's day, for Michaelmas or All Saints' day. In these assemblies the king received his subjects' petitions and examined them or had them examined. We find him taking

---

[1] We have no complete list of the members of the council in Edward I's reign. The council, before which Llewellyn was sentenced for contumacy on the 12th November 1276, contained the archbishop of Canterbury, six bishops, four abbots, the prior of the Hospitallers, nine earls, seventeen other persons described by name "and the other lords of the king's council, the judges and other faithful servants of the king" (*Parl. Writs*, I, p. 5). Among the *placita coram rege* of the octave of Michaelmas of the same year there is a sentence given upon the earl of Gloucester, *in pleno consilio regis*, in the presence of the archbishop of Canterbury, five bishops, three earls and thirty other persons, including the Bolognese legist Francesco Accursi (*ibid*. I, p. 6). The council, before which the bishop of Byblos appeared on the 5th April 1305, comprised the treasurer, two bishops, three earls, twenty-four persons described as "knights" (ten of whom had been summoned as barons and eight as councillors), three clerks and three "discreet persons," namely the master of the wardrobe and two royal secretaries (*Memoranda de Parliamento*, ed. Maitland, p. 299–300). Maitland tried to reconstruct the list of the members of the council in 1305 by using the lists of persons summoned to parliament, the parliament rolls and the charters granted during parliament's session and attested by persons in attendance on the king. By these means he arrived at a total of 70 (*ibid*. p. cvi sq.). This figure, we believe, may be taken as a maximum. We have no proof that all those who attested charters or even all those who were present at the council were sworn councillors.

measures to have the petitions classified and to have them referred either to the judges who were members of the council, or to the barons of the exchequer, or to special commissions; so that only the most important were reserved for the personal inspection of the king. In these assemblies also were tried those suits *coram rege et consilio*, the records of which, together with the texts of petitions and their answers, fills the greater part of the parliament rolls of Edward I. In them also the king, either "by his council" or even by his sovereign authority without mention of the council, promulgated legislative measures which seem to have had the same validity as the statutes promulgated "in full parliament." Indeed many such measures are included in the collection of Statutes of the Realm.

Such assemblies formed the high court of parliament and entirely correspond with the well-known and contemporary statement of *Fleta*, "The king has his court in his council, in his parliaments, in the presence of the prelates, earls, barons, lords and others learned in the law, where doubts with regard to sentences are determined, where new remedies are provided for new injuries that have occurred, and where justice is meted out to each according to his deserts[1]."

Edward I's council is, then, in itself a parliament[2].

---

[1] "*Habet enim Rex cur[iam] suam in concilio suo, in Parliamentis suis, praesentibus praelatis, com[itibus], baron[ibus], proceribus, et aliis viris* (or *iuris*, see Maitland, *Memoranda*, Introd. p. lxxxi) *peritis, ubi terminatae sunt dubitationes judiciorum, et novis injuriis emersis nova constituuntur remedia, et unicuique justitia, prout meruit, retribuetur ibidem*" (*Fleta*, Lib. II, cap. 2, sec. 1).

[2] Since the publication of the French edition of this essay, Professor A. F. Pollard (*The Evolution of Parliament*, p. 47–58) has clearly brought out the importance of the council under Edward I and shown "that a session of the king's council is at first not merely, as Maitland has said, the core of every parliament, but the whole

To this small parliament the king, when he sees fit, adds a more or less considerable number of his tenants-parliament" (p. 33). But he goes further. He observes that, if the occasional meetings of tenants-in-chief are called parliaments by the chroniclers, they are not described by that name in the writs of summons before 1300; that the prelates, barons, knights and burgesses "are summoned to a *colloquium* or a *tractatum*, but not to parliament"; that the business of these assemblies is not recorded in the *Rotuli parliamentorum*, which contain only the petitions and pleas heard by the king and his council in parliament; that the sessions of the great assemblies summoned by royal writs do not, before 1298, coincide with the sessions described as parliaments in the rolls. He concludes (p. 47) that "the gatherings convoked by these so-called 'parliamentary' writs were not parliaments; and the meetings called parliaments in the rolls were not summoned by the writs to which the name has since been given."

This somewhat paradoxical conclusion provokes criticism. That assemblies composed exclusively of the king and his council were indeed parliaments is indisputable. But it does not follow that the great assemblies were not parliaments because their writs had the word *colloquium* instead of *parliamentum*. Further, contrary to Professor Pollard's opinion, the clerks of the chancery did use the word *parliamentum*, not only in their marginal notes (see above, p. 127), but also in the writs themselves long before 1300. When the king informs the sheriffs, in the writs of the 26th December 1274, that he has prorogued the *generale parliamentum* to the morrow of the octave of Easter and orders them to provide for the arrival of knights and burgesses on that date *ad tractandum una cum magnatibus regni nostri de negociis ejusdem regni*, it cannot be denied that these representatives were summoned to a parliament. Similarly, in the summons of the 1st September 1275 the king recalls that he has required the magnates to be present "at our parliament that we shall hold...at Westminster fifteen days after Michaelmas," and orders the election of two knights, *cum...expediens sit quod duo milites de comitatu predicto...intersint eidem parliamento*. The assembly of the 1st August 1295, which contained no representatives of the commons but many barons and clergy, is also called a *parliamentum* in the writ of summons. This assembly coincided with a session of what Professor Pollard calls a "parliament of the rolls" (cf. *Rotuli*, I, p. 132 sq.), and there are other examples of such coincidence before 1298. The absence of all mention of the great assemblies in the *Rotuli parliamentorum* during a large part of Edward's reign is to be explained not only by the incomplete character of those records, but also in another way. There is no

in-chief and faithful servants, whom in the circumstances he considers it necessary to summon to suit of court. These consist of the bishops, or some of them, and a varying number of abbots, earls and barons. Sometimes, as at Salisbury in 1297, only laymen are summoned; sometimes, as in 1294, only ecclesiastics. It occasionally happens that he also summons representatives of the inferior clergy.

During the earlier part of his reign, he sometimes summons knights representing the communities of the counties (1275, 1283, 1290, 1294); while in 1275 and 1283 he similarly calls up representatives of the towns. From 1295 knights and burgesses are usually summoned at the same time; yet only the knights come to the parliament of October 1297, while only the delegates of the greater towns are summoned to the assembly of 1303, at which the king wishes to secure consent to the augmentation of the customs.

At first these new-comers are sometimes summoned, like the prelates and barons, "to give counsel" (*ad*

doubt that the chief function of the king "in his council, in his parliaments" was to administer justice by means of judgements given in particular cases or by ordinances and more general statutes. It was essential to keep a record of such procedure, of which litigants might demand extracts. With regard to the great assemblies, on the contrary, there was usually little to record, except sometimes the result of the deliberations, *e.g.* a statute, such as the statute of Westminster the first, which the king made "*par son conseil e par le assentement des erceveskes, eveskes, abbes, priurs, contes, barons, et la communaute de la tere ileokes somons*" (Stubbs, *Select Charters*, p. 442), or a writ for the collection of a fifteenth or twentieth that had been granted. When the deliberations had produced no practical result or when they bore on questions of a non-legal character, such as foreign affairs, the chancery clerks had nothing to record and therefore recorded nothing. Thus it happens that we only know of a parliament, whose deliberations were of such a kind, from the writs of summons and the descriptions of chroniclers. But it was none the less a parliament.

consulendum, consilium impensuri); but the formula is soon changed and they are only summoned "to consent to" and "to do" what shall be decided by common accord. It may well be that the earlier formula was nothing but a form of words copied from the writs of summons of the magnates and having no precise meaning. It is doubtful if the delegates of the counties and boroughs were really called upon to "give counsel." We know that the house of commons has never shared the judicial powers of the early *curia*, the council, the great council and the house of lords[1]. The fact is of the utmost importance with regard to the original position of the knights and burgesses in parliament. We know also that in legislation the house of commons does not intervene to counsel the king, but acts indirectly by way of petition. Everything goes to prove that at the end of the thirteenth century the knights and burgesses are *before the council*, in the capacity of assessors and petitioners, but that, unlike the prelates and barons, they are not truly *councillors*.

For the knights and burgesses the expressions "to come before the king and his council," "to come before the council," are synonymous with "to come to parliament." In 1294 the writs that order the election of knights have in the margin of the roll "On behalf of the king, concerning the election of knights and sending them to the council[2]." In 1295 the sheriff of Lincoln-

---

[1] The house of commons has rather the character of the grand jury of the nation, as Professor Pollard points out (*Evolution of Parliament*, p. 79, 112). In this connection he quotes the words of Prynne, who speaks of the commons as being "informers, prosecutors, grand jurymen." This conception is found in the procedure for impeachment.

[2] *Pro rege, de militibus eligendis et mittendis ad concilium* (*Parl. Writs*, I, p. 26).

shire, after giving the names of the knights and burgesses whose election he has superintended, adds that they have full powers "to do before the king and his council what this writ demands[1]." Similarly in 1305 the sheriff of Middlesex communicates the names of two knights who have been elected by the consent of the whole county "to be before the king and his council at the time and place mentioned in the writ[2]." In this same year 1305 the list of knights and burgesses, who received writs for the payment of their expenses, has upon it the following official minute: "These were summoned before the council and came. They may therefore have writs for their expenses...[3]." We have already encountered similar formulae earlier, in 1254 and 1265.

The position of the representatives of the counties and towns was, therefore, quite different from that of the prelates and barons. But at that period and in parliaments of such varying composition there could be no question of a regular division into two houses, such as subsequently obtained. Parliament under Edward I was essentially a single whole, even though its component groups might on occasion hold separate meetings. In ordinary parliaments the prelates and barons probably deliberated together, except perhaps on matters specially concerning one or the other order. In the great parliaments, which Stubbs calls "parliaments of estates" and which indeed in some respects resemble the estates general of Philippe le Bel, the division into

---

[1] *Ad faciendum coram domino rege et ejus consilio quod hoc breve requirit* (*Parl. Writs*, I, p. 39).

[2] *Essendi coram domino rege et ejus consilio ad diem et locum in brevi contentum* (*ibid.* I, p. 147).

[3] *Isti fuerunt vocati coram consilio et venerunt. Ideo habeant brevia pro expensis suis...* (*ibid.* I, p. 158).

clergy, nobility and third estate seemed the most natural and might have been established in the end, had not the clergy abandoned parliament, where they sat with laymen, and retired to their own convocations. But in Edward I's reign the distinction between the three orders was far from being clear cut, as it was in France[1]. The bishops and abbots were barons, bound, like the lay barons, to furnish their contingent of knights when the king summoned the feudal host. If they met the inferior clergy in provincial synods, in the ordinary parliaments they constantly sat with the barons. On the other hand, the knights of the shires did not belong to the third estate, and everything goes to show that at this time they considered themselves to be part of the baronage.

Thus a great parliament, like those of 1295 and 1305, was formed of five different groups, in addition to the council: the dignified clergy (bishops and abbots), the earls and barons, the inferior clergy, the knights of the shires, and the citizens and burgesses of the towns[2]. The members of the first two groups were directly summoned by royal writ addressed to each of them personally; while the other three groups were indirectly summoned, the inferior clergy through their bishops, the knights and burgesses through the sheriffs. The knights, the burgesses and a portion of the inferior clergy were elected, and represented the community of a county, the community of a town or the parochial clergy of a diocese. In the midst of these five groups

[1] See Pollard, *Evolution of Parliament*, p. 61 sq., "The myth of the three estates."
[2] This is the division indicated by the author of the *Modus tenendi parliamentum* (Stubbs, *Select Charters*, p. 503), who differentiates six *gradus parium*, one of which is the king.

the judges and officials, who formed the permanent part of the king's council, appear to have guided the activities of parliament.

The clergy had their peculiar interests. They were subject not only to the king, but also to the pope. They owed obedience not only to the law of England but also to that of the church. When they were faced with the need for granting a collective aid or making a collective decision, they no doubt deliberated apart. Bartholomew Cotton represents them as acting thus at the parliament at Bury St Edmund's in 1296 in the anxious days when they were trying to reconcile the papal orders given in *Clericis laicos* with the fears inspired in them by the king. The chronicler even appears to say that in their parliamentary sessions the clergy adopted that division into four sections (bishops, abbots and religious, canons and other dignitaries, delegates of the parochial clergy) which we find in their synods[1]. The distinction between the clergy, as an order, and the rest of parliament is clear cut. It has been pointed out that the writs to the sheriffs for the election of knights and burgesses mention the presence of the earls and barons, but not of the clergy, at an approaching parliament. The conclusion has sometimes been drawn that Edward I thought of forming two assemblies, one ecclesiastical and the other lay.

But the bishops and abbots were, as we have said above, barons as well as clergy. They received or might receive personal summons to parliament, even when the other clergy were not convoked. We see them regularly granting the king the same aid as do the barons. With the baronage they henceforth formed another sub-

[1] Cotton, *Hist. Angl.* p. 314–315. Cf. *Ann. Dunstable*, p. 405.

division of parliament, the germ of the later house of lords. The distinctive mark of this group of prelates and barons was that all its members were individually summoned by the king[1], a right accorded by Magna Carta to the great barons (*majores barones*). This individual summons became the test of nobility amongst the barons, and those not thus summoned, whatever their birth, sank *ipso facto* into the ranks of the *commun*[2].

⁎⁎

There remain the knights and burgesses to whom we must pay peculiar attention, since the house of commons is the later outcome of their assemblies. Despite striking differences the two groups have certain similarities. Both consist of elected representatives. As we have seen, it is arguable that there was no actual election of the representatives to attend certain assemblies before 1265 or the assembly of 1265 itself. Their election in Edward I's reign is undoubted.

We know little about the method of election of the knights. The writ of summons to the parliament of October 1275 expressly orders the sheriff to provide for their election "in full county court with the assent

---

[1] Irregular summons addressed only indirectly to the bishops through the archbishops aroused protests in 1282.

[2] We need not investigate the principle on which the king selected the barons whom he summoned to his parliaments. Originally all who held their lands of the king *per baroniam* may have had the right—or rather the duty—of coming to the king's court. But none did suit of court without being summoned, and at any rate by the end of the thirteenth century the king only summoned the barons whose presence he considered necessary. The idea of a hereditary peerage was certainly quite unknown at that time and remained so till a much later period. (Cf. Pollard, *Evolution of Parliament*, p. 81 sq., "The fiction of the peerage.")

of the said county[1]." Later the formulae vary and are less explicit, but the elections continued to take place in the same way; the sheriffs' returns are the proof. The knights are elected "by the whole community of the county" (Gloucestershire, 1290), "in full county court" (Oxfordshire and Berkshire, 1290), "in full county court by the assent of all the county" (Lincolnshire, 1290), "by the consent of all the county" (Lancashire, 1295), "in full county courts of Somersetshire and Dorsetshire by the community of the said counties" (1295)[2]; and similar formulae are constantly used in connection with subsequent parliaments. Nothing lends support to the now discredited theory[3] that the right to elect was confined to the tenants-in-chief of the king and that the knights represented only those lesser vassals of the crown who, by article 14 of the Great Charter, were to have been summoned to the great council by the sheriffs whenever the king demanded an aid from his vassals. Moreover, such a restriction would have been, as we shall see later, entirely contrary to the policy followed by Edward I.

However, if it is clear that the knights were elected by the county court, the composition of the county court which elected the knights towards the close of the thirteenth century is most uncertain. It would be most rash to offer a solution of this problem. Only detailed research in the local records of England, when those records are better known and better classified, will be able to throw some light on the matter. We will

---

[1] *In pleno comitatu tuo de assensu ejusdem comitatus eligi facias dictos duos milites*. The word *comitatus* can be used both for the county and the county court.   [2] *Parl. Writs*, I, p. 22, 23, 38, 41.

[3] This theory seems to have been that of the authors of the *Reports on the Dignity of a Peer* (cf. I, p. 188).

therefore confine ourselves to a statement of essential facts in so far as they affect our subject. The instructions given to sheriffs on the occasion of a visit to their counties by the itinerant justices tell us what the composition of the county court was in theory. The sheriff was to summon all the archbishops, bishops, abbots, earls, barons, knights and freeholders of the county, the reeve and four lawful men from each vill, and twelve burgesses from each borough[1]. But clearly such a gathering was exceptional. A county court of these dimensions could not be assembled every month, in accordance with article 35 of the Great Charter of 1225[2]. Also the statute of Merton (1236) allowed every freeman owing suit to the county court to empower an *attornatus* to represent him in his absence[3]. Magnates were represented by their stewards (*senescalli*), and in many localities it became customary to grant land on condition that the grantee did suit of county court in place of the individual or community making the grant. Maitland's researches in the *Rotuli Hundredorum*[4], which contain

[1] See above, p. 15.
[2] Article 35 of the Great Charter of 1217 and 1225 (Bémont, *Chartes des libertés anglaises*, p. 57): *Nullus comitatus decetero teneatur, nisi de mense in mensem; et, ubi major terminus esse solebat, major sit.* The documents published by C. Gross, *Select cases from the coroners' rolls* (Selden Soc. 1896), show that the court did indeed meet every month or every four weeks. An action in 1226 (*Bracton's Note Book*, ed. Maitland, No. 1730) shows that at that time the county court of Lincolnshire only met every forty days.
[3] *Statutes of the Realm*, I, p. 4. The authenticity of this article, which is mentioned neither in the writs addressed to the sheriffs (*Statutes of the Realm, ibid.*) nor in the accounts of Matthew Paris and the *Annals of Burton*, is not unassailable. But of the custom there is no doubt.
[4] *English Historical Review*, 1888, p. 417–421, The suitors of the county court (reprinted in Maitland's *Collected Papers*, I, 1911). See also Pollock and Maitland, *History of English Law*, I, p. 522 sq.

the results of the great inquest ordered by Edward I at the opening of his reign, brought to light a large number of instances in which the service owed by an individual, a borough, a hundred, a vill, was performed by one whom the records describe as an *attornatus feoffatus*. The obligation to "follow" the county court on behalf of the grantor of a fief might even be divided amongst several persons, each of whom attended a certain number of meetings of the court in the course of a year.

To attend the county court, then, was not a privilege, but an obligation, to be avoided if possible. The *Calendar of charter rolls*[1] show a large number of charters in which exemption from the county court is conspicuous among the advantages accorded to towns or individuals.

Despite the increasing subdivision of fiefs, the number of those who attended the county court does not seem to have risen. Indeed the number of suits owed by a fief seems to have been held to be fixed and unalterable, even if the original fief should become divided between several persons. Thus the number of suitors of the county court was likely to diminish. In 1258 the complaint is made that not enough knights attend for the dispatch of regular business[2]; and probably Maitland was right in thinking that at the end of the thirteenth

[1] See the words *county court* and *shire* in the Index. In 1258 one of the criticisms on Henry III's administration was that he had granted too many exemptions (cf. n. 2, below). And Henry III, in a letter of the 22nd June 1255, had himself ordered an inquest on those *qui sectas debent ad comitatus illos et ad curias nostras in eisdem comitatibus et qui subtraxerunt se ab hujusmodi sectis faciendis sine waranto* (in H. Cox, *Antient parliamentary elections*, p. 49, from Pat. 39 H. III, m. 9 d.; cf. *Calendar of patent rolls*, 1247–1258, p. 438).

[2] Article 28 of the Petition of the Barons of 1258 in *Ann. Burton*, p. 443 (Stubbs, *Select Charters*, p. 378).

century the county court was not a numerous body, at any rate at its ordinary sessions. All the freeholders of the county were doubtless convoked and had the right to attend; but they took care not to avail themselves of this "right," the exercise of which they would only have found vexatious. The number of suitors of the court must have been further reduced by the statute of the 13th December 1293, which was framed at the request of the common people (*mediocris populi*) and ordered the sheriffs to summon to juries, inquests and recognitions (except for the assizes and on certain other occasions) only those who had at least forty shillings of annual revenue from land[1].

Thus constituted, the county court acted in the name of the county, under the supervision of the sheriff. It judged suits; it answered for its decisions before the king's court; on the king's demand, it elected the persons to assess royal taxes and the coroners[2]. It also sent knights up to Westminster to appear before the king's judges or the council and to deal in the county's name with all sorts of matters judicial and administrative. There is nothing to show that the composition of the

[1] *Statutes*, I, p. 113; *Rot. Parl.* I, p. 117; Riess (*Geschichte des Wahlrechts zum englischen Parlament im Mittelalter* (1885), p. 47, 48), on the contrary, thinks that between 500 and 1000 persons attended. But the facts which he cites are not convincing, at any rate for our period. The only case that refers to our period is one of 1278 (*Parl. Writs*, I, p. 214). The sheriff of Northumberland assembles the county court after receipt of an order to make all those provide surety who have land of £20 annual value and ought to become knights. The prospective knights, with their sureties, number 149 persons. This, Riess suggests, leads us to suppose that the number of all present at the court was very large. But clearly the assembly in question was quite exceptional.

[2] According to C. Gross, *Select cases from the coroners' rolls*, p. xxxv, the method of election of coroners was the model for the parliamentary elections.

county court, when summoned to elect delegates to parliament, differed in any way from its ordinary composition. The majority of knights and freeholders, as we shall see, had no reason to take much interest in these elections. In 1297 the sheriff of Surrey and Sussex, referring to the elections for the parliament of Michaelmas, writes, "I assembled before me at Southwark the knights and freeholders of the county of Surrey, who elected...," and uses the same terms with regard to Sussex[1]. As we have said, a general summons was probably issued. But probably those, who owed suit of court in any case, formed the majority of those who answered the summons. In 1290 the sheriff of Lincolnshire, reporting the election of three knights "in full county court by the assent of all the county," adds that the third knight had not been present and that no one had been willing to act as surety for him, but that "the stewards and suitors of the court" (*senescalli et sectatores*) had refused to elect another and had given full powers to the first two knights to act for the county, should their colleague not appear[2]. On this occasion, therefore, the body of electors seems only to have included the agents of the magnates and those performing obligatory suit of court.

The composition of the body of electors may have varied according to circumstances. If the election coincided with an exceptional assembly, due to a visit of the royal justices, then the attendance would be more than usually large. On the other hand, the sheriff of Northumberland would be obliged to simplify the pro-

---

[1] *Venire feci coram me apud Suwerk milites et libere tenentes de comitatu Surrey qui elegerunt,... (Parl. Writs*, I, p. 60).

[2] *Parl. Writs*, I, p. 22.

cedure for election, if, as was the case in 1297, he had only eight days in which to convene the court, carry out the election and cause both the names of the elect and the elect themselves to reach Westminster[1].

The electoral franchise was so little valued at this time that there was no need to define it with precision. That was only done early in the fifteenth century, when the activities of the house of commons had already become extremely important[2]. A century earlier the electors avoided the exercise of their "right," in order to escape paying their share of the knights' expenses. The candidates do not seem to have been any more enthusiastic than their constituents. The sheriff had to make them provide surety or to take part of their possessions as security for their appearance. Under such conditions the influence of the sheriff and of a few magnates, who were either present in person or represented by their stewards, would be decisive; all the more since the election was presumably by acclamation and the names of the candidates were proposed by the sheriff[3]. It was the sheriff, too, who returned the names of the elect to the chancery. In 1319 we find a knight com-

[1] *Parl. Writs*, I, p. 60. The sheriff states that he received the writ on Saturday, the vigil of Michaelmas (28th September); and the knights were summoned to appear at Westminster on the 6th October.

[2] Statutes of 1406 and 1430. The latter statute (*Statutes*, II, p. 243) provides that henceforth the knights of the shires "*soient esluz en chescun counte par gentz demurantz et receantz en icelles, dount chescun ait frank tenement a le valu de xl s. par an al meins.*" Thus the obligation of suit of county court, imposed by the statute of 1293 on forty shilling freeholders, was transformed into a privilege.

[3] On this point see Riess, *Wahlrecht*, p. 51–52. The terms of the writ of summons (*de discrecioribus et ad laborandum potencioribus*) would authorize the sheriff to intervene in the choice of candidates.

L

plaining that, although he had been nominated by the court, the sheriff had substituted another name in place of his[1]. In 1376 a petition, presented to the king by the commons, demands that the knights be elected by "common election on the part of the better persons" of the counties (*par commun election de les meillours gentz des ditz countees*) and not be "certified" by the sheriffs without a regular election[2]. On the other hand, it sometimes happened that a county court refused to carry out the wishes of the sheriff and elected, for example, persons absent from the court, despite the sheriff's protests[3].

About the elections of deputies from the towns we have, if possible, even less information than about the elections of knights of the shires. Edward I's chancery ceased to summon the towns direct, as had been done for the parliament of 1265 and was again done for the parliament of Shrewsbury in 1283[4]. In 1275 the king summoned the towns through the sheriffs. In 1295 and for subsequent parliaments the same writ orders the sheriff to provide for the election of two knights "and two

[1] *Parl. Writs*, II, ii, App. p. 138. The knight in question declares that he was elected by "*le evesque de Excestre, Sir Williame Martyn par assent des autres bones gentz de cel conté.*"

[2] *Rot. Parl.* II, p. 355.

[3] As in Lincolnshire, 1290 (*Parl. Writs*, I, p. 22); and in Surrey, 1297 (*ibid.* p. 60). Riess (*Wahlrecht*, p. 52–53) thinks that the names written by the sheriff on the reverse side of the writ of summons, some of which are in some cases erased and replaced by others, are the names of the candidates proposed for election; that, if a candidate were rejected, the sheriff struck out his name and inserted that of another knight; and that the sheriff finally made a fair copy of the names of the elect along with their sureties. The hypothesis is plausible; but the names erased may be those of knights who refused the responsibility thrust upon them.

[4] London is an exception. It was treated as being a county and summoned direct.

citizens from each city and two burgesses from each borough." The sheriff transmitted the order to the bailiff of the hundred or the liberty in which a town lay or to the magistrates of the town itself. He received a reply and communicated it to the chancery along with the result of the election of knights of the shire. The sheriff of Oxfordshire writes in 1295: "In Oxfordshire there is no city or borough except the town of Oxford. And the writ which reached me has been returned to the bailiffs of the liberty of the aforesaid town, who have the return of all sorts of writs. And they have replied to me that with the assent of the community of the town of Oxford the two undermentioned burgesses have been elected in accordance with the terms of the writ...[1]." We find many similar reports in connection with subsequent parliaments. When a town made no reply, as frequently happened, the sheriff was usually careful to note that such and such a town had not replied.

With regard to what actually happened in the towns, we must confess that we know nothing. We do know that in London the aldermen and four men of each ward held a meeting on the 26th September 1296, and elected two delegates for the parliament of that year. On the 8th October, in the presence of the guardian of London[2] and ten aldermen, there was a meeting of the community (*i.e.* an assembly composed of "six of the better and more discreet persons from each ward"), which elected the same delegates[3]. In 1298 the two deputies from London were elected by the mayor

[1] *Parl. Writs*, I, p. 40.
[2] London was administered by a guardian named by the king from 1285 to 1296 (inclusive).
[3] *Ibid.* I, p. 49.

and aldermen[1]. On the 3rd February 1300 "the six better and more discreet persons of each ward" were summoned to elect two citizens, in the presence of the mayor and aldermen. The assembly elected two aldermen and two others, "so that the four said persons may have full powers from the aforesaid city, and that what is done by them the aforesaid community shall hold to be agreed and confirmed." But a commission, dated the 28th February and addressed to the king, states that *the two aldermen* have full powers[2]. The record of the election of 1312 runs: "On the Saturday next after the feast of SS. Peter and Paul...there met here at the Guildhall T. Romayn, N. de ffarendon and John de Wengave, in place of the Mayor who was ill, aldermen [ten names], Richard de Welleford, the sheriff, and from each ward twelve good men etc., to elect two or four good men for the business contained in the said writ etc. And for this purpose there were elected...." The names of four persons follow[3]. In 1314 the mayor, the aldermen and the good men of each ward chose three persons, from whom the mayor and aldermen chose two; the community also chose three persons from whom two were selected. These four persons, or any two of them, had full powers[4].

The method of election does not seem to have become fixed; and it did not err on the side of simplicity. Further, it is impossible to generalize from the particular case of London; and with regard to the other towns the texts tell us nothing. We cannot tell who composed the community that elected the deputies

[1] *Parl. Writs*, I, p. 72.
[2] *Ibid.* I, p. 85.
[3] *Ibid.* II, ii, p. 74.
[4] *Ibid.* II, ii, p. 129.

in each town. If we can argue from later practice, the towns probably differed widely from each other in electoral methods.

Some documents suggest that the deputies of the towns were sometimes elected in the county court. That is the impression given by the report of the sheriff of Somersetshire and Dorsetshire in 1295: "In full county courts of Somerset and Dorset, by the community of the said counties, I have had four knights elected, and by each city two citizens and by each borough two burgesses, according to the tenor of this writ; their names and the names of those who are sureties for their appearance before you on the day mentioned in the writ, are contained in the schedule attached to this writ...[1]." But the sheriff may be only alluding to a practice, which later became general, namely, that a deputation from each town officially proclaimed in the county court the names of the burgesses elected by their town[2]. Possibly also the words "in full county courts" only refer to the election of the knights.

[1] *Ibid.* I, p. 41.

[2] A deed containing the record of the election was drawn up between the sheriff on the one hand and the members of the deputation on the other. This deed was made obligatory by the statute of 1445. There has been much argument over the powers and functions of these deputations, which seem sometimes, in the fifteenth century, actually to have elected the burgesses in the county court (cf. H. Cox, *Antient parliamentary elections*, p. 125 sq.; Stubbs, *Const. Hist.* III, p. 427 sq.). In our period the documents clearly represent the sheriff as, directly or indirectly, transmitting the order to elect burgesses to the towns and awaiting their replies, which sometimes were late in coming (*Parl. Writs*, I, p. 143 and 157, Colchester; II, ii, p. 46, Scarborough) or even never came at all. But Riess (*Wahlrecht*, p. 104–105) has pointed out a remarkable fact; sometimes the knights and the burgesses of several towns in the same county had the same sureties. This can only be explained by supposing that at least the final details of the elections were completed in the county court. See Appendix III, note M.

Burgesses and knights alike were summoned through the sheriff, were elected by their neighbours and were the representatives of communities, whether of towns or counties. Another characteristic also was in time to draw them together. In parliament they formed a new group, clearly inferior to the meeting of prelates and barons which had always formed the king's court. Even after 1295 they were only summoned occasionally. When they attended parliament, no time was lost in dismissing them to their localities as soon as they had done what was required of them. We have seen that the writs for the payment of their expenses were sometimes dated on the very day fixed for the meeting of parliament. Their consent to a legislative measure is only clearly stated on two occasions, in 1275 and 1307, and then, as we shall see, for special reasons. In 1305 the more important matters were discussed after their departure. The chroniclers do not mention them, and the rolls, on which the chancery clerks copied the petitions, pleas and enactments of parliament, allude to their presence only at a late date and accidentally. Finally, both knights of the shires and deputies of the towns were not summoned to parliament to deliberate, but to "do that which shall be ordained by common counsel."

These common characteristics were bound in time to effect a close association of knights and burgesses. But in Edward I's reign the points of difference between them were more marked than those of resemblance. The two groups belonged to different social classes. As country gentry or as relatives of the great magnates, the knights naturally looked down upon the commercial bourgeoisie. By birth, upbringing, manner of life, they were much more closely associated with the barons than with the townsmen. In fact, nothing distinguished them from the baronage, except that they did not receive the king's personal summons to parliament and that they represented the interests not only of themselves and their vassals, but of all the freemen of their county. When they granted the king an aid, the amount was always the same as that granted by the barons. Finally they were summoned to parliament without the burgesses several times before 1295 and again in 1297; while in 1307 they probably continued to attend parliament after the departure of the burgesses, who seem to have been dismissed at once[1].

The comparative insignificance of the burgesses is evident. They were of little importance in parliament, despite their numbers (220 from 35 counties in 1295, 156 from 34 counties in 1298, 187 from 37 counties in 1305, 176 from 35 counties in 1307). Most of the towns were on royal demesne and therefore subject to tallage; and the aid granted by the towns was usually at a higher rate than that granted by the knights and barons. In 1294, although they had not been represented in parliament, they were bidden to supply a sixth, whereas the rest of the laity only paid a tenth. In 1295 the towns on demesne granted a seventh, whereas the barons and

---

[1] The writs for payment of expenses for the knights of 26 shires and the burgesses of 19 towns are dated the 20th January 1307, the day fixed for the meeting of parliament. "Then the said knights, because of the long stay which they made at the said parliament by order of the king," received new writs in which the king ordered account to be taken of the distance that they had come and the length of their stay, which had lasted from the octave of St Hilary (20th January) till Palm Sunday (19th March). But we have seen that there was no question of new writs for the deputies of the towns (*Parl. Writs*, I, p. 190–191).

knights gave an eleventh, and the clergy a tenth. In 1296 all the towns alike paid an eighth; the barons and knights a twelfth. In 1297 an attempt was made to make them pay a fifth, whereas "the earls, barons, knights and other laity" were only to pay an eighth; and it was only after considerable haggling that the ninth, granted by parliament on condition of the confirmation of the charters, was accepted from the towns as well as from the other classes. When in 1306 the king knighted his son, the aid granted by the barons and knights was a thirtieth; the burgesses gave a twentieth.

The record of this last parliament was published by Brady[1]. Although the session was extremely short, for the knights and burgesses were dismissed on the day fixed for their arrival, this record is of interest for several reasons and in particular because it shows us that the burgesses were still sharply separated from the knights.

The document first states the object of the king in assembling the magnates of the realm and the representatives of the counties and towns before himself and his council. Then follows a list of the great lords spiritual and temporal who had in fact appeared on the appointed day, whether in person or by proxy. It is also stated that two knights from each shire attended and two burgesses from each city or borough, "elected by the communities of the counties, cities and boroughs to treat, ordain and consent to the aforesaid demands in the name of the said communities."

---

[1] In *Introduction to the old English History* (1684), App. p. 29, and in *An historical treatise of cities and burghs* (ed. 1777), App. p. 26. See below, Appendix II, p. 234 sq.

All were assembled before the king's council, who, on behalf of the king, explained that on such an occasion an aid should be granted and emphasized the heavy expenses incurred in repressing Robert Bruce's rebellion. "The prelates, earls, barons and other magnates and the knights of the shires" deliberated on the matter (*tractatum super hoc cum deliberatione habentes*) and unanimously decided, on behalf of themselves and of the whole community of the realm (*pro se et tota communitate regni*), to grant the king a thirtieth of their movable property.

The burgesses discussed the matter separately: "The citizens and burgesses of the cities and boroughs and the others of the royal demesne gathered together and discussed the said questions. Considering the charges which the king had to bear, as has been said above, they unanimously granted the lord king, for the said reasons, the twentieth part of their movable goods...."

The inferior position of the burgesses comes out also in the sum allowed to them for their daily expenses. We have not indeed any table of allowances for Edward I's reign. Until the early years of Edward II the writ given to deputies only ordered that they should be repaid their "reasonable expenses." But in 1315, to put an end to dispute on the matter, the sums payable to deputies were fixed, and a burgess's time was then valued at two shillings a day, or half the value of a knight's time (four shillings a day)[1]. In subsequent years the amounts of the payments varied, but the proportion between the two rates remained almost unchanged. When the knights received three shillings

---

[1] *Parl. Writs*, II, ii, p. 149–150.

or forty pence, the burgesses had to be content with twenty pence[1].

Even the formation of the house of commons did not affect the inferiority of the burgesses. They long remained less respected and less influential than the representatives of the counties. Till 1533 the speaker of the house of commons was invariably a knight[2].

It is, therefore, certain that in Edward I's parliaments the knights and burgesses did not form a single group. The different rates of the aids which they granted prove that they did not deliberate together. Had anyone at that time cared to foretell the future development of parliament, no doubt he would have considered a division into four houses—clergy, barons, knights and burgesses—the most natural result of Edward I's innovations; unless indeed he preferred to believe that the knights would end by joining the barons. Such a prophet would have been most unlikely to foresee that happy accident of the English constitution, known as the house of commons.

[1] In May 1322 the knights were paid three shillings a day and the burgesses twenty pence. In November the knights received four shillings a day and the burgesses two. In March 1324 the knights received three shillings and four pence and the burgesses twenty pence (*Parl. Writs*, ii, ii, p. 258–259, 277–278, 313–314). The cost of the journey to parliament was naturally reckoned according to distance.

[2] See Appendix iii, note N.

CHAPTER V

THE REASONS FOR SUMMONING THE DEPU-TIES OF THE COMMONS TO PARLIAMENT

WHATEVER motives may have impelled Simon de Montfort to convoke representatives of the counties and towns in 1265, it is certain, as we have seen, that the very aristocratic constitution, by which he proposed to limit the king's power, did not provide for similar assemblies in the future. It was Edward I who conferred membership of his parliament on these representatives, without however making them a necessary element of that assembly. Under Edward I what had been exceptional became normal. Throughout his reign the composition of parliament continued to vary. But these gatherings of representatives, which began with Edward's first parliament and became increasingly frequent, nevertheless appear so systematic as to suggest a deliberate plan.

They were not forced upon the king by an alliance of the nobility with the gentry and townsfolk. We have no record of any such alliance. The one document, in which the baronage appear to insist on the right of the knights and burgesses to be summoned to parliament, is article 1 of the *Statutum de tallagio*, in which the king undertook not to levy tallages and aids without the consent "of the archbishops, bishops and other prelates, the earls, barons, knights, burgesses and other freemen of our realm." But we know that this so-called statute is no more than a petition presented by the earls' supporters at the parliament of October 1297, that is to say, two years after the "model" parliament of 1295 and twenty-two years after the first summons of knights and burgesses to parliament by Edward I. Also the importance of the demand is much diminished by the circumstances in which it was made. The malcontent barons were forced to seek allies in every class of the community. But the necessity for the consent of all freemen to the taxes levied by the king interested them so little that in this same parliament of October 1297 they granted an aid of a ninth, which was collected in the towns although the latter had not been represented at the parliament. And a few years later the same barons, who in 1297 had presented this apparently liberal petition, submitted another petition at the parliament of 1305 asking for the right to tallage those portions of the ancient royal demesne which were in their possession, in the same manner in which the king had just tallaged the towns and estates of his demesne.

Nor was it in response to the aspirations of the lesser gentry, the townsmen or the mass of freemen that Edward I decided to call their representatives to parliament. We find no trace of any such aspirations, whether in chroniclers like Hemingburgh who have "whig" leanings or in official documents. On the contrary, the communities of the counties and towns were so little disposed to put forward such pretentions that they sometimes tried to escape from the obligation to send deputies to parliament.

We have mentioned above the remarkable practice of securing each deputy's attendance in parliament by a certain number of sureties[1]. These sureties (*manu-*

[1] This practice, which does not seem to have been prescribed by any special order, was probably connected with the early

captores) were never less than two; they were sometimes three or even four. When no sureties were provided, the sheriff took a portion of the deputy's goods as security. "They are bound over in all their goods and chattels to be present on the day, etc.," says the sheriff of Essex, speaking of the two knights elected by the county in 1290[1]. Sometimes the nature and value of the security were defined. In 1298, whereas one of the knights of Bedfordshire had four sureties, the other "is bound over in eight oxen and four draught horses" to appear in parliament on the appointed day[2]. If the sheriff received the names of the deputies of a town without the necessary sureties, he demanded that this deficiency should be made good. In 1298, after inserting the names of the two deputies of Chichester, the sheriff of Sussex adds: "The bailiffs of the said city were ordered to see that they (the deputies) had good surety, but they have made no reply to the order[3]." Similarly, he protested when the county court insisted on electing absentees for whom no one would stand surety[4]. When the goods of a deputy were in some liberty, which the sheriff could not enter and whose bailiff refused to give any undertaking, the sheriff repudiated responsibility by carefully noting the facts in his report[5].

custom of demanding surety from those summoned before the king's court whether as accused or as litigants or even, in some cases, as jurors.

[1] *Parl. Writs*, I, p. 22: *districti sunt per omnia bona et catalla sua quod sint ad diem, etc.*

[2] *Ibid.* I, p. 66: *districtus est per octo boves et quatuor afros.*

[3] *Ibid.* I, p. 76: *mandatum fuit ballivis civitatis predicte ad ponendum eos per bonam manucapcionem; unde nihil responderunt.*

[4] See above, p. 146, the case of Lincolnshire in 1290. Similar case in Sussex in 1297 (*ibid.* I, p. 60).

[5] *Ibid.* II, ii, p. 271, 273 (1322).

The king therefore literally constrained the deputies to appear in parliament. If they could not be present, they had to send excuses: if they were ill, they had to report the fact[1]. When the king prorogued parliament, without dissolving it, the knights and burgesses were instructed to be prepared to return instantly when summoned[2]—"under pain of the appropriate penalty" (*sub poena quae decet*), says a document of the beginning of Edward II's reign[3].

These precautions were not superfluous, for suit of court in parliament was considered by the communities much more as a duty than as a right. This was true of the counties, although the knights were on the whole more ready than the burgesses to obey the royal summons. It is true that we have only discovered one case of a county court refusing to elect representatives; that of Sussex in 1297. The knights and freeholders declared that, "in the absence of the archbishop of Canterbury and others, as well bishops, earls, barons and knights as other persons employed in the service of the king oversea and elsewhere," they would not proceed to an election[4]. But a more common occurrence was the determination of a county court, despite the sheriff's opposition, to impose attendance at parliament on an absentee, who could not easily be bound over. Thus, also in 1297 and in the presence of the same sheriff, the electors of Surrey chose a knight who was then employed on the king's service in the county of Southampton and who consequently would not appear;

---

[1] Lists of 1298 and 1307 with *infirmus* opposite the names of deputies excused on the ground of ill-health.

[2] As in 1305 (*Memoranda*, ed. Maitland, p. 4).

[3] *Parl. Writs*, II, ii, App. p. 53 (1312).

[4] *Ibid.* I, p. 60.

and "they would not elect another in his place," says the sheriff[1]. The election of an absentee as their third knight by the county court of Lincolnshire in 1290 (of which we have spoken above[2]) is to be explained by the same motive.

In the towns passive resistance was more easy than in the counties, since the sheriff passed on the royal order and awaited the town's reply. The town might send no reply. Also the towns, as we shall see, had a greater interest than the counties in avoiding the obligation that was being thrust upon them. In connection with the parliament of 1298 we find the sheriffs reporting that certain towns, to whom they had transmitted the summons, had made no reply[3]. The phrases *nihil responderunt, nullum dederunt responsum* become more and more common in subsequent elections for parliament[4]. Not only little country towns, but important centres, such as Bristol, did not always reply[5]; and some towns, like Yarmouth and Orford, habitually refused to reply[6].

---

[1] *Parl. Writs*, I, p. 60: *Venire feci coram me apud Suwerk milites et libere tenentes de comitatu Surrey qui elegerunt Willelmum Ambesas qui manucaptus est per Willelmum le Cartere et Willelmum le Pestur de Kersaulton venire etc. Et elegerunt Johannem de Aubernun alium militem qui stat in obsequio domini Regis in comitatu Suthamptonie per preceptum domini Regis etc. et ipsi alium loco suo eligere noluerunt.*

[2] See above, p. 144.

[3] Some towns may have failed to reply in 1295 and 1296. But the returns for 1296 are not extant, and those for 1295 are only copies.

[4] For example, Wiltshire, 1298: *Et retornatum fuit constabulario Merlebergie et ballivis libertatum de Kalne et Worthe qui nullum inde dederunt responsum* (*Parl. Writs*, I, p. 77).

[5] Parliament of 1302, Gloucestershire: *Et pro burgo Bristoll retornatum fuit istud breve ballivis burgi Bristoll qui habent returnum omnium brevium qui nullum mihi inde dederunt responsum* (*Parl. Writs*, I, p. 121).

[6] On Yarmouth, cf. *Parl. Writs*, I, p. 72 (1298), 123 (1302); on Orford, Riess, *Wahlrecht*, p. 33, n. 2.

But it is not possible to arrive at the number of towns which made no reply to the summons for any given parliament by running over the lists printed in *Parliamentary Writs* and counting the cases in which the sheriff expressly says that such and such a town made no reply. Riess has pointed out[1] that certain sheriffs were in the habit of endorsing the writ with shortened forms of the names of those towns to which they had transmitted the summons; but that the number of towns thus indicated is often larger than the number of towns represented in parliament, for the sheriffs did not always mention that the unrepresented towns had failed to reply. Take, for example, the case of Yorkshire. In 1295 eleven towns in Yorkshire were represented (York, Beverley, Ripon, Scarborough, Pickering, Malton, Hedon, Pontefract, Thirsk, Yarm and Tickhill). Two other towns (Northallerton and Boroughbridge) were represented in 1298 and 1300 respectively, and two others again (Kingston-upon-Hull and Ravenser) in 1305. This gives a total of fifteen towns whose deputies appeared at one or more of the parliaments of Edward I. Yet for the parliament of 1306 the sheriff only reports election results for two towns, York and Scarborough, and does not mention any town as having failed to reply. It might, therefore, be supposed that summons had been sent only to these two towns. But a reference to the sheriff's endorsements shows that Beverley, Ripon, Pickering, Tickhill, Kingston-upon-Hull, Ravenser, Northallerton, and probably Pontefract and Hedon should have received the writ of summons, not to mention Whitby and Howden, which also appear

---

[1] Riess, *Wahlrecht*, p. 18-19.

on the list and which never sent deputies to parliament in Edward I's reign[1].

When the magistrates of a town received the writ of summons direct from the sheriff, it was not easy for them to disregard it. But if the writ reached them through the bailiffs of the hundred or the liberty in which the town lay, then as a rule the town eventually escaped from parliamentary obligations[2]. The sheriff dropped the subject or was replaced by a successor more negligent or more open to persuasion; and the town disappeared from the list of boroughs, either permanently or temporarily[3]. To the parliament of 1295 Worcestershire sent the deputies of six boroughs and the city of Worcester. In 1306 the city of Worcester and one borough only were represented. In 1307 the sheriff writes that in his county there is only the city of Worcester, and no boroughs[4]. Similarly, in 1325 the sheriff of Yorkshire, which had sent representatives from fifteen towns to Edward I's parliaments, writes that the county contains no other cities or boroughs but York and Scarborough[5].

[1] Cf. *Parl. Writs*, I, p. 168–169. The wapentakes of Osgodcross (containing the liberty of Pontefract) and of Holdernesse (containing that of Hedon) appear amongst the endorsements.

[2] This point seems to us to be on the whole established by Riess (*Wahlrecht*, p. 32–35). But cf. the comments of Prothero, *English Hist. Review*, 1890, p. 153.

[3] It was the object of a statute of 1382 to remedy this abuse: "*Et si ascun Viscont du Roialme soit desore necligent en faisant les retournes des briefs du Parlement ou qu'il face entrelesser hors des ditz retournes aucunes citees ou burghs, queux sont tenuz et d'auncien temps soloient venir aux Parlement, soit puniz en manere q'estoit acustumez d'estre fait en le cas d'auncientée*" (*Rot. Parl.* III, p. 124; *Statutes*, II, p. 25).

[4] *Parl. Writs*, I, p. 44, 177, 187.

[5] *Ibid.* II, ii, p. 337. Other examples in Brady, *An historical treatise of cities and burghs* (ed. 1777), p. 114, and in Riess, *Wahlrecht*, p. 23–24.

The number of towns summoned and of towns represented gradually diminished. A hundred and ten towns, without counting those of Norfolk and Suffolk, were represented at the parliament of 1295; and 166 were represented in one or more of Edward I's parliaments. But Riess calculates that the average number of towns summoned under Edward I was only 83, and that of towns represented was 75. Under Edward II the average of towns summoned sank to 67 and of that of towns represented to 60[1].

The towns never protested when they no longer received a summons; except in one case. At the parliament of January 1315 the town of St Albans presented a petition to the king complaining that the sheriff of Hertfordshire, at the instigation of the abbot of St Albans, had refused to transmit the writ of summons to the town or to inform the chancery of the names of the burgesses elected to represent the town in parliament. The burgesses of St Albans declared that they held of the king in chief; that they discharged their service to the king by sending two burgesses to parliament; that they and their ancestors had done this service in the times of king Edward I and his ancestors as under the reigning king until the parliament recently assembled; and that by his conduct the sheriff had prevented them from doing their service, in contempt of the rights of the king and to the great prejudice of the burgesses themselves. In reply the council ordered the rolls to be examined, to see whether or no the burgesses of St Albans had been accustomed to come to parliament in the times of the king's ancestors[2].

---

[1] Riess, *Wahlrecht*, p. 19–21.
[2] *Rot. Parl.* I, p. 327.

This petition from St Albans raises all kinds of
problems. In the seventeenth century it was used
to support the argument that the origins of the
house of commons were considerably more ancient
than was generally supposed, since these burgesses
claimed to have sent deputies to parliament under
Edward I's ancestors[1]. It has given rise to the opinion
that only the towns on the royal demesne were summoned to parliament[2]. It might well suggest that the
towns set great store by the parliamentary summons
and considered themselves seriously injured by being
deprived of it (*in...burgensium predictorum prejudicium
et exheredacionis periculum manifestum*).

In reality the petition proves nothing of the kind.
Madox saw clearly[3] that the position of St Albans was
merely that of a town which was trying to escape from
the control of its lord in order to come under the direct
lordship of the king. The town formed part of the demesne of the abbey of St Albans in the time of Domes-
day Book and continued to do so till the destruction of
the monasteries. But at the beginning of the fourteenth
century it made a prolonged effort to escape from this
dependence. The effort failed. The town indeed in 1327
obtained letters patent from Edward III confirming
an agreement between the abbot and the people of

[1] On this argument, see W. Petyt, *The antient rights of the
Commons*, p. 7 sq., and Brady, *Introduction to the old English
History*, p. 38.
[2] The authors of the first *Report on the Dignity of a Peer* (1,
p. 386–387) seem to have accepted this view.
[3] *History and antiquities of the Exchequer* (ed. 1711), p. 520 sq.
Madox thinks that the townsmen were moved to action because
they were more heavily tallaged by a vassal of the king than they
would be by the king himself. He quotes cases similar to that of
St Albans.

St Albans, by the terms of which the town was recognized as a borough and the inhabitants as burgesses having the right to elect two deputies to parliament as well as other privileges. But this agreement was no doubt invalid, for five years later, on the demand of the people of St Albans themselves, its concessions were declared null and void, and the seal of the town was destroyed in the presence of the town's representatives[1]. St Albans fell back under the lordship of the abbot.

The petition of 1315 must therefore be regarded as an episode in the struggle between the abbot of St Albans and the townsfolk. The latter, regarding the right of sending deputies to parliament as an argument for the immediate lordship of the king, declared that they held of the king by this service; and, in order to give greater weight to their contention, they attributed remote antiquity to their connection with parliament. Representatives of St Albans had indeed appeared at the parliament of 1307. But the townsmen, who in 1315 showed so lively a desire to do suit of court to the king, had not always displayed the same enthusiasm. In connection with the parliaments of January 1301 and February 1305 St Albans is included amongst the towns which made no reply to the writ of summons[2]. The eagerness for the parliamentary summons which the townsmen of 1315 displayed arose

---

[1] *Reports on the Dignity of a Peer*, App. II, p. 991. Cf. *Report*, I, p. 379. The letter patent is dated the 14th April, 1327; the annulment the 13th April 1332. See also *Calendar of patent rolls*, 1327–1330, p. 93; *Calendar of close rolls*, 1330–1333, p. 558; *Gesta abbatum monasterii S. Albani*, ed. Riley (Rolls S.), p. 155 sq., 166 sq., 259 sq. At the time of the revolt of 1381 the townsfolk forced the abbot to grant them a new charter (cf. Petit-Dutaillis, *Studies supplementary to Stubbs*, II, p. 294).

[2] *Parl. Writs*, I, p. 95, 143.

solely from their desire to escape from the lordship of the abbot[1].

The towns, then, laid little store by electoral "rights." When they were placed on the sheriff's list and were ordered to elect deputies, they not infrequently left it at that and omitted to send the deputies to parliament. The attendance at the great parliaments of Edward I was probably considerably smaller than an examination of the sheriffs' lists of elected representatives might lead us to suppose. The full number of knights of the shires was not always present, and burgesses sometimes failed to appear, in spite of all the precautions taken. The number of knights and of burgesses who received writs for the payment of their expenses was much smaller than the number of representatives elected. In 1306 the former number only contained 36 knights from 19 counties, and 8 burgesses from 4 towns. In 1307 it contained 43 knights from 26 counties and 31 burgesses from 19 towns[2]. These lists are no doubt incomplete, and, further, we know that the knights and burgesses could forego their writs for expenses or accept a smaller indemnity. But to the list for 1305, on which appear only 39 knights and 23 burgesses, is attached a note, which we have already quoted and which leaves little room for doubt. "These have been called before the council and have come. Let them therefore have writs for their expenses, upon the community of the counties,

[1] Barnstaple also, in 1344, claimed the right to send deputies to parliament, in virtue of a charter of Athelstan. Barnstaple's case is similar to that of St Albans, with this difference, that the inhabitants of Barnstaple did not scruple to use fraudulent methods in their attempt to escape from the lordship of Lord Audley. Cf. *Reports on the Dignity of a Peer*, 1, p. 381 sq., where the case of Barnstaple is discussed in detail.

[2] *Parl. Writs*, 1, p. 177–178, 190–191.

as well within liberties as without[1]." For the parliament of 1298 at York we have even more decisive documentary proof. Concerning the 33 counties (and the city of London), whose lists we have, there are notes telling us which deputies failed to appear and which attended the parliament. Thus we learn that from eight counties no one appeared, neither knights nor burgesses. From ten other counties some of the representatives, burgesses for the most part, failed to appear[2].

One of the principal reasons why the "right" to send deputies to parliament was not considered a privilege was that the inhabitants of a town or county were required to pay their representatives' reasonable expenses. This practice was not new at the end of the thirteenth century, for in 1258 the knights, who came before the king's council bringing the complaints of the shires against the sheriffs, had received repayment of their expenses at the cost of the community[3]. In 1265 the payment due to the knights of the shires had been assessed by a jury of four knights[4]. But an occasional payment, like those of 1258 and 1265, was one thing,

---

[1] *Parl. Writs*, I, p. 156–158. Cf. above, p. 136, n. 3.

[2] *Ibid.* I, p. 66 sq. In spite of the care taken to make them give security for their appearance, defaulting deputies do not seem ever to have been penalized, as was sometimes the case with the barons. The *Modus tenendi parliamentum* (Stubbs, *Select Charters*, 8th ed. p. 509), indeed, says that cities and counties paid a fine of £100 if their representatives did not attend parliament; and boroughs a fine of 100 marks. But the doubtful authority of that document is well known. However, cf. *Statutes*, II, p. 25.

[3] The writ, addressed to the sheriff of Huntingdonshire, is in R. Brady, *Introduction to the old English History* (1684), p. 141. See above, p. 32, n. 1, and Appendix, p. 231. Its form suggests that the practice was not new in 1258. See also, for another writ of the same date, with reference to the parliament at Easter, *Reports on the Dignity of a Peer*, II, p. 7.

[4] *Ibid.* App. I, p. 35.

and a regular payment, to be met every year or every other year, was another.

We cannot tell exactly what was the amount payable for parliamentary expenses under Edward I, for the writs only order that the deputies are to be repaid the reasonable expenses of their journey and their attendance at the parliament, "as has been customary in such a case." In 1315 it was decided that the knights who had attended parliament should receive four shillings a day and the burgesses two shillings, together with the expenses of their journey which were to be calculated by the distance traversed[1]. The rate varied slightly in subsequent years, but four and two shillings became the regular amounts under Edward III. The rate was probably much the same in the opening years of the fourteenth century. Indeed we find evidence of this in the record of a suit which is among the *placita* of the thirty-fifth year of Edward I. It is there recorded that, for the parliament of 1305, which lasted from the 28th February to the 20th March, the sheriff of Northumberland had to pay each of the knights of his shire the sum of 100 shillings[2]. We can estimate the actual value of this amount by comparing it with the prices fixed for livestock at that time. In the valuation of chattels, made at Colchester for the payment of a seventh in 1295 and a fifteenth in 1301, a cow is taken as worth five shillings[3]. According to the maximum prices, fixed

[1] *Parl. Writs*, II, ii, p. 149 (writ of the 9th March 1315).
[2] *Ibid*. I, p. 192.
[3] *Rot. Parl*. I, p. 228 sq., 243 sq. The valuation seems to have been an underestimate of the actual value. The same is probably true of the valuation made in the hundred of Blackbourne (Suffolk), for a thirtieth in 1283; according to which a cow was valued on the average at a little less than 4 shillings, an ox at 4s. 3½d., a sheep at 11½d. (E. Powell, *A Suffolk hundred in* 1283, p. xxiv–xxv).

at the request of parliament in 1315, the best cow is valued at twelve shillings, and a fat sheep with its fleece at twenty pence[1]. The rate of payment for parliamentary expenses, therefore, was relatively high.

The payment seems to have been from the first very unpopular. In the counties, where it was spread over a very numerous community—for villeins paid as well as freemen[2]—it was often very difficult to collect the amount. The royal writs declared that the rate was to be collected within liberties as well as without, but the sheriffs could only transmit the order to the bailiffs of liberties, and these latter made little haste to reply; indeed sometimes they made no reply.

In reporting the names of the deputies who were to attend parliament in 1301, the sheriff of Gloucester explained in detail all the difficulties which he had encountered and which had prevented him from remitting to the deputies what was owed to them on account of the previous parliament[3]. In this same year the king had to remind many sheriffs that the payments to deputies for the parliament of 1300 were long overdue[4]. Throughout the fourteenth century deputies were continually presenting petitions to the king asking that the burden of payments due to the knights of the shires should be distributed over the whole county, with the

---

[1] *Rot. Parl.* I, p. 295.

[2] In 1307 the king ordered the sheriff of Cambridgeshire not to demand the rate for the payment of the knights of the shire from the villeins of John de la Mare, since the latter had been present in person at parliament (*Parl. Writs*, I, p. 191). The document indicates that villeins habitually paid, except perhaps when their lord had been summoned to parliament. The exemption does not, however, seem to have applied to John de la Mare's free tenants.

[3] *Parl. Writs*, I, p. 95. See also a suit pleaded before the exchequer, 2 Edw. II, in Madox, *Firma burgi*, ed. 1726, p. 100, n. *u*.

[4] *Parl. Writs*, I, p. 101.

exception of prelates, dukes, earls and barons, and their villeins. The king no less continually replied that in such a matter the established custom should be followed[1]. In 1313 a section of the county court of Kent refused to pay, on the ground that they held in gavelkind, which mode of tenure carried with it no obligation in the matter[2]. In the end the whole burden was, in Kent, placed upon the knights' fees[3]. Elsewhere the free-holders of the old royal demesne, the free tenants of barons and prelates who were personally summoned to parliament and the inhabitants of liberties also claimed to be free from contribution, and sometimes succeeded in making good their claim[4]. As Stubbs says[5], almost every conceivable plea was alleged in order to escape the obligation of contributing to the payment of parlia-mentary deputies.

If this parliamentary burden was disliked in the counties, it was still more resented in the boroughs. Not all the English towns were as rich as London, which in 1296 granted ten shillings a day to each of the deputies representing her at the parliament of Bury St Edmund's and in 1298 a payment of a hundred shillings to those who attended the parliament of York. Many of the boroughs summoned to Edward I's parliaments

[1] *Rot. Parl.* II, p. 258 (1354), 287 (1364), 368 (1377); III, p. 44 and 53 (1378). The commons demand that contributions be raised from liberties and from the free tenants of barons and prelates.

[2] *Parl. Writs*, II, ii, p. 91.

[3] See the petition presented by the "*gentils et autres gentz*" of Kent in 1414 (*Rot. Parl.* IV, p. 49). Cf. *Reports on the Dignity of a Peer*, I, p. 364.   [4] See references quoted in note 1 above.

[5] *Const. Hist.* III, p. 500. But it does not follow from that, as Stubbs seems to think, that only those who contributed to the payment could participate in the elections. The stewards of the great lords took part in the elections and it is highly probable that they did not contribute to the payment.

were quite small market towns, upon whose resources a payment of a hundred shillings for a parliament like that of 1305 would have been a very heavy burden. It was no doubt for this reason that Edward I, contrary to custom, allowed the smaller boroughs to send only one representative in 1306. The towns preferred to send none at all, whenever possible. It was to their advantage to avoid representation. The rate of taxation levied on the counties was usually lower than that paid by the boroughs, and small towns which sent no representatives to parliament could always hope that they would be taxed not as boroughs but as parts of their counties. But this hope appears to have been usually frustrated[1].

It seems, then, that the representation of the counties and towns in parliament was not a right claimed by the knights and burgesses with the support of the nobility, but an obligation imposed by the king and accepted more or less submissively by his subjects. In Edward III's reign (1368) the inhabitants of the little town of Cheping Toriton (Torrington, in Devonshire) even presented a petition complaining that the burden of sending representatives to parliament was maliciously imposed (*malitiose...oneratis*) upon them; and, after an inquest, they succeeded in obtaining their release from the obligation[2]. The deputies elected sometimes refused to

[1] Cf. Riess, *Wahlrecht*, p. 25–26.

[2] *Rot. Parl.* II, p. 459. The reason urged by the inhabitants of Torrington was that the town had received no summons before the 24th year of Edward III. This was untrue, for the town had been summoned in the reign of Edward I (cf. *Parl. Writs*, I, p. 35, 36, 119). In the fourteenth century other towns obtained temporary permission not to send representatives, for financial reasons. Under Richard II Colchester was dispensed for five years from this burden, because the town had just been building its walls (*Rot. Parl.* III, p. 395). Cf. Cox, *Antient parliamentary elections* (1868), p. 156–157.

undertake the reponsibility thrust upon them. In 1322 the mayor and community of Lincoln informed the master of the rolls that their fellow-citizen Thomas Gamel, elected to represent them in parliament, "would not go for anything that they could do" and that they had had to elect another to "act and assent on behalf of the said city[1]." Even later, when the commons had attained to some importance in parliament, to be excused from suit of court by the king was still considered a privilege[2].

***

What motives induced Edward I thus to compel representatives of the lesser gentry and the freemen of the counties and towns, as well as the prelates and barons, to do suit of court? Did he really perceive, as Stubbs suggests, that "a strong king must be the king of a united people" and that a people, "to be united, must possess a balanced constitution, in which no class possesses absolute and independent power, none is powerful enough to oppress without remedy[3]?" Was he chiefly concerned to obtain the consent of his subjects to the increasing taxes which he imposed on them? Such has been, since the seventeenth century[4], the view

[1] Brady, An historical treatise of cities and burghs (ed. 1777), p. 154 (15th May).

[2] See in Rymer, Fœdera, III, p. 257 (20th April 1353), Edward III's letter, excusing James de Audley for his lifetime from suit of court and military service (quod ipse...quietus sit de veniendo ad parliamenta et concilia nostra); and in Reports on the Dignity of a Peer, App. I, ii, p. 707, Richard II's letter, excusing Thomas Camoys de officio militis ad dictum parliamentum venturi, as being a banneret (7th October 1383).

[3] Const. Hist. II, p. 305.

[4] Riess traces this theory back to De Lolme. But it is to be found in Brady, An historical treatise of cities and burghs, p. 53 (ed. 1777. The first edition appeared in 1690).

of a large number of historians. Or did he merely wish to reform administration, to be informed about his sheriffs, to receive petitions addressed to the crown, and to provide for the collection of aids? This theory, which very much reduces the importance of the earliest representatives of the commons, has been put forward by Riess and supported with arguments that are not without force[1].

Historians have often quoted and highly praised that passage in the writ of 1295, addressed to the prelates, in which Edward I says: "As a most just law, established by the careful providence of the holy princes, orders and decrees that what affects all should be approved by all, even so very evidently should common dangers be met with means provided in common[2]." Edward then dwells on the dishonest seizure of Gascony by the king of France and concludes with an order to the bishops to attend parliament accompanied by their clergy.

The phrase "*quod omnes tangit ab omnibus approbetur*" is, according to Stubbs, a summary of Edward's policy. The gathering of deputies from counties and towns to the parliament of 1295 was but an application of this principle. Deliberately for twenty years Edward prepared for this innovation. He perceived that the English people desired to take its place in the constitution of the country; and, when the appropriate moment seemed to him to have come, he called the whole nation to participate in the government of the

---

[1] Riess, *Wahlrecht*, p. 1–14.

[2] *Sicut lex justissima provida circumspectione sacrorum principum stabilita hortatur et statuit ut quod omnes tangit ab omnibus approbetur, sic et nimis evidenter ut communibus periculis per remedia provisa communiter obvietur*... (*Parl. Writs*, 1, p. 30. See Stubbs, *Select Charters*, p. 480).

realm. Two years later, it is true, he seems to have wished to retrace his steps. A violent conflict broke out between him and his subjects over his proposed expedition to Flanders. Edward confiscated the wool, seized ecclesiastical property and tried to levy aids to which parliament had not agreed. But that was because at the moment he was at war with Scotland and France and was also at odds with Boniface VIII. In these exceptional circumstances he tried to assume dictatorship and "failing, he yielded gracefully[1]."

If Edward I really entertained the designs attributed to him, he should not be compared, as he is by Stubbs, to Alfonso the Wise, to Philippe le Bel, or to Saint Louis, but to one of those great men of rare political genius, who have at intervals appeared in human history, to Julius Caesar or to Augustus. But such designs are so utterly opposed to the conceptions of Edward's time and to his own authoritarian temperament as not even to have an air of probability . In 1305 Edward obtained the pope's cancellation of the Great Charter and his own release from all his promises to his people. How can we believe that, in calling the representatives of the counties and towns to his parliament, he desired of his own free will to share his power with the nation? We may further observe that the phrase, which is held to summarize Edward's whole policy, does not appear in the writ ordering the sheriffs to proceed to elections, but only in that addressed to the prelates. If, therefore, we wish to give it any precise significance, it can only be applied to the representatives of the inferior clergy. But in reality the phrase seems to have been a common-place of thirteenth century political literature, bor-

[1] Stubbs, *Const. Hist.* II, p. 305 sq.

rowed, as Stubbs himself points out[1], from Justinian's Code. It is but a part of that store of philosophical maxims and flowers of rhetoric, on which English chancery clerks loved to draw, especially when addressing the clergy, who seemed to them more capable than the laity of appreciating elegance of style. Edward was so little disposed to see that what concerned all should be approved by all, that after 1295, as before that date, he often reserved the most important questions for the consideration of his barons or merely of his council, without calling representatives of the commons to a parliament[2].

It is clear that Edward's object, in assembling deputies of the counties and towns, was not to make them participate in his legislative activities. Legislation was a royal prerogative[3], in which subjects took no part, except to give counsel, when the king demanded it of them. In the preceding chapter we saw that a considerable number of ordinances or statutes—there was then no precise distinction between these two terms— were promulgated by the king alone and as concessions to his subjects. Others were promulgated by the king, on the advice of his council. Others were promulgated by the king, on the advice of the prelates and barons. So little importance was attached to the presence and the

[1] Stubbs, *Const. Hist.* II, p. 133, note 4; cf. Riess, *Wahlrecht*, p. 2.
[2] See Appendix III, note O.
[3] To the Middle Ages the idea of "making" laws was almost unknown and a new law appeared rather as a codification, renewal or development of an ancient custom. A judicial decision and a piece of legislation were both "declarations" of the law. Even in the sixteenth century the passage of a bill is called "judicium" in the journals of the houses (cf. Pollard, *Evolution of Parliament*, p. 24, 92). The essential function of the king in his high court of parliament was to declare the law, whether in a suit or in the form of an ordinance or statute. See Appendix III, note P.

opinion of the commons that in 1290 the statute *Quia emptores*, although it affected the knights, was promulgated a week before the delegates of the counties arrived at the parliament. Even when the knights and burgesses were present, it was not considered necessary to mention the fact. The statute of merchants of 1283, whose object was to facilitate the recovery of debts and which was drawn up at the parliament of Shrewsbury probably after consultation with the burgesses, contains no allusion to any such participation. The *Articuli super cartas* were promulgated in 1300, at the close of a parliament, at which representatives of the counties and the towns had been present, but probably after their departure[1]. Only prelates, earls and barons are mentioned. The only laws of Edward I, in which the consent of the community or communities of the realm is mentioned, are the first and the last of his reign, the statute of Westminster of 1275 and the statute of Carlisle of 1307. As regards the latter statute, the king did not wish to have trouble with the Roman curia and therefore no doubt thought it best to shelter himself behind the united opinion of the whole nation. He accordingly decided to add "the communities of the realm" to the list of those on whose counsel he had acted. It had been impossible to place the clergy on the list, but the mention of the communities gave increased authority to the decision taken. But too much importance should not be attached to this addition. In 1307, as in 1275, in the writs sent to officials for the execution of the law all mention of the communities of the realm

[1] The letter in which the king transmitted to the sheriffs the text of the articles, granted by him, "of his special grace," for the good of his people, is dated the 15th April. Cf. Rymer, *Fœdera*, I, p. 920.

has disappeared. The writs speak only of earls and barons[1].

Neither did Edward I summon the delegates of the commons in order to consult them on questions of general policy. This is so evident that it seems hardly necessary to waste time proving it. A few examples will suffice. In 1294 the decision to engage in war with France was taken in a parliament of barons in June; the knights of the shires were only summoned to the parliament of November. In 1301 the letter addressed to the pope, on the rival claims of the papacy and the English king on Scotland, bears only baronial names and seals and is dated the 12th February, thirteen days after the departure from parliament of the representatives of the counties and towns[2]. In 1305 the parliament of February was specially summoned, according to the text of the writs, to consider the affairs of Scotland. The king ordered the bishop of Glasgow, the earl of Carrick and John de Mowbray jointly to consider what steps should be taken to consult representatives of Scotland, who should appear at a subsequent parliament. On the 26th March the committee thus appointed presented a report submitting that two bishops, two abbots, two earls, two barons and "*deus pur la comune*" would be an adequate representation and that an assembly should be held to elect them[3]. The king then acted in the matter and decided that the parliament, at which the organiza-

---

[1] For 1275 see the writs addressed to the mayor and sheriffs of London and to the judges of the earldom of Chester (*Statutes*, I, p. 39); for 1307, the writs sent to the sheriffs and the superiors of certain monasteries (*Rot. Parl.* I, p. 217, 218).

[2] The writs for the payment of expenses are dated the 30th January. Cf. *Parl. Writs*, I, p. 101–103.

[3] *Memoranda de Parliamento*, ed. Maitland, p. 14–16.

tion of Scotland would be regulated, should be held on the 15th July in London. The assembly was subsequently postponed to the 15th September at Westminster, and, as we have seen above, it was then that the ordinance *Super stabilitate terre Scotie* was drawn up in the presence of the Scottish delegates and several members of the council. Now we have already shown that on the 21st March—five days before the discussion on these important matters began—the deputies of the counties and towns and those barons and clergy who were not of the council had received leave to depart[1].

Discussion of questions of general policy was long to remain reserved for the prelates and barons or even for the king's council alone.

The desire for financial support, on the contrary, has been considered by most historians to have been the principal cause for the convocation of deputies of the commons. Edward I, like his contemporary Philippe le Bel, was always short of money. The royal demesne was impoverished. The government of the kingdom was becoming more and more complex and more and more costly. The great undertakings of the reign, the conquest of Wales, the conquest of Scotland, the war with France, were very expensive. The king was thus forced by financial pressure to summon the representatives of his counties and good towns in order to obtain the necessary aids from them; and they used their financial power to diminish the royal prerogative by gaining ever-increasing concessions in matters of legislation and policy.

This theory is attractive. There is often a clear connection between the convocation of the knights and

[1] See above, p. 120, 121.

burgesses and the financial demands of the king. The concession made by them (or by the knights alone) is mentioned in the writs that order the collection of an aid in 1275, 1283, 1290, 1294, 1295, 1296, 1297 and 1301. A marginal note on the roll even tells us that the two assemblies of 1283, at Northampton and York, were expressly summoned *de subsidio petendo*. Unfortunately, we know that similar formulae are found in the writs of Henry III, although they were apparently not preceded by any convocation of representatives of the counties and towns. We are therefore forced to discount the value of the consent granted by the knights and burgesses. Further, Edward I, especially in the latter part of his reign, often assembled the delegates of the commons without apparently making any pecuniary demand from them. Such was the case in 1283 (at Shrewsbury), 1298, 1300, 1302, 1305 and 1307. The question is therefore not so simple as it might appear at first sight[1].

It seems even more complicated when we come to examine the circumstances in which the summons of the knights and burgesses to parliament were issued. In 1297 the barons showed their conviction that they could not rightfully be required to pay any aids but such as they had freely granted. Consent to aids was indeed an undoubted principle of feudal law, and, although the articles touching aids had been struck out of the Great Charter after John's death, we know that they had been observed in practice by the royal government at any rate in relation to the baronage. As an

---

[1] Riess is well aware of the difficulties. See especially *Der Ursprung des englischen Unterhauses* (*Hist. Zeitschrift*, 1888), p. 18, 19, where the problem is clearly stated.

order, the clergy were as little disposed as the baronage to submit to what ecclesiastical writers called the "extortions" of kings, although they more than once had to yield to force. But it is far from certain that the mass of freemen were equally convinced that they possessed such rights or that they attached the same importance to the question. A very large proportion of the freemen were not the immediate tenants of the king. They could not, like the barons, invoke the principle of aids by consent; nor, like the clergy, plead the privileges of the church and the orders of the pope. Throughout the period during which aids were granted by the barons alone, we do not find that the freemen ever complained that such a practice was unlawful. In 1220, when the barons' stewards in the county court of Yorkshire refused to pay the aid demanded of them, they did so not in the name of the county, but on behalf of their lords, who had not been summoned to parliament[1]. Even in 1297, when the county court of Worcestershire refused to pay an aid that had not been granted in parliament, it did so not because the aid had not been voted by its delegates, but for a wholly different reason. The king was demanding the aid in return for promises which no sanction compelled him to keep and which his father, Henry III, in similar circumstances, had not kept. "Therefore," concluded the members of the court, "when we are in enjoyment of these liberties, we will freely give the money mentioned[2]." What really interested the lesser gentry of the countryside, much more than did constitutional machinery[3], was that the

[1] *Royal Letters*, ed. Shirley (Rolls S.), I, p. 151.
[2] *Ideo quando habuerimus libertatum saisinam, gratis dabimus pecuniam nominatam* (*Ann. Wigorn.* p. 534). See above p. 107.
[3] There is an interesting illustration of this indifference, of slightly

amount of the aid should not be too large and that an aid should remain, as in the past, an exceptional expedient of the crown.

The position of the towns was peculiar. Although, in article I of the *Statutum de tallagio*, the burgesses appear amongst those without whose consent the king could not levy an aid, yet no one then denied that the towns on royal demesne, that is to say, the great majority of the English towns, could be tallaged at the king's pleasure. London, which offered resistance under Henry III[1] and again under Edward II, nevertheless agreed in 1312 that, if London were not tallageable, all the other towns of the demesne were[2]. Further, the citizens of London seem to have paid the tallage of 1304 without protest.

We may well ask, therefore, how Edward I could have thought it necessary to summon to parliament, for a grant of aids, the representatives of those townsfolk of his demesne whom he could tallage at will.

So far we have only spoken of the claims and rights of the king's subjects. It remains to examine the views of the sovereign himself on this question of aids. Edward's ideas are clearly illustrated by his whole conduct. He did not look upon himself as a mere feudal

later date. In 1324 the county court of Derbyshire complained that the sheriff had chosen two deputies without the assent of the county. But the burden of the complaint was not precisely that the sheriff had violated the rights of the electors. It was that he had chosen two men for whom he had thereupon levied parliamentary expenses to the amount of £20, whereas the county could have had *sufficientes homines ad eundum ad parliamentum* for 10 marks or £10 (*Parl. Writs*, II, ii, p. 315).

[1] Cf. Madox, *Exchequer* (ed. 1711), p. 491.

[2] *Licet Dominus Rex pro voluntate sua talliare possit dominica sua civitates et burgos, tamen intelligunt quod ipsi de civitate London non sunt talliabiles* (*Parl. Writs*, II, ii, App. p. 84).

overlord. He never admitted that what he called the rights of his crown did not authorize him to levy, not merely on the towns but on all his subjects, taxes to which they had not consented. He tried to do so and even to a large extent succeeded in the attempt in 1297, despite his final defeat[1]. If it is true, as Hemingburgh asserts[2], that the text of the *Statutum de tallagio* was sent to him in Flanders, he was careful not to set his seal to a document which would have so definitely limited his rights. What he did accept was the French text of the Confirmation of the Charters, in which he undertook not to levy "such manner of aids, mises or prises," save with the consent of the community of the realm and for the common profit of the realm. And he himself remained the judge of what was to be understood by the common profit of the realm and of what constituted the community of the realm[3]. He also reserved the ancient, due and customary aids and prises, thus leaving himself considerable freedom of action in view of the legal chicanery practiced by the royal lawyers and by Edward himself. Further, we know to what subterfuges the king had recourse, after his return to England, in order to avoid a renewed and more solemn confirmation of the charters. When, at the parliament of March 1299, the magnates demanded

[1] According to Professor Pollard (*Evolution of Parliament*, p. 50) the fifteenth of 1290 was also imposed by the king and his council, without the assent of any representative assembly. The *Annals of Osney*, whose author frequently complains of the exactions of the royal treasury, attribute this tax to the evil councillors of the king (p. 326; Stubbs, *Select Charters*, p. 427). But the *Annals of Dunstable* (p. 362) regard it as having been regularly granted in exchange for the expulsion of the Jews (Stubbs, *Select Charters*, p. 427. See above, p. 93, 94). The tax does not seem to have aroused any opposition.

[2] *Chronicon de gestis regum Angliae*, ed. Hamilton, II, p. 152.

[3] Cf. Bémont, *Chartes des libertés anglaises*, p. 88 and 98.

the confirmation so often promised, he first took his departure and then replied through his council that he would confirm the charters, saving the rights of his crown[1]. Into the *Statutum de finibus levatis*, in which he ordered an inspection of the forests, he inserted the same reservation[2]. A similar clause appears at the end of the *Articuli super cartas* of 1300[3]. Finally, we have seen that at the end of 1305 he succeeded in persuading the pope to grant him release from his oaths and the annulment of the Great Charter. "Thus the best king of the thirteenth century," says M. Bémont, "had acted like the worst; like John Lackland, Edward I had acknowledged that he had voluntarily and of his own accord granted the Great Charter; in reality neither the one nor the other ever believed that he had surrendered the least particle of his authority[4]."

This same Edward I, who not only disowned his promises of 1297, but refused to recognize the Great Charter, of his own accord summoned in 1275 representatives of the counties and towns, in 1295 knights, burgesses and clerical proctors, and continued to summon them to the end of his reign, even after Clement V's bull had released him from his oaths. Is it likely that he would have been willing to admit that they had a right of freely granting aids; a right which the commons did not claim and which the king, two years after 1295, only granted to the "community of the realm" in vague

[1] *Salvo jure coronae nostrae* (Hemingburgh, II, p. 183).

[2] *Salvis semper juramento nostro, jure corone nostre et racionibus nostris atque calumpniis ac omnium aliorum* (*Statutes*, I, p. 126).

[3] *En totes les choses desus dites, e chescunes de eles, voet le Roi e entent, il et soen consail, et touz ceus qui a cest ordenement furent, qe le droit et la seignurie de sa coroune savez lui soient par tout* (*Statutes*, I, p. 141; Bémont, *Chartes des libertés*, p. 108).

[4] *Chartes des libertés anglaises*, p. xlviii.

terms and under reservations? Above all, is it likely that he would have wished to give this right to the deputies of the towns, when the towns remained tallageable after 1295 as before?

•.•

Difficulties of this sort induced Riess to explain the convocation of representatives of the commons by putting forward a wholly different theory. According to Riess, there was no connection between consent to aids and Edward I's summons of knights and burgesses; the undertakings given by the king in 1297 in the Confirmation of the Charters applied only to the magnates of the kingdom, as is shown by a passage in Hemingburgh[1]; much later, under Edward III (1376), the commons demanded that no aid should be levied without their consent, which proves that their rights in the matter were then not yet formally recognized[2].

Riess's theory is that Edward's innovation was chiefly intended to serve an administrative object. The king proposed:

1. More closely to supervise the administration of

---

[1] According to Hemingburgh (II, p. 182) the king undertook *quod nullum auxilium vel vexationem a clero et populo peteret vel exigeret in posterum absque* magnatum *voluntate et assensu.* It is obvious that these words have not the precise significance that Riess attributes to them.

[2] Cf. *Historische Zeitschrift*, 1888, p. 16–18. The text of the petition is in *Rot. Parl.* II, p. 365: "*Ne que en temps a venir voz dits prelatz, contes, barons, communes, citiszeins et burgeaux de votre roialme d'Engleterre ne soient desore chargez, molestez ne grevez de commune aide faire ou charge sustiner, si ce ne soit par commune assent des prelatz, ducs, contes et barons et autres grantz (gentz?) de la commune du vostre dit roialme d'Engleterre et ce en plain parlement....*" It is clear that, if we accept Riess's interpretation of this passage, the king would then be granting the right of consenting to taxation not only to the commons but also to the magnates.

the sheriffs in the counties and to obtain exact information concerning that administration.

2. To use the knights of the shires for collecting aids,
for bringing petitions to parliament, for transmitting
the council's replies to those concerned, and in general
for making known to the provinces the various measures
taken by the government.

Certainly the supervision of the sheriffs had long
been one of the cares of the royal government. The
sheriffs, often taken from amongst the great landlords
of the counties, did not always obey the orders of the
king or respect the rights of his subjects. In 1170
Henry II had made a great inquest of sheriffs, which
was long remembered. Similar inquests, local or
general, took place several times during the thirteenth
century. In each county a committee of knights was
nominated or elected to make the inquest. Sometimes,
as for instance in 1226, 1227 and 1258, the king summoned the knights before his council to give account of
their work. Already we have something that is almost a
parliament, similar to those assembled in the early part
of Edward I's reign. Edward himself several times took
measures against the absolutism of the sheriffs. He
dismissed a large number of them at the beginning of
his reign[1], and further changes were made in 1278[2].
In 1285 he took steps to prevent them from abusing
their power in matters of law[3]. In the *Articuli* of 1300

---

[1] *Ann. Dunst.* p. 263. At the end of 1274 twenty-one sheriffs
administering thirty counties were superseded. Cf. *List of sheriffs
from the earliest times to* 1831 (Public Record Office, 1898). Several
articles of the great inquest ordered in 1274, the results of which
are recorded in the *Rotuli Hundredorum*, refer to the administration
of the sheriffs.   [2] *Ann. Dunst.* p. 279.

[3] *Illi qui timent malitiam vicecomitum liberent brevia sua originalia
et judicialia in pl/no comitatu vel in retro comitatu (Statutes*, I, p. 90).

he granted the inhabitants of the county the right to
elect their sheriff, wherever the office was not of fee
and so presumably heritable[1].

Further, it is certain that parliaments were sometimes used for the presentation of complaints against
the sheriffs. Ought we, then, to conclude, with Riess[2],
that the use thus made of Edward's new institutions
to denounce sheriffs and remedy their exactions
shows us what was Edward's conscious purpose? Even
if the facts adduced by Riess were numerous and
weighty, the answer would be uncertain. It is a common practice to-day, in countries governed under a
parliamentary system, for deputies to complain of the
behaviour of executive officials. Yet we do not therefore
argue that they were elected for that particular purpose.
But the facts adduced by Riess are neither very numerous
nor very weighty. They are mostly taken from the
reigns of Edward II and Edward III, and therefore
prove little about the intentions of Edward I. For the
reign of Edward I only three petitions are quoted as
characteristic examples. Of these the first is a petition
presented in 1290 in the name of a large number of
inhabitants of London, who "say that as long as the
existing clerks and officers in the city of London remain
in office there will be no justice for litigants, on account
of their plots and subterfuges and because of the
favour...." The second is a petition presented in 1305
by the community of the county of Cumberland
complaining of their sheriff. The third is a petition of

[1] *Le Roi ad granté a son poeple q'il eient esleccion de leur viscontes
en chescun comté ou visconte ne est mie de fee, s'il voelent* (*Statutes*, 1,
p. 139; Bémont, *Chartes des libertés*, p. 104; Stubbs, *Select Charters*,
p. 438).
[2] *Geschichte des Wahlrechts*, p. 4.

1306, in which several villages in Yorkshire protest against the action of their sheriff in taking oats for the queen's stables without payment[1]. The first of these petitions is beside the point. Since 1285 London had been in the king's hands and administered by a royal guardian. The Londoners seem to have disliked this state of affairs; but it was certainly not in order to allow them to complain of it that Edward decided to require them to send deputies to parliament. The petition from Cumberland is more important. But, even in conjunction with that from the Yorkshiremen, it is not, in our opinion, an adequate support for a thesis with no solid foundation. Further, if a wish to supervise the sheriffs was one of the principal reasons—the principal reason, Riess almost says—for the assembling of deputies, how are we to account for the summoning of deputies of the towns? For we know that many towns had very little to do with the sheriffs.

The employment of knights of the shires as collectors of aids, on the contrary, is a fact firmly established by numerous examples. In 1352 the knights demanded that none of their number should be made *coillour de l'eide*, no doubt because they found the duty very burdensome. The council replied that they did not find the petition reasonable[2]. To support his argument Riess has chosen the parliaments of 1297 and 1316, when a considerable number of knights were placed on the list of collectors[3]. He might also have taken the parliament of 1295 at the close of which, in 21 counties out of 35, the collector was a deputy and usually one of the

[1] *Rot. Parl.* I, p. 48, 164, 195. Cf. Reiss, *Wahlrecht*, p. 5, n. 1.

[2] *Rot. Parl.* II, p. 240.

[3] Reiss, *Wahlrecht*, p. 7–8.

deputies of that county in which he was required to collect the aid. But here, too, we must be on our guard against exaggeration and hasty conclusions. In other parliaments comparisons between the lists of deputies and the lists of collectors give quite different results. With regard to the aid of 1306 the number of collectors is 86, of whom only 14 appear in the list of the knights who had just been representing the counties. In 1309 there are only 16 names common to both lists and in 1313 only 7[1]. In the year 1297 itself, on the occasion of the unsuccessful attempt to collect an aid irregularly granted, the instructions for collection expressly state that the two knights "*taxurs et quilleurs*" for each county should be selected from outside the county and from those who hold no land therein[2]; a provision absolutely at variance with the intentions that Riess attributes to Edward I. It was natural for the king often to choose deputies as collectors of his aids, since they were amongst the prominent persons of the county and would have local influence. Indeed, collectors had long been chosen from the knightly class. But there is nothing to prove that it was for collecting purposes that the king decided to summon the knights of the shires to parliament. If it was so, the nation mistook his intentions; for one of the articles of the bill of 1301 demanded that the fifteenth granted by parliament should be collected by knights *elected by the county*[3], which shows that that was not supposed to have been the method of collection

[1] Lists of the collectors in *Parl. Writs*, I, p. 178; II, ii, p. 38, 39, 117. In 1306 the list of deputies only refers to 34 counties, while that of collectors refers to 37. There may therefore have been two or three more deputies amongst the collectors.

[2] *Parl. Writs*, I, p. 54.

[3] *Ibid.* I, p. 105.

previously in use. Edward acceded to the request, but did not repeat the experiment in 1306.

Finally, on the hypothesis that the collection of aids was one of the determining motives in the convocation of the commons, as on the hypothesis which attributes their convocation to the king's desire to control the sheriffs, it is impossible to account for the presence of the burgesses in parliament.

Riess's theory, then, in the unqualified form which he gives to it, seems to us untenable. It was not for the special purpose of supervising the sheriffs, nor for that of collecting taxes that Edward I decided to convoke representatives of the counties and towns. But it is none the less true that between the collection of aids and the general administration of the realm on the one hand, and the convocation of the knights and burgesses on the other, there was a connection, the nature of which must be exactly defined.

First let us see how the summons to parliament can be connected with the collection of aids.

By the time of Edward I the aid had become the usual form for taxes levied by the king. Scutage, which John had wished to make one of the ordinary sources of royal income, now produced only an insignificant amount and was only occasionally levied[1]. But the king, whose ordinary revenue did not increase[2], was

---

[1] The scutages of 1279, 1285 and 1303 were levied at the rate of forty shilling on the knights' fee. We can get an idea of the amount raised by such a tax, when we consider that the aid *pour fille marier* granted in 1290 and levied at the same rate brought in £3061 (Ramsay, *Dawn of the Constitution*, p. 527).

[2] Sir J. H. Ramsay (*Dawn of the Constitution*, p. 533) estimates the ordinary revenue of Edward I at an average of £30,000 *per annum*. Such a revenue seems to be a little less than that of John or of Henry III (cf. *ibid.* p. 293, and *Angevin Empire*, p. 504). But the comparison is very difficult to establish.

obliged to meet the costs of his almost uninterrupted campaigns and of an administrative service ever becoming more expensive. He found himself unable to pay his officials[1]. At whatever sacrifice of his pride and his authoritarian principles, he was frequently obliged to appeal to his subjects for supplementary grants of aids.

Until the reign of Edward I aids seem to have been always, except in 1254, granted by the magnates alone. But, when aids became more frequent, practical considerations led the king to demand also the consent of the knights and burgesses, about which he had not hitherto concerned himself.

An aid was based on the value of movable goods. It amounted to a tenth, or a fifteenth, or a twentieth of those goods. To assess the sum payable towards each new aid, it was necessary to make an inventory of the goods of each inhabitant of the kingdom. These inventories were extremely detailed, as is shown by the rolls of the borough of Colchester for the seventh granted in 1295 and the fifteenth granted in 1301[2]. A well-staffed bureaucracy, had it existed, would with difficulty have accomplished such a task.

For such assessments juries of inquest had long been used. From the numerous *formae taxationis* which have come down to us, we know the method of procedure in Edward I's time.

The king began by nominating a certain number (two to four as a rule) of knights as *taxours et quilleurs* in each county. They were ordered to assess the tax, to

---

[1] *Memoranda de Parliamento*, ed. Maitland (Rolls S.), No. 80.

[2] The rolls of the seventh are in *Rot. Parl.* I, p. 228–238; those of the fifteenth, *ibid.* p. 243–265. See also the roll of a village in Bedfordshire in 1297 in H. Hall, *Formula book of English historical documents*, II, p. 46; and that of a hundred in Suffolk in 1283 in E. Powell, *A Suffolk hundred in 1283* (1910).

collect the amount and to pay it in to the exchequer. Sometimes some of these *taxours* were taken from amongst the delegates who had represented the county in parliament. In 1301, at the request of parliament, they were elected by the county. On the other hand, we have seen that in 1297 the king feared that his financial projects would encounter resistance and therefore decided that the knights *taxours* should be taken from outside the county in which they were to function and from among those who held no land in that county.

The collectors thus nominated had to draw up the roll of the tax, and for that purpose had to rely on the inhabitants of the county. The writ of the 24th October 1275, which orders two knights under the direction of the dean of Salisbury to assess and collect a fifteenth in Devonshire and Cornwall, expressly states that the amount shall be fixed "by oath as well of knights as of other good and lawful men from whom the truth may best be known." The sheriffs were commanded to bring the knights and other honest men (taken from within liberties and without), who would be best able to give exact information, before the collectors at the times and places indicated by the latter and in as large numbers as should be necessary[1].

The instructions given in 1294 for the collection of the tenth have been preserved by Bartholomew Cotton[2]. The method used was particularly complicated. In each county the knights, to whom the king had confided the task of assessing and collecting the

[1] *Parl. Writs*, I, p. 3.
[2] *Historia Anglicana*, ed. Luard (Rolls S.), p. 254–256. The organization seems to have been the same in 1290 (cf. *Parl. Writs*, I, p. 24).

tax, were to go from hundred to hundred and to call before them as many as they wished of the honest men of the hundred, "from whom they can elect a dozen of the more worthy of the hundred." The twelve honest men, thus selected, were in their turn to call up the reeve and four lawful men in each *villa*, who, under their direction, were to go from house to house and make inventories of the movable goods of the people. The knights and their clerks were to exercise a general supervision. The instructions contain a list of the articles not to be subjected to the tax.

In 1297, for the collection of the eighth and the fifth, which, however, were never paid, the two knights, or the knight and the sergeant, nominated in each county, were to provide for the election by each *villa* of either two or four lawful men, according to the importance of the *villa*, and these men were to swear "that they will lawfully assess and tax all goods in the vills where they make the taxation[1]." The organization was the same in 1301 (except that the knights *chefs taxours et quillours* were elected) and in 1306[2].

Thus, in a case like that of 1294, to take the most complicated example, the exchequer supervised and controlled the collectors general of each county[3]; the collectors general supervised the juries of twelve honest men who operated in each hundred; the twelve honest men in turn supervised the reeve and his four lawful men. All who took part in drawing up the roll of the tax, all who handled the king's monies, had to take an

---

[1] *Parl. Writs*, I, p. 54–55.
[2] *Ibid.* I, p. 105, 178–179.
[3] It was sometimes stipulated that the goods of these collectors should be taxed by the exchequer.

oath. The formula of the oath is usually appended to the instructions for collecting the tax.

The formula of the oath taken in 1290 by the twelve jurors who were ordered to fix the amount of the fifteenth in each hundred is given in *Parliamentary Writs*. It was repeated, with some unimportant modifications, in the years following. The twelve honest men were to swear to tax the goods and movables of each man "well and lawfully to the best of their power and knowledge." They promised to allow themselves to be influenced neither by love, nor by favour, nor by hate, nor by gifts, nor by promises, and to discharge their office without sparing any, so that there should be no fraud and the king should not suffer loss[1].

These precautions show clearly what the royal government feared. And in fact, despite all the oaths, the king could do little if the juries deliberately made too low an estimate, or if, as in 1297, a whole county court refused to pay the sum demanded[2].

For the satisfactory payment of an aid, therefore, it was essential that the king should be able to count on the goodwill and co-operation of the governing class of the counties, that is, the class of knights. And so during the earlier part of Edward's reign the knights were fairly frequently summoned to parliament without the burgesses. In 1275 the burgesses were summoned to the parliament in April because they were to agree to the *nova custuma* on wool and leather, which it would have been difficult to collect without the consent of the merchants[3]. But, at the parliament in October, when a

---

[1] *Parl. Writs*, I, p. 24. Cf. p. 55, 105.

[2] See above, p. 179.

[3] This is shown by the instructions for the collection of the custom (*Parl. Writs*, I, p. 1).

general aid of a fifteenth was granted, only the presence of the knights was considered necessary. The consent of the knights was, in some respects, as important as that of the magnates, for it was they who assessed and collected the taxes even on the demesnes of the great lords. The experiment made by Edward in October 1275 seems to have had excellent results from a fiscal point of view[1], and the king continued to demand the co-operation of the knights of the shires in subsequent years.

It is more difficult to understand how the convocation of deputies from the towns could serve the financial interests of the king, since most of the English towns were on the royal demesne and therefore tallageable at the king's pleasure. But in practice a tallage differed from a granted aid much less than might be supposed. This explains why the two expressions were frequently used interchangeably in current speech. A tallage might be imposed *separatim*, *per capita*, that is to say, on the property of individuals, the rate of the tallage being fixed by the royal government. In this case the assessment of the tallage was made by a jury of burgesses, exactly as for an aid. If the burgesses refused to discharge the duty of jurors, as in London in 1255[2], the government was in a difficult position. On the other hand, a tallage might be imposed in common. The town and the king's representatives came to an agreement on the amount of the tallage and then the town distributed the stipulated obligation amongst the towns-

---

[1] The *Annals of Waverley* (ed. Luard, Rolls S. p. 386) speak of the tax of 1275 as having been imposed *ad unguem, inaudito more*.
[2] Madox, *Exchequer* (ed. 1711), p. 491.

folk. The principle of a tallage might be different, but the procedure was exactly like that used in the case of a granted aid. The difference between an aid like that of 1294 and a tallage like that of 1304 is much more apparent than real. Thus the king made no great sacrifice in summoning the representatives of the towns to parliament along with the knights of the shires, and the previous consent of the representative burgesses might be of use to him when it came to collecting the money. He also avoided such long and troublesome negotiations as we have seen that he conducted in 1282 and 1294.

It is, therefore, inexact to say that the king assembled the delegates of the knights and burgesses in order that they might grant him aids. Aids had previously been collected without their views being asked and they had not claimed any right to sit in parliament with the prelates and barons. But, for greater facility in collecting the aid, it was to the king's interest that delegates of each county and town should undertake in advance that it should be paid. Edward had no thought of surrendering the rights of the crown, when he summoned the plenipotentiaries of the counties and towns before his council to demand this undertaking from them; any more than he believed that he was surrendering his rights by permitting his officials to argue with the magistrates of a town over the amount which they should pay for a tallage in common, as in 1304, or for an aid, as in 1282 and 1294.

The deputies were essentially the plenipotentiaries of a county or a town, in the name of which they could make valid undertakings. They were to be furnished with full powers, so that the matter, on account of which the royal writ summoned them, "may not remain unfinished for want of sufficient powers." When ordering the collection of an aid, the king sometimes reminded a county that its representatives had promised that it should be paid. Thus, in 1283, he thanked the freemen and all the community of Northamptonshire for the subvention that they had promised "by the four knights sent to Northampton on behalf of the community," just as though the delegates of Northamptonshire had appeared alone before the king's representatives[1]. He wrote in the same way to Cheshire, which was not summoned to parliament and made separate arrange-ments with the king[2]. In 1301 the writ addressed to the knights, freemen and all the community of Lincoln-shire begins as follows: "Since, like the other com-munities of the other counties of our realm, at our parliament at Lincoln you have granted us the fifteenth of your movable goods...[3]" In 1294 a note, written on the schedule attached to the writ ordering the collection of a tenth, gives the names of two persons appointed by the king to collect "the tenth, which has been granted to the king, as a subvention for his war, by the whole community of the county of Warwick[4]."

The number of delegates sent by each county or town mattered very little. The minimum was usually fixed at two, because every legal transaction required two wit-nesses. But in 1290 the king required the counties to

[1] Writ of the 8th February (*Parl. Writs*, 1, p. 13).
[2] *Parl. Writs*, 1, p. 4, 391 (writs of the 3rd November 1275 and of the 6th August 1292).
[3] Writ of the 8th October (*Parl. Writs*, 1, p. 106).
[4] *Rot. Parl.* 1, p. 226. As one of the persons named had not yet taken his oath, the king ordered that he should take the same oath as his colleague.

send two or three knights (most of the counties only sent two); in 1275 the towns had to send four or six burgesses; in 1306 the boroughs, according to their importance, were to send one or two delegates. On these occasions the counties and towns seem to have been left quite free to send either the larger or the smaller number of delegates, and they sometimes exceeded the limits of the freedom accorded to them by the royal writ[1]. We may also notice that no attempt was ever made to regulate the number of deputies in proportion to the importance of the community which elected them[2]. Rutlandshire, like Sussex or Norfolk, had its two knights; and no more deputies were demanded from London than from the most insignificant little borough in Wiltshire or Cornwall.

₊

Nevertheless, the desire to obtain the preliminary consent of the counties and towns to the levying of aids and the co-operation of knights and burgesses in collect-

---

[1] In 1290 the sheriff of the counties of Essex and Hertfordshire sends the names of four knights for Essex and two for Herts. He adds that two of the knights for Essex are already *in curia* and that the other two *districti sunt per omnia bona et catalla sua* (*Parl. Writs*, I, p. 22). In the same year Lincolnshire elects three knights, but if one of the three does not appear, the other two have full powers (*ibid.*). In 1295 the sheriff of Bedfordshire and Buckinghamshire sends three names for the former county and two for the latter (*ibid.* p. 34); the writ only asks for two knights. In the same year the county of Southampton has four knights (*ibid.* p. 42). Amongst towns London usually elects four deputies, although only two are demanded.

[2] The instance of 1306 is only an exception in appearance. It was not in order to make the number of delegates proportionate to the importance of the town that the king allowed the smaller towns to send one delegate only, but in order to lessen their expenses.

ing them was not the sole nor even the principal purpose for which Edward I assembled them. The right of voting the budget has become so much the most important prerogative of modern parliaments that we are naturally inclined to suppose that financial questions played the chief part in their origins. On certain occasions, indeed, as for example in 1294 and 1306, the representatives of the commons seem to have been summoned for the sole purpose of being asked for an extraordinary grant. But we know that these representatives were summoned by Edward to numerous parliaments (1283, 1298, 1300, 1302, 1305, 1307), at which no demand of a financial kind seems to have been made by the king.

The documents published in the collection of *Rotuli Parliamentorum* and, for the parliament of 1305, in the *Memoranda* of Maitland show us that in these parliaments, as in nearly all the parliaments of Edward I, most of the work consisted of hearing the suits which the king had reserved for himself in parliament and examining the petitions presented to the king and his council. Important questions of policy and legislation might be dealt with in conferences between the king and the *fideles* whom he summoned, but suits and petitions were the normal business of parliamentary routine. Thus parliament, in its essential functions, appears as the continuation of the old *curia regis*, as the high court of justice of the realm, capable of redressing wrongs which could not be redressed by the common law.

The part which the knights and burgesses could take in the hearing of *placita* was evidently very small. The documents do not mention their presence. In 1305 suits were determined after their departure[1]. Indeed, as we have already said, the house of commons has never claimed a share in the judicial functions of the house of lords. If knights or burgesses were summoned before the king in a judicial matter, they came as individuals, to provide information, or as pleaders, to further the interests of a town or county. Thus at the parliament of 1305 amongst the four citizens, to whom Salisbury entrusted the conduct of its litigation against its bishop in the king's court, were the two deputies of that city[2].

For our purpose the petitions are of much greater importance than the *placita*; an importance that has not wholly escaped the notice of Riess, who devotes a few lines of his monograph to it, but does not adequately dwell on this point, which to us seems essential.

The practice of approaching the king and his council to complain of an injustice or to demand a favour dates back to a period long before the reign of Edward I. But it seems that in earlier times the petitioner appeared in person before the council and explained the nature of his demand orally. By the end of the thirteenth century this form of procedure was rendered impossible by the great number of petitions and the enlarged activity of the royal administration. Attendance in person and oral demand were supplanted by written petition. It was even found necessary to systematize the filing and examination of these petitions, many of which were of

---

[1] All those who were not of the king's council received leave to depart on the 21st March. The case of Nicholas de Segrave was determined on the 29th. That between the citizens of Salisbury and their bishop on the 6th April.

[2] *Memoranda*, ed. Maitland, p. 266. The city of Salisbury contested the bishop's right to tallage it.

very little importance and only wasted the time of the king and his councillors. In the eighth (1279–1280) and the twenty-first (1292–1293) years of Edward I measures were taken to classify the petitions and to reserve for the king's personal attention only those matters which were so important that they could not otherwise be dealt with[1].

In 1305 the king, being then absent from London, gave instructions in advance to the chancellor, commanded a public proclamation to be made in the great hall of Westminster, in West Cheap and at the Guildhall, requiring all with petitions to submit to present them before the first Sunday in Lent (7th March), and ordered that as many petitions as possible should be examined before his return[2].

The number of petitions presented at this parliament, on which we have exceptionally complete information, was about 450. They were received and classified by a commission of four persons: a judge, a high official of the exchequer, and two clerks of the chancery. When parliament met, a special commission was appointed to examine the petitions concerning Scotland, another those of Gascony, a third those of Ireland and the Channel Islands. Similar commissions were probably nominated for the English petitions. The king himself went vigorously to work. On Sunday, the 7th March, thirty-two petitions were examined before him[3].

The status of the petitioners and the nature and importance of the petitions varied considerably. Most of the petitions (over 400) were presented by individuals,

---

[1] The texts are given in Stubbs, *Const. Hist*, II, p. 276, nn. 2 and 3.
[2] Cf. *Memoranda*, ed. Maitland, p. lxi.
[3] *Ibid.* p. 48.

and most of these, as Maitland points out, could not have been debated in an assembly. For example, the prior of Bridlington complains that Thomas de Monceaux will not allow him, or his people, or the people of the district, to cross his land, as has always been their custom, to go to the king's market at Kingston-upon-Hull. The university of Cambridge begs the king to found a college. Thomas de Moriley asks the king to restore to him his father's fiefs in Cumberland; which fiefs had been confiscated because his father had been hostile to the king in the Scottish war; but the petitioner had ever been loyal to the king. Robert Treyfot, imprisoned for having allowed a prisoner, whom he had been ordered to deliver to the sheriff of Essex, to escape, implores the king to pardon him. Alice, the divorced wife of John de Beaumont, protests that her late husband has returned, ravaged her domains and seized her charters and jewels[1]. In many cases the council or the commissioners appointed to examine the petition confine themselves to informing the petitioner as to his line of procedure—he should obtain a writ from chancery, he should appear before the exchequer, he should await the results of an inquest, etc.

But some of these petitions are of more general interest. Simon le Parker complains that the jury, ordered to pronounce on the facts on account of which he is in prison, has been challenged out of pure malice, and consequently he is still in the prison of Canterbury. The king and council reply with a ruling, which is later considered to be an ordinance and as such appears in the *Statutes of the Realm*[2]. Possibly the ordinance of

---

[1] *Memoranda*, ed. Maitland, Nos. 49, 50, 92, 97, 105.
[2] *Ibid*. No. 10. *Statutes of the Realm*, I, p. 143.

trailbaston, which was also made at this parliament, originated similarly in a private petition[1].

None of those sent to the parliament of February 1305 as representatives of a county or a town figure among the members of the commissions which were nominated to examine petitions and whose composition is known to us. Some may have been included in the commissions for English petitions; but it is unlikely. The council may sometimes have consulted knights and burgesses on the petitions that concerned their county or town. It would have been a convenient method of verifying the statements of the petitioners. But it was above all as being themselves petitioners that the knights and burgesses came to parliament and appeared before the council.

The parliament rolls of 1305 contain eight petitions presented by counties (including one from the community of the bishopric of Durham, which had no representative in parliament) and 23 presented by twelve towns (all, it appears, represented in parliament)[2]. Like the petitions of individuals, amongst which they are enrolled, these petitions from communities deal with the most varied topics. They contain many pecuniary claims, which are usually referred to the exchequer. The people of Cumberland demand payment for the provisions taken by the sheriff for the king's larder. They also complain that the collectors of the fifteenth[3] have restored nothing on account of the amounts which the king ordered to be repaid. Carlisle also claims the value of the barley and oats "borrowed" by the king

[1] The petition numbered 90 in Maitland's edition. The ordinance is in *Rot. Parl.* I, p. 178.

[2] We omit the Scottish and Irish towns.

[3] The reference, no doubt, is to the fifteenth granted in 1301.

for his army in Scotland. Dunwich asks for assistance towards the repair of her harbour, which has been wrecked by a storm, and that against her dues to the king shall be set a credit for the enormous losses in ships and men, which she has sustained in the king's wars. The people of York complain that the exchequer is demanding the price of a quantity of wine, which they had bought from the king's cellarer in the time of Henry III and for which they had paid[1].

Numerous petitions refer to the privileges of counties and towns and request their confirmation or extension. The community of the bishopric of Durham claim a charter which has remained in chancery. Carlisle demands the return of her liberties, which had been suspended after the burning of the city's charters. Cockermouth asks permission to establish a right of pontage for the repair of her bridge. Worcester asks permission to establish a right of murage. Norwich wishes her right of murage prolonged for seven years (the king only prolonged it for five). Several towns (Appleby, Dunwich) complain of illicit markets established in their neighbourhood. Newcastle's petition on this point is characteristic. The people of Newcastle declare that the prior of Tynemouth has established a market which attracts commerce so that the king's revenues suffer diminution; already, in the nineteenth year of the reign, the burgesses had prosecuted the prior and won their case. This petition was given special attention. The burgesses of Newcastle were instructed to appear before the king, with their charters, in the fortnight after Easter; and meanwhile to demand from Gilbert de Roubiry the record of the suit and its decision, to

[1] *Memoranda*, ed. Maitland, Nos. 137–140, 187, 168.

which they had appealed, so that they might submit it to the king in his parliament. The burgesses of Norwich, who claim the view of frankpledge in the village of Newgate, do not fail to point out that it was through them that the king had recovered the village from the prior of Norwich[1].

Two petitions from the borough of Bristol are particularly interesting. The first refers to the tallage of 1304. The town, which had doubtless agreed to a tallage in common, asks that the Templars shall be subjected to the tallage like the other inhabitants of Bristol, since they profit by the same markets and enjoy the same privileges as the burgesses. The king decided that this request should be granted. The second deals with the difficulties arising between the burgesses of Bristol and two neighbouring magnates, Thomas and Maurice de Berkeley, of whom the former had been summoned to this parliament in the capacity of a baron. These two eminent persons, who held the village of Redcliff in the suburbs of Bristol, claimed the right to compel the burgesses of Bristol to do suit of their court, and, as the burgesses refused, molested them in a number of ways. The mayor and other persons of the borough had been assaulted and beaten, and things had come to such a pass that the inhabitants no longer dared to leave the town to attend the markets of the neighbourhood. The king replied by nominating a commission of three persons of good sense who, with the constable of the castle of Bristol, were to make an inquest and act as they considered necessary. If they encountered difficulties which they could not solve

[1] *Memoranda*, ed. Maitland, Nos. 8, 103, 78, 159, 187, 167, 59.

without the king's help, they were to submit them to him at his approaching parliament[1].

Amongst the other petitions presented by communities to this parliament of February 1305, we may quote that of Northumberland, which asks that judges *de banco* should visit the county, hold assizes and take inquests; that of Lancashire, requesting the nomination of a commission of two persons to hold an inquest on the malefactors who trouble the king's peace[2]; those of Cumberland which refer to the deforestations effected since 1301 and have a more general interest. The inhabitants of the deforested parts of the forest of Allerdale complain that they are still obliged to furnish poture to the foresters. The king replies that he upholds the deforestation, but that the land shall remain a warren and that the right of poture shall continue[3]. Cumberland's and other similar petitions were probably the origin of an ordinance of the forest, in which the king does not conceal a lively irritation against those who had forced him to agree to undesirable deforestations and in which he clearly warns the inhabitants of the deforested districts that they must either renounce the advantages attaching to a forest or else revert to the full forest *régime*[4].

The parliament of 1305 affords us other examples of

---

[1] *Memoranda*, ed. Maitland, Nos. 214, 213.

[2] *Memoranda*, Nos. 20, 26. Lancashire submitted the names of Thomas de Burnham and John Biroun for the king's choice. The king accepted John Biroun, but substituted Milo de Stapelton for Thomas de Burnham.

[3] Poture or puture was a charge levied for their board by foresters.

[4] Cumberland's petition is numbered 6 in Maitland's edition; the ordinance of the forest 461. This ordinance is also in *Statutes of the Realm*, I, p. 144.

collective petitions besides those from towns and counties. There is a petition in which "the poor men of the land of England" demand measures against those who are entrusted with the making of inquests or form part of assizes and juries and allow themselves to be corrupted by litigants; and another against the ordinaries of dioceses who are usurping the functions of the king's judges. These are probably petitions from all the representatives of the commons, knights and burgesses together[1]. Two other petitions were presented in the name of the earls, barons and community of the realm. Their object was to prevent religious houses, both of men and women, from sending money abroad to the superiors of the mother-houses of their orders. To these petitions, which he may have himself suggested, the king replies that in full parliament, "with the consent of the prelates, earls, barons and others of the realm," he has provided for the matter in a statute "in the following form." But on the roll the space that follows remains blank. The statute *De asportatis religiosorum* was only promulgated two years later at the parliament of Carlisle[2].

During the three weeks which they passed at this parliament of 1305 one of the chief functions of the knights and burgesses was certainly the presentation of the petitions of their county or town and the defence of these petitions before the council. We saw above[3] that they took their leave before the discussion on Scottish affairs began. The only question of general importance on which the king seems to have consulted

---

[1] *Memoranda*, No. 472.
[2] *Ibid.* No. 486.
[3] See above, p. 177.

them was that of the tallage paid by English religious
to foreign houses. Later on the Articles of 1309 also
show us that in the presentation of petitions the representatives of the commons saw one of the essential
reasons for their presence in parliament. They complain that "the knights and the men of the cities,
boroughs and other towns," who come to parliament
at the king's order, on behalf of themselves and the
people, "and have petitions to submit on account of
wrongs and oppressions done to them that cannot be
redressed by the common law or in any other way
except by special warrant," find none to receive their
petitions; which is contrary to the custom of parliament
under Edward I[1]. The king decided to meet their
wishes. At the parliament of Lincoln in 1316 the organization of parliamentary business was almost the same
as in 1305[2]. Gradually collective petitions presented
by the whole body of the representatives of the commons
assumed greater importance and wider application till
they became in fact bills, which only needed the royal
approbation to become statutes. In this way, during
the fourteenth century, the character of parliament
continued to change. The presentation and examination
of private petitions passed more and more into the
background, and that function of parliament was in-
herited by the council. Meanwhile parliament itself,
by means of collective petitions, developed from a
court of justice into a legislative assembly[3].

[1] *Rot. Parl.* I, p. 444.
[2] *Parl. Writs,* II, ii, p. 156.
[3] This view has been excellently stated by Professor Pollard
(*Evolution of Parliament,* esp. p. 118, 127–130). Even to-day, as
he points out, a parliamentary bill is a petition up to the moment
at which it is transformed into an act by the royal assent.

There is no doubt that Edward I did not foresee such a development of the system of petitions; and that he did not summon knights and burgesses to parliament in order to allow them to submit fully prepared legislative proposals in the form of petitions. To redress wrongs and oppressions done to his subjects certainly appeared to him one of the first duties of the king; but the prerogatives of the king could not fail to gain by these periodic "great days," at which all his subjects brought their complaints before him. The petitions of the communities, counties and towns, gave him exact information on the state of the kingdom. They enabled him to supervise the smallest details of the behaviour of his officials, to repress encroachments by great lords or abuses of their authority by the clergy. If Thomas de Berkeley tried to force the burgesses of Bristol to do suit to his baronial court, the people of Bristol complained. The king then made an inquest and announced his decision. If the ordinaries of dioceses brought into their courts causes that should have been reserved for the royal judges, and if they levied charges that should have gone to the treasury, the "poor men of the land" complained, and the king decided that in such cases a writ of prohibition should be demanded from chancery. If the prior of Tynemouth established a market without royal authorization, the king was at once informed of the matter by the inhabitants of Newcastle, who protested at the wrong done to them and at the same time to the royal treasury. By means of such petitions, the king kept a firm hand upon the general administration of the realm. All favours came from him. No decision of any importance could be made without his consent or that of his ordinary councillors. No evil custom could be established to the detriment of his subjects and of himself. We may notice the precision with which Edward, ever careful not to diminish the rights of his crown, limited the duration of the concessions that he saw fit to make. When Norwich asked for a prolongation of its right of murage for seven years, only five years were granted. When the earl of Warwick demanded the same right for the town of Warwick for twelve years, he only obtained it for seven. Edward I, unlike his father, cannot be reproached for having allowed the inheritance of his royal ancestors to be diminished by imprudent concessions.

.

This brings us to an idea which was, we believe, one of the bases of Edward's policy. The convocation of deputies of the commons was the outcome not only of practical needs and administrative requirements, but also of a new conception of the relations that should exist between the king and his subjects. If we did not hesitate to use terms which are anachronistic, we would be tempted to say that, throughout his reign, Edward's object was to transform his vassals and sub-vassals into subjects and feudal aids into taxes; and that the convocation of deputies of the commons was one of the most effective means which he employed to carry out that transformation.

Edward had the most exalted idea of his own authority. He claimed to be not only the suzerain of his vassals, but the king of all his subjects. Although he availed himself to the utmost of every legal advantage given him by feudal custom, he did not respect one of the fundamental principles of that custom, namely the distinction between immediate vassals and sub-vassals. That distinction he set aside whenever he thought it necessary to do so. Indeed he set himself systematically to destroy it.

His reign opened with the great inquest whose results were entered in the *Rotuli Hundredorum*. The object of the inquest was that the king might be exactly informed on the extent of the rights of the crown and the nature of the encroachments which those rights had suffered. The commissioners were to obtain information on the lands which were then in the king's possession and on those which had once been in his possession and were so no longer. With regard to the lost lands, they were to discover who held them and by what title (*quo warranto*). They were similarly to enquire into those lands which had once been held immediately of the king but had passed into the hands of sub-vassals. They were to take note of lands, which had once been held by military tenure, but had passed to religious houses or become fiefs of some religious house. Where a hundred was not in the king's hands, they were to discover the authority for its present condition; and similarly with regard to every "liberty impeding the common course of justice[1]."

Despite their protests the holders of liberties had to produce their title-deeds. Inquests *Quo warranto*, regulated by the Statute of Gloucester (1278), were carried on without interruption during a large part of the reign.

[1] *Fœdera*, I, p. 517; *Rot. Hundredorum*, I, p. 13–14 (11th October 1274). Cf. Stubbs, *Select Charters*, p. 421. The *Rotuli Hundredorum* have been published by the Record Commission; also the *Placita de quo warranto* which followed the inquest. On the sequence of the inquests from the beginning of the reign, see H. Hall, *Formula book of English historical documents*, II, p. 216 sq.

The royal judges at first displayed an exaggerated severity, picking holes in the terms of charters granted by previous kings and refusing to take account of prescription. It is true that they were obliged to diminish their pretentions[1]; but, even if they failed to recover for the crown the lands and rights that had been formally ceded, their efforts at least succeeded in preventing the formation of new liberties and in checking the movement which threatened to withdraw a considerable portion of the land from the direct authority of the king. On one essential point the king successfully imposed his will; in 1290 the statute *Quia emptores* put an end to subinfeudation.

Subinfeudation was highly objectionable from the point of view of royal authority. When fiefs were so multiplied that, in some cases, each one was no more than a twentieth or a fortieth of a knight's fee, the services, which his tenants-in-chief owed the king, were not forthcoming. Indeed sometimes the principal object of subinfeudation seems to have been to avoid the services due to the capital lord; as, for example, when a tenant alienated his fief to an abbey, only to resume it as the vassal of that abbey[2]. Such practices had resulted in a very considerable reduction in the number of knights that the tenants-in-chief were bound to bring to the king's military service and in the number of knights' fees on which the king could levy scutage or the three regular aids. Earlier calculations, which were still accepted in the middle of the thirteenth

[1] Cf. Maitland, Introduction to *Select pleas in manorial courts*, p. xx, lxxvii.

[2] The statute *De religiosis* (Mortmain) was promulgated in 1279 in order to put a stop to such practices. Stubbs, *Select Charters*, p. 451.

century but seem to have had no basis in fact, reckoned the number of knights' fees in all England at 32,000. In reality the tenants-in-chief of Edward I do not seem to have been required to provide the king with more than 7000 knights[1]. But even this figure is much in excess of the obligation which Edward's tenants-in-chief recognized. The aid *pour fille marier*, granted in 1290 and collected in 1302 at the rate of £2 on the knight's fee, brought in a sum of £3061; which would give a total of 1530 knights' fees. In 1277, according to the very detailed investigations of Mr J. E. Morris on the Welsh wars, the feudal host contained 228 barons and knights and 294 sergeants, or the equivalent of 375 fees. According to the same author, the summons to the host in 1282 brought to Rhuddlan 123 barons and knights and 190 sergeants, representing altogether 218 fees, to whom must be added a certain number of knights and sergeants operating elsewhere in Wales. Mr Morris, indeed, points out that the king, for various good reasons, was not anxious to assemble the whole feudal array of England, that he preferred mercenary troops and that it had become an established custom for the feudatories to send military contingents far smaller than their due number of knights. But the

[1] Round (*Feudal England*, p. 292), arguing from the inquest of 1166, estimates the *servitium debitum* under Henry II at about 5000 knights. For Edward I's reign, J. E. Morris (*The Welsh wars of Edward I*, p. 41) arrives at a total of slightly less than 7000 fees liable to scutage; S. K. Mitchell (*Studies in taxation under John and Henry III*, p. 302) gives 6500. On this question, which we cannot examine in detail, see also Madox, *Exchequer* (ed. 1711), p. 422, 450–451, 472; Stubbs, *Const. Hist.* I, p. 468; Pollock and Maitland, *History of English Law*, I, p. 254 sq.; J. H. Ramsay, *Dawn of the Constitution*, p. 341–342, 527; Miss H. M. Chew, *Scutage under Edward I*, in *English Hist. Rev.* XXXVII, p. 321 sq. and XXXVIII, p. 19 sq.

feudatories ought to have paid the customary fine of 40 shillings for each knight not supplied, and many, especially among the more powerful, did not pay. Thus we find that in 1277 the countess of Devon confessed to holding 2½ fees and paid on that number, whereas in Devonshire alone she possessed 89. During the wars of 1282–1283 the whole of the fines levied seems to have amounted to £2959, which, at 40 shillings on the fee, would represent 1479½ knights' fees. If we add the knights and sergeants serving with the host, we do not reach a total of 2000, out of the 7000 fees, which the country then contained[1].

The situation is set out with extreme candour in a petition presented to Edward II at the parliament of January 1315.

The great lords of England, as the prelates, earls and barons who hold their baronies in chief of our lord the king, —to which baronies many fees are appurtenant—depend and do service for fewer fees than the number they hold of the king, so that *he who is lord of a hundred fees does service for five or for six*; and some for more and others for less...[2].

They therefore considered themselves outraged by the exchequer's attempt to make them pay scutage on all their fees, since their ancestors had always done service for less than the number of fees that they held of the king.

After this petition an attempt was made, by means of declarations by the persons concerned, to discover the number of fees for which they defended themselves in the king's service. But the obstruction was such that the project seems to have been dropped[3].

---

[1] See J. E. Morris, *Welsh wars*, p. 43, 45, 46 sq., 166, 168, 173–174, 197. Cf. *Parl. Writs*, I, p. 197, 228 sq.
[2] *Rot. Parl.* I, p. 292.   [3] Cf. *Rot. Parl.* I, p. 455.

Subinfeudation and the diminution of service which was its almost inevitable consequence had two results. The feudal host became inadequate for a serious campaign and the king was obliged to have recourse to mercenaries paid by himself; while the old feudal taxation, when levied, only produced an insignificant amount. For these reasons the king in 1290 promulgated the statute *Quia emptores*, by the terms of which the purchaser of land became the vassal not of the vendor, but of the vendor's overlord[1]. The magnates, who composed the parliament, accepted the measure because it appeared to them to serve their interests as well as those of the king, and perhaps also because the king granted them certain concessions[2]. In the same year Gilbert de Umfraville, earl of Angus, asked permission to enfeoff his eldest son with the manor of Overton, which the son should hold of his father during the latter's lifetime and subsequently of the capital lords. The king's reply was emphatic: *Rex non vult aliquem medium et ideo non concessit*[3].

The king went much further in his efforts to extirpate mesne lords and to bring all his subjects under his immediate authority. It was in pursuance of this policy that he took steps on several occasions to force those of his subjects—as well sub-vassals as tenants-in-chief—who had revenue of a certain amount, to become knights and serve in the host when he summoned them. Similar orders had several times been issued in the reign of Henry III, but appear to have been applied only to

[1] Stubbs, *Select Charters*, p. 473–474.
[2] By the statutes *De quo warranto* (*Statutes*, I, p. 107).
[3] *Rot. Parl.* I, p. 54. The petition was presented at the parliament of Michaelmas, and therefore after the promulgation of the statute *Quia emptores*.

tenants-in-chief[1]. Under Edward I this distinction disappeared. In 1278 he ordered the sheriffs to compel all those to assume knighthood who had land of £20 annual value or a whole knight's fee of that value, from whomsoever they held, and who ought to have been knights and were not. This command was to be carried out before Christmas and the king returned to the attack in the next year to secure its complete execution[2]. The prospective knights had to pledge a part of their lands as security or provide sureties[3]. In 1282, at the time of the Welsh war, all £30 landowners, without distinction of tenure, were summoned to provide themselves with arms and a war-horse. A few weeks later another writ remitted this obligation in return for a payment to the royal treasury[4]. At the end of the year the writ, which summoned the delegates of the counties and towns to Northampton and York, ordered the sheriffs also to command the attendance before the king or his representatives of all the £20 landowners in their counties, who were capable of bearing arms[5]. The object of this order was probably to make these landowners pay a special contribution to the costs of the war. The

---

[1] In 1255 the king ordered the sheriffs to summon all tenants-in-chief for an expedition to Scotland. Sub-vassals were also requested to come "as they loved the king and their own honour and desired to earn his grace and favour." As far as they were concerned, therefore, the summons was not obligatory (*Fœdera*, I, p. 326).

[2] *Parl. Writs*, I, p. 214 (writ of the 26th June 1278); cf. p. 219. Stubbs, *Select Charters*, p. 448–449.

[3] The list of persons distrained to knighthood in Northumberland, with their sureties, is in *Parl. Writs*, I, p. 214 sq.; the number of tenants-in-chief declared subject to this obligation is seven, that of sub-vassals 33; but the latter list is probably incomplete.

[4] Writs of the 26th May and the 22nd June 1282 (*Parl. Writs*, I, p. 226).

[5] Writ of the 24th November 1282 (*ibid.* p. 10).

measures taken in 1278 and 1282 were mitigated in 1285. In consideration of the good service done by the community of the realm, the king pardoned those who were £20 landowners but had not undertaken the duties of knighthood. The obligation was only imposed on the holders of land of £100 annual value[1]. Yet in 1292 writs similar to those of 1278 imposed the duties of knighthood on all £40 landowners[2]. In 1297 all £20 landowners, whether tenants-in-chief or not, whether their lands were in a liberty or not, received a preliminary order to provide themselves with horses and arms[3]; and on the 15th May they were summoned to appear in London on the 7th July, with horses and arms, prepared to cross the sea with the king. The summons was repeated a few days later[4].

These experiments, which were not always crowned with success, are to be in part explained by the king's financial needs. The imposition of the duties of knighthood on as many of his subjects as possible was a means of obtaining a larger revenue from fines. But we believe that it would be wrong to reduce a policy pursued by Edward I with so much perseverance to mere financial sharp practice. With regard to military service the king proposed to abolish the existing distinction between tenants-in-chief and sub-vassals[5]. By summoning

[1] Writ of the 6th May 1285 (*ibid.* p. 249).

[2] Writ of the 6th February 1292 (*ibid.* p. 257). Measures were taken in the next year against defaulters (cf. the writ of the 2nd January 1293, in *Parl. Writs*, I, p. 258, and H. Hall, *Formula Book*, II, p. 77 sq.).

[3] Writ of the 5th May 1297 (*Parl. Writs*, I, p. 281).

[4] Writs of the 15th and 24th May 1297 (*ibid.* p. 281, 285).

[5] In France, under Philippe le Hardi and Philippe le Bel, the crown similarly claimed the right to issue direct summons to sub-vassals. Cf. P. Guilhiermoz, *Essai sur l'origine de la noblesse en France au Moyen Age* (1902), p. 269–270, 296.

representatives of the knights and burgesses to his parliament, he abolished that distinction with regard to suit of court. In the one case as in the other he was destroying the feudal framework of society.

In the earlier part of the reign, suit of court was imposed much more frequently on the knights than on the burgesses. Owing to the division of fiefs there had grown up in rural England a class of large landowners, who were usually knights only in name and of whom many were not tenants-in-chief of the crown. It was this class which, under the supervision of the sheriff, was in fact governing the shires. Accustomed by attendance at the county court to juridical discussions, accustomed by the practice of the county court to representative institutions, these knights were marked out as the natural representatives of the freemen of the county. In accordance with a custom already long established by the end of the thirteenth century, some of them would appear before the king to defend the county, whenever the county needed defence. The method of assessing and collecting aids brought them into touch with the financial department of the king's court. More than once the king had summoned two, three or four knights from each county before his council, in order to have a "parliament" with them, as with the prelates and magnates. Under Edward I such assemblies became frequent and systematic. The king distrained to suit of court two knights from each county, on behalf of the whole legal body of the county, just as he distrained to military service all those who had lands of £20 annual value, without distinction of tenure.

It has sometimes been erroneously supposed that the

knights of the shires at a parliament only represented the lesser tenants-in-chief of the king and that consequently their convocation was ultimately due to article 14 of the Great Charter. Such a restriction would have been entirely contrary to the policy pursued by Edward. Moreover, there is no trace of it in the documents, which only say that the knights were elected in full county court by the consent of all the county[1].

The summoning of representatives of the towns is connected with ideas similar to those which led to the summoning of the knights of the shires. Here also we are confronted with a new class, the bourgeoisie, whose importance had grown considerably during the thirteenth century. Here also Edward dealt with the urban communities, as he did with those of the counties, without reference to the feudal hierarchy. Just as it has been supposed that the elected knights represented only tenants-in-chief, so it has been suggested that the towns summoned by the king were exclusively towns on the royal demesne. But the documents will not permit of this view. The writs of summons sent to the sheriffs order them to provide for the election "of two citizens from every city and two burgesses from every borough." The words *de qualibet civitate*, *de quolibet burgo*, left the selection of the towns to the sheriffs, and certainly the sheriffs at first interpreted these terms more or less generously and somewhat capriciously[2]. But nothing authorizes us to think that the towns not of the royal demesne were deliberately excluded. Further, as was

[1] Cf. Stubbs, *Const. Hist.* II, p. 240–241.
[2] Thus in 1295 (*Parl. Writs*, I, p. 35) the sheriff of Cornwall interpreted the word *burgus* as including the *villae mercatoriae*, which had been summoned in 1275, but of which the new summons made no mention.

shown by John Allen in 1821, in the learned article which he contributed to the *Edinburgh Review*[1], on the occasion of the reports by the house of lords on the peerage, it is certain that towns not of the royal demesne were included in the first convocations. Amongst these were Lynn (summoned to the parliaments of 1283, 1298, 1301, 1302 and 1305), which belonged to the bishop of Norwich; Salisbury (summoned to the parliaments of 1295, 1298, 1300, 1301, 1302, 1305, 1306 and 1307), which belonged to its own bishop; St Albans (summoned to the parliaments of 1300, 1305 and 1307) and Evesham (summoned to the parliament of 1295), which formed part of the demesnes of their respective abbots; Tonbridge (summoned to the parliament of 1295) and Bletchingley (summoned to the parliaments of 1295, 1298, 1300, 1301, 1302 and 1307), which were on the demesne of the earl of Gloucester; Arundel (summoned to the parliaments of 1295, 1302, 1305 and 1307), which was in the honour of Arundel. Cox gives a whole list of towns that were in the same position[2]. Stubbs and Riess have added further names to the list[3]. The question may therefore be considered as closed. In summoning the representatives of the towns, as in summoning those of the counties, Edward I deliberately broke with feudal custom.

His policy not only aimed at assuring the direct authority of the king over all his subjects, in all ranks of the feudal hierarchy; it also furthered his financial interests.

Especially was this true with regard to the towns.

[1] *Edinburgh Review*, vol. xxxv, March 1821, p. 36–37 (*History of the English Legislature*).

[2] *Antient parliamentary elections*, p. 150–152.

[3] *Const. Hist.* ii, p. 245; *Wahlrecht*, p. 26–27.

The towns of the demesne, which were tallageable, frequently paid an aid at a higher rate than the rest of the kingdom. We have seen that in 1294, for example, after separate negotiations with each town, the towns of the demesne paid a sixth of movable goods, whereas the rest of the kingdom only paid a tenth[1]. Now, by summoning to parliament the deputies of towns situated on the demesnes of his vassals, the king was able easily to induce such towns, which were relatively few in number, to accept the higher rate habitually demanded from the towns on royal demesne. This change was effected step by step, but very rapidly. In 1294 the king negotiated with the towns of his demesne and imposed higher rates on them than on the rest of the kingdom. In 1295 he called to parliament the representatives of all the cities and all the boroughs of England; but only the towns on his demesne paid a seventh, the rest of the kingdom paying an eleventh[2]. In 1296

[1] See above, p. 97.
[2] See above, p. 101, n. 2. Stubbs (*Const. Hist.* II, p. 245–246) suggests that the formula used in 1295 was an old one, reproduced without alteration although no longer corresponding with the facts. But there is no ground for such a hypothesis. On the other hand, Professor Tait, in his review of the original edition of the present work (*English Historical Review*, vol. XXIX, p. 753) maintains that all the towns had to pay the seventh in 1295. According to him, the word *dominicis* in the writ for the collection of the taxes granted in 1295 (*cives, burgenses et alii probi homines de dominicis nostris civitatibus et burgis*) is not an adjective, but is, as usual, a noun and refers to the rural manors of the demesne. He therefore suggests that the words *dominicis nostris* should be followed by a comma or an *et*. We find difficulty in accepting this interpretation. In the documents concerning the sixth of 1294, published by Brady (see above, p. 97; and below, Appendix I), the word *dominicis* is certainly an adjective; and there is no doubt that only the towns on the demesne paid the sixth. The writ addressed to Robert de Ratford for the counties of Kent, Sussex, Surrey and Southampton says: *assignavimus vos ad petendam huiusmodi sextam partem in*

all the towns of the kingdom, *de quorumcumque tenuris aut libertatibus fuerint*, and all the demesne gave an eighth of their movable goods, while the rest of the kingdom gave a twelfth[1]. Again in 1306 all the towns and the demesne contributed at the rate of a twentieth to the aid granted for the knighting of the king's son, whereas the rest of the kingdom only gave a thirtieth[2].

Nor was the assembly of the knights of the shires, representing the lesser tenants-in-chief and sub-vassals, without importance for the treasury. It enabled the king to transform the ancient feudal aids, which were only due from tenants-in-chief and no longer had any value, into general aids payable by all. Thus in 1290 he had obtained an aid *pour fille marier* of 40 shillings on the knight's fee from a number of magnates present in parliament. But they had only been willing to promise this on behalf of the community of the realm "as far as in them lay." The king postponed the collection of this aid, summoned representatives of the counties to the parliament, promised to expel the Jews, and obtained the grant of a fifteenth, which

singulis dominicis civitatibus et aliis villis nostris...et ideo vobis mandamus quod...ad singulas dominicas civitates et alias villas nostras personaliter accedatis. And the roll adds: *per consimiles litteras assignantur infrascripti ad petendam huiusmodi sextam partem in singulis dominicis civitatibus et aliis villis regis in comitatibus subscriptis.* Again, if a precedent for imposing the same rate on all the towns, whether on demesne or not, had been established in 1295, why was it thought necessary in 1296 to write: *et cives, burgenses et alii probi homines de singulis civitatibus et burgis regni nostri de quorumcunque tenuris aut libertatibus fuerint*? Possibly, however, despite the terms of the writ, the agents of the king tried to levy the higher rate on all the towns in 1295 and in some cases succeeded.

[1] See above, p. 103. In 1297 the king tried to levy the higher rate again from all the towns. The demesne does not seem to have had any separate representation.

[2] See above, p. 123.

brought in £120,287[1]. The aid *pour fille marier*, when collected later, produced, as we know, £3061. The financial advantages of the new policy were even more apparent in 1306. The aid for knighting his eldest son, which the king wished to levy, was only payable by the tenants-in-chief and would no doubt have produced the same amount as had the aid *pour fille marier*. But Edward assembled not only the prelates and barons but also the knights of the shires and the representatives of all the towns; and, as we have just said above, the burgesses granted a twentieth, the others a thirtieth. We do not know the exact product of this tax (Sir J. H. Ramsay puts it at £40,000[2]), but certainly the king did not lose by the new method. The magnates made no attempt to oppose it, no doubt because they were not sorry to transfer to the whole kingdom a charge which hitherto they alone had had to support.

Finally, we ought to add that, in summoning the representatives of the gentry and the bourgeoisie to suit of court, Edward I probably counted on obtaining their support against the magnates, should he need it. That this was his intention is not easy to prove, because we know almost nothing of what happened in parliament; but it is at least probable. Perhaps it was because this manœuvre had not succeeded as well as he had hoped that the king was so exasperated by the knight who presented the prelates' and barons' bill to him in the parliament of 1301. Perhaps also in the last years of his reign he was not sorry to associate the community

---

[1] Ramsay, *The dawn of the Constitution*, p. 536. Stubbs, *Select Charters*, p. 470–473.

[2] *Ibid.* According to E. Powell, *A Suffolk hundred in 1283*, p. xiv, the product of the thirtieth of 1283 from the whole kingdom, except Durham and Cheshire, had been £42,765. 10s. 1¼d.

of the realm with himself in the struggle which, like his contemporary Philippe le Bel, he was conducting against the pope. This would provide a further point of resemblance between the constitutional innovations of these two kings, both of whom intended not to surrender any part of their sovereignty to their respective nations, but to strengthen the royal power against domestic opponents and foreign enemies.

CONCLUSION

OUR investigation has shown us that the convening of representatives of the counties and towns in parliament was essentially the work of the crown. This convening is to be traced to remote origins. The custom of summoning four knights, on behalf of the county, before the king's court appeared to us to have been firmly established in the reign of Richard I. And parliament is only an amplified form of the king's court. In the thirteenth century the kings gradually adopted the custom of summoning several counties at once, and even all the counties of England together. Through the sheriffs they summoned before themselves and their council two, three or four discreet knights to represent a county and to speak in its name. Sometimes, when the circumstances seemed to demand it, they particularly ordered that these knights should be elected by the county court. On other occasions the sheriffs were merely commanded to provide for the attendance of four knights, as in the case of an ordinary judicial citation. The purpose of the summons was not always the same. The knights might be required to give evidence in an inquest on the administration of the sheriffs. Or their assent might be required for an aid, the collection of which would be difficult without their co-operation. Lastly, in its struggles against the magnates, the crown was not above seeking the help of the numerous and powerful class of gentry, who held a large portion of the land of England and in the county courts administered the countryside.

At a moment of crisis, when nearly all the magnates were opposed to him, Simon de Montfort, then ruling in the king's name, summoned to parliament not only representatives of the county communities, but also representatives of the town communities.

For the counties and towns, as for the prelates and barons, the summons was in the nature of a feudal obligation. Attendance at the king's parliament was not a right, but a duty or, to adopt the contemporary expression, a service—the service, or suit, of court. As regards the knights and burgesses, the compulsory character of the summons is very clearly shown by the practice of demanding security for their appearance; a practice which was in use from the beginning of Edward I's reign and does not seem to have been then an innovation. We never find the counties and towns claiming to be summoned to parliament as of right. The knights and burgesses were by no means anxious to repair to London, York or Shrewsbury in order to waste valuable time over the king's business and to play a part of but small importance in the king's assembly. Even if the knights, long accustomed to such summons, discharged their service without much grumbling, the towns offered a passive resistance which in the end often defeated the perseverance of the sheriffs and the wishes of the king.

The formation of the house of commons has long been represented as the last step in a development which began with the Great Charter, was continued by the Provisions of Oxford and the great parliament of 1265, and ended in the "model" parliament of 1295. This development was held to have been caused by the alliance of the magnates, gentry and bourgeoisie, who

all united to oppose the excessive power of the crown
and succeeded in limiting the royal authority. But the
study of the documents has led us to quite other conclusions. The nation did not demand representation in
the king's parliament. It was the king who imposed on
his subjects the duty of sending him their representatives.

Edward I changed an occasional expedient into a
regular custom, not in order to associate the whole
nation with himself in the work of government, but in
order to strengthen the royal power. He only summoned
the representatives of the commons when such a course
seemed to him to serve his own interests; and often the
most important agenda were discussed in their absence.
If in the end he made a practice of summoning them
almost regularly, this was because he perceived that the
previous consent of the knights and burgesses greatly
facilitated the collection of aids and even enabled the
government to collect rather more than would otherwise
have been possible. Another reason was that the petitions,
in which the delegates of the communities begged him
to redress wrongs irremediable by the ordinary processes
of the law, gave him full information on the condition
of his kingdom and enabled him to make all aware of
the strength of the royal arm. Every abuse of power by
a great lord, every injustice by a servant of the crown,
every invasion of the royal rights was denounced before
the king's court; and thus the sessions of the full
parliaments carried on the grand inquests of the beginning of the reign. Lastly, the assemblies of representatives from counties and towns embodied one of the
fundamental ideas of Edward's policy. In parliament,
as formed by him, the old feudal distinction between

tenants-in-chief and sub-vassals was entirely abolished. The king had before him only subjects. Despite its feudal form, the summoning of the commons was an essentially anti-feudal measure, the object of which was to strengthen the central power and to subject all the inhabitants of the realm, of whatever rank in the feudal hierarchy, to the direct authority of the monarch[1]. In this respect Edward continued the policy of Henry II and emulated Philippe le Bel.

But Edward's plans did not succeed; or rather they succeeded only in part. The assembly of representatives from counties and towns did indeed rapidly achieve the destruction of the feudal system of society. But it did not result in an increase of the royal power, as Edward had hoped.

About the middle of the fourteenth century the house of commons, which existed only in embryo in the model parliaments of Edward I, assumed the character of an established and clearly defined institution. We may ask why the knights associated themselves with the burgesses. Between these two groups, which were elected by the communities of the realm and represented the "poor folk of the land" and whose constituents paid the greater part of the royal taxes, was there any natural affinity drawing them together? Or were the knights excluded from the baronage by the growing tendency towards the constitution of an hereditary peerage? It is difficult to say. Anyhow, in the early years of Edward III's reign, we clearly see the two groups of representatives drawing together. It is uncertain whether the knights and burgesses united in

[1] The same idea is to be noted in the summons of the clergy, who were brought to Edward's parliaments almost by force.

one body at the parliaments of March and September 1332[1]. It is almost certain that they did so at the parliaments of December 1332 and January 1333[2]. Undeniably they did so in 1339 and 1341[3]. At first

[1] At the parliament of March 1332 the king asked the advice of all the prelates, earls, barons and other magnates with regard to suitable measures for the restoration of the king's peace in the counties. "The prelates and proctors of the clergy went apart by themselves to take counsel on the aforesaid matters, and the said earls, barons and other magnates by themselves." The proposals of the magnates were then read before the king "and the prelates, the knights of the shires and the *gentz du commun*," and approved. The knights and burgesses were then given leave to go, but the full parliament continued in session (*Rot. Parl.* II, p. 64). In September 1332 the prelates deliberated "by themselves and the said earls, barons and other magnates by themselves and also the knights of the shires by themselves"; but it is not clear whether the knights deliberated with the burgesses. The latter are only mentioned when it comes to the grant of the aid. "The said prelates, earls, barons and other magnates and the knights of the shires and all the *commune*" granted the king a fifteenth "to be levied on the *communalte*" and a tenth "to be levied on the cities, boroughs and demesnes of the king." At the request of the prelates, earls, barons and knights of the shires, the king consented to withdraw the commissions issued for the tallage of the towns and the demesne (*Rot. Parl.* II, p. 66).

[2] In December 1332 the prelates deliberated "with the clergy by themselves, and the earls and barons by themselves, and the knights and men of the shires and the men of the *commune* by themselves" (*Rot. Parl.* II, p. 67). At the parliament of January 1333 it was decided by all in full parliament that a certain number of great persons, who seem to have been of the king's council, should treat "of the same matters by themselves, and the other prelates, earls, barons and proctors by themselves, and the knights of the shires and men *de commune* by themselves" (*Rot. Parl.* II, p. 69). Plenary sessions were held as well as sectional discussions.

[3] At the parliament of October 1339 the archbishop of Canterbury, who had come "overseas from our lord the king as a messenger to inform the magnates of the land and them of the *commune* concerning the state of our lord the king yonder," explained the situation "to the said magnates and to them of the *commune*." To the demand for an exceptional aid "the magnates gave their reply in a schedule in the following form.... And they of the *commune* gave their reply in another schedule...." In the latter docu-

the co-operation between the two elements, of which the new institution was formed, was not perfect. The bourgeoisie were an inferior class, subject to heavier charges than was the community of the realm. Sometimes the royal government still negotiated separately with them, as before. But the distinction between the knights and burgesses gradually became a mere question of their respective degrees of influence in parliament.

Parliament long retained the appearance of a single whole. As councillors of the king, the lords remained in the great hall of the council. They did not form a separate chamber; and the term "house of lords" does not appear till the sixteenth century. Even the deputies of the commons, although they established themselves in the chapter-house of Westminster Abbey and there deliberated apart, formed a committee of parliament (as Professor Pollard has pointed out) rather than a real "house." From time to time they crossed the road to appear "in parliament," their speaker at their head. It was only very slowly that the original unity of parliament ceased to have any real existence and was reduced to a mere form; and even more slowly did the commons come at last to play a decisive part in the English constitution.

ment "the men who are here at this Parliament on behalf of the *commune*" refused to give any undertaking and demanded fresh elections (*Rot. Parl.* II, p. 103, 104). In 1341, at the parliament held a fortnight after Easter, the distinction between the magnates and the commons is perhaps even more pronounced. The rolls of parliament tell us that the king "in an emphatic manner ordered and requested the said magnates and others of the *commune* to treat together and discuss; that is to say, the magnates by themselves, and the knights of the shires, citizens and burgesses by themselves..." (*Rot. Parl.* II, p. 127).

But the amalgamation of the knights and burgesses in the house of commons is one of the facts that have determined the development of that constitution. Without the knights the house of commons would have formed a very feeble third estate, and would have cut a sorry figure beside the king and the haughty and turbulent aristocracy that arose from the ruins of the old feudalism. But the nobility and the crown had to reckon with the knights, whose wealth, legal knowledge and influence in the counties rendered them formidable alike to the royal officers and to the liveried swash-bucklers of the great lords.

Another fact which had a decisive effect on the development of English institutions was the secession of the clergy, who, as an order, gradually ceased to attend parliament and retired to their convocations, just at the time when the house of commons was being formed. As has often been observed, the secession of the clergy destroyed that system of three estates, which would have rendered difficult the development of parliamentary institutions. The lords and the commons alone remained to face the king.

The lords and the commons were not always allied. Nor, on the other hand, did the commons always support the king's government, as Edward I had hoped, and as they did during part of Richard II's reign. Between the nobility and the king they more than once played the part of arbiters, sometimes without glory, but not always without profit. They also took advantage of the king's continual need of money, arising from the great campaigns and glorious victories in France. Still using the formulae of an extreme humility, they forced the kings to grant their petitions by only consenting to aids on certain conditions or at the end of the parliamentary session. Very slowly, by a series of precedents, they established their supremacy in financial matters and circumscribed that royal prerogative, which had previously been almost unlimited.

At the end of the fifteenth century, when the nobility had been destroyed and the monarchy seemed to have become all-powerful, in reality it was too late for the establishment of absolute power in England. The old forms, consecrated by two centuries of practice, survived the despotism of the Tudors; and in the seventeenth century the instrument, which Edward I had intended to make one of the weapons of the royal authority, was turned against the king.

APPENDIX

DR PASQUET *desired that the documents quoted from*
BRADY *(see* pp. 32, n. 1, 97, n. 5, 152, n. 1, 166, n. 3,
and 219, n. 2, *above) should be reprinted. The documents
are of importance and have not been printed since* BRADY
published them. Further, BRADY'S *transcriptions are not
complete.*

MR HILARY JENKINSON, *of the Public Record Office,
kindly put me in touch with* MISS E. SALISBURY, *to whom
I am much indebted for the transcriptions. Unfortunately*
BRADY'S *reference for the writ addressed to the sheriff of
Huntingdonshire (see* p. 32, n. 1, *and* p. 166, n. 3, *above)
seems incorrect. The writ could not be found.*

R. G. D. L.

I

WRITS FOR THE COLLECTION OF THE SIXTH IN LONDON
AND FOR THE NOMINATION OF COMMISSIONERS,
NOVEMBER, 1294.

See p. 97, n. 5, and p. 219, n. 2, above.

K.R. Memoranda Roll 68, rot. 73.

De sexta   Rex dilectis et fidelibus suis Custodi, Vicecomi-
parte Regi   tibus, Aldremannis, et toti Communitati ciuitatis
concessa in   sue London' salutem. Cum Vos in forma, in
Lond'.   qua nuper nobis quintamdecimam concesseratis,
sextam partem bonorum et mobilium vestrorum[1] in subsidium guerre nostre nobis concesseritis liberaliter et libenter,
Nos, vt illa sexta pars ad minus dampnum et grauamen vestri
et singulorum Ciuitatis eiusdem leuetur et colligatur prouidere
volentes[2], assignauimus dilectos et fideles nostros Iohannem

[1] sextam . . . vestrorum *interlined*.
[2] prouidere volentes *interlined*.

de Banquelle, Thomam le Romeyn, Hamonem Box, Willelmum de Betonia, et Gilbertum de Marchia vna cum dilecto
Clerico nostro Magistro Willelmo de Wymund-
ham, quem ad hoc duximus assignandum, ad
dictam sextam partem infra Ciuitatem predictam
et extra infra totum procinctum eiusdem Ciuitatis, quatenus ad Ciuitatem ipsam pertinet, assidendam et taxandam, leuandam et colligendam,
et ad scaccarium nostrum portandam et ibidem
soluendam ad terminos infrascriptos—Videlicet,
Vnam medietatem citra festum Purificationis
beate Marie proximo futuro et aliam medietatem citra festum
Pentecostes proximo sequens. Et ideo vobis mandamus quod
dictis Iohanni, Thome, Hamoni, Willelmo, et Gilberto, et
eorum singulis vna cum Clerico antedicto in premissis sitis
intendentes, respondentes, consulentes, auxiliantes, et obe-
dientes in forma predicta prout ipsi et singuli eorum vobis
scire facient ex parte nostra. In cuius rei testimonium Has
litteras nostras fieri fecimus patentes, Teste venerabili patre
etc. xxvj die Nouembris, Anno xxiij⁰.

Marginal note: Compotum in magno Rotulo de anno xxxiiij Regis Edwardi filij Regis Henrici Rotulo compotorum.

Marginal note: [26 *Nov.* 1294.]

Rex dilecto et fideli suo Roberto de Ratford
salutem. Cum Ciues et probi homines nostri
London' sextam partem bonorum suorum mobilium nobis in subsidium guerre nostre gratanter concesserint, vt aliis qui sunt de dominicis
villis nostris exemplum prebeant ad consimile
subsidium faciendum, Assignauimus vos ad petendam huiusmodi sextam partem in singulis
dominicis Ciuitatibus et aliis villis nostris in
Comitatibus Kanc', Sussex', Surr', et Suth' secundum taxacionem decime iam nobis in regno nostro concesse. Et ideo
vobis mandamus quod, assumptis vobiscum vicecomitibus
locorum, ad singulas dominicas Ciuitates et alias villas nostras
personaliter accedatis, et homines earundem Ciuitatum et
villarum ad concedendum et prestandum nobis predictam
sextam partem iuxta taxacionem predictam diligenter ex parte
nostra requiratis, et efficaciter inducatis modis quibus vide-
bitis magis expedire. Et quid inde feceritis nobis aut Thesaurario et Baronibus nostris de scaccario sine dilacione con-
stare faciatis. In cuius rei testimonium has litteras nostras fieri

Marginal note: De diuersis assignatis ad petendum consimilem sextam in dominicis villis Regis in diuersis Comitatibus.

fecimus patentes, Teste venerabili patre etc. xxj. die Nouem- [21 *Nov.*
bris, Anno xxxiij⁰. 1294.]

Per consimiles litteras assignantur infrascripti ad petendum
huiusmodi sextam partem in singulis dominicis Ciuitatibus
et aliis villis Regis in Comitatibus subscriptis—videlicet,

Willelmus de Ormesby in Comitatibus Norff', Suff', Essex',
Hertf', Cant', Hunt'.
Magister Petrus de Lek in Comitatibus Nothampt', Leyc',
Warr', Rotel', Lync'.
Iohannes de Litegremes in Comitatibus Ebor', Norhumbr',
Cumbr', Westm', Lanc'.
Magister Iohannes Louel in Comitatibus Wyltes', Somers',
Dors', Deuon', et Cornub'.
Iohannes de Bosco in Comitatibus Notingh', Derby, Salop',
Staff', Wygorn'.
Radulfus de Broghton' in Comitatibus Oxon', Berk', Bedef',
Buk', Glouc', Heref'.

Teste vt supra etc.

Et mandatum est vicecomiti Kancie in hac forma: cum as-
signauerimus dilectum et fidelem nostrum Robertum de
Ratford ad petendum subsidium ad opus nostrum de dominicis
Ciuitatibus et aliis villis nostris in balliua tua et te associa-
uerimus eidem, prout in litteris nostris patentibus ei inde
confectis plenius continetur, tibi precipimus quod prefato
Roberto in premissis viriliter et diligenter assistas, prout
ipse tibi scire faciet ex parte nostra et cum ab ipso super hoc
fueris requisitus. Et hoc nullatenus omittas. Teste Thesaurario etc. xxj⁰. die Nouembris, Anno predicto.

Consimili modo mandatum est singulis vicecomitibus Comitatuum predictorum, in quibus predictus Robertus et alii
supradicti assignantur, Teste Thesaurario ut supra.

II

RECORD OF THE PARLIAMENT OF TRINITY, 1306

See p. 152, n. 1, above.

L.T.R. Memoranda Roll 76, rot. 43.

Adhuc communia de termino
Sancte Trinitatis anno regni
Regis Edwardi xxxiiij^{to}
Recorda.

Anglia.
De auxilio
concesso ad
Miliciam
filii Regis.

Memorandum quod cum nuper dominus Rex
ordinasset quod Edwardus filius suus primo-
genitus in festo Pentecostes Anno regni sui
Tricesimo quarto cingulo Milicie decoraretur, et
mandatum esset Archiepiscopis, Episcopis, Abbatibus, Prioribus, Comitibus, Baronibus, et aliis magnatibus
regni quod essent coram ipso domino Rege et consilio suo
apud Westmonasterium in crastino Sancte Trinitatis proximo
sequentis ad tractandum et ordinandum de auxilio Regis
faciendo ad Miliciam predictam et ad consenciendum hiis,
que vlterius ordinarentur in hac parte, vel quod procuratores
aut attornatos suos sufficienter instructos ad premissa loco
eorum facienda mitterent tunc ibidem, Ac eciam preceptum
fuisset singulis vicecomitibus Anglie quod eorum quilibet
venire faceret de Comitatu suo ad prefatos diem et locum
duos Milites et de qualibet Ciuitate Balliue sue duos Ciues et
de quolibet Burgo eiusdem Balliue sue duos Burgenses vel
vnum etc. ad tractandum, ordinandum, et consenciendum
sicut predictum est,—Venerunt personaliter coram Rege et
consilio suo apud Westmonasterium ad diem illum Antonius
Bek' Patriarcha Ierosolomitanus, Episcopus Dunolmensis,
W. de Langeton' Couentrensis et Lichefeldensis, Radulfus de
Baldok' Londoniensis Episcopi, H. de Lacy Comes Lincolnie,
I. de Warenna Comes Surreie, R. de Monte Hermeri Comes
Gloucestrie et Hertfordie, H. de Boun Comes Herefordie,
G. de Bello Campo Comes Warr', Robertus filius Walteri,
Hugo le Despenser, Iohannes de Hastingges, Hugo de Veer,

Willelmus Martyn, Henricus le Tyeys, Iohannes Louel,
Rogerus de Mortuo Mari, Iohannes de Mohun, Alanus La
Zousche, Willelmus de Leyburn', et Robertus de Burghersh
Custos quinque Portuum cum quibusdam Baronibus portuum
eorundem, Ac eciam per procuratores et attornatos Robertus
Cantuariensis et Willelmus Eboracensis Archiepiscopi, Thomas
Exoniensis, Ricardus Herefordensis, Iohannes Wyntoniensis,
Iohannes Cicestrensis, Thomas Roffensis, Robertus Elyensis,
Iohannes Norwycensis, Iohannes Lincolniensis, Simon Sarum,
Willelmus Wygorniensis, Walterus Bathoniensis et Wellensis,
et Iohannes Karliolensis Episcopi, Abbates Westmonasterii,
Sancti Edmundi, Sancti Augustini Cantuarie, Sancti Albani,
Glastonie Burgi, Sancti Petri Rammeseye, Thorneye, Seleby,
Malmesbury, Sancti Petri Gloucestrie, Rogerus Comes Norff'
et Marescallus Anglie, Thomas Comes Lancastrie, Edmundus
Comes Arundell', et quamplures alii prelati, Magnates, et
proceres regni, necnon de quolibet Comitatu regni eiusdem
duo Milites et de qualibet Ciuitate duo Ciues et de quolibet
Burgo duo Burgenses electi per communitates Comitatuum,
Ciuitatum, et Burgorum eorundem ad premissa loco com-
munitatuum (*sic*) eorundem tractandum, ordinandum, et
consenciendum similiter venerunt. Quibus predictis omnibus
congregatis coram consilio Regis predicto, ipsisque ostenso
per idem consilium ex parte Regis quod de iure Corone Regie
auxilium domino Regi fieri debuit in casu predicto, Ac eciam
quod expense multiplices et alia quamplura onera eidem
domino Regi incumbunt ad rebellionem et maliciam Roberti
de Brus proditoris ipsius domini Regis et sibi in partibus
Scotie adherencium, qui aduersus ipsum Regem iam in illis
partibus guerram mouere presumpserunt reprimendas, iidem
prelati, Comites, Barones, et alii magnates, necnon Milites
Comitatuum tractatum super hoc cum deliberacione habentes
considerantesque auxilium deberi, vt predictum est, et quamplura onera Regi incumbere propter guerram predictam,
tandem vnanimiter domino Regi concesserunt pro se et tota
communitate regni tricesimam partem omnium bonorum
suorum temporalium mobilium que ipsos habere continget
in festo Sancti Michaelis proximo futuro habendam pro
auxilio eidem domino Regi competente ad Miliciam filii sui
predicti Ac eciam in auxilium Misarum quas est facturus circa

guerram predictam; Ita tamen quod ista concessio ipsis vel
eorum successoribus aut heredibus futuris temporibus nullatenus cedat in preiudicium, nec in casu huiusmodi trahatur
in exemplum; Et quod in taxando bona predicta excipiantur
omnia, que in taxacione quintedecime a communitate regni
domino Regi anno regni sui. xviij°. concesse propter exilium
Iudeorum fuerunt excepta. Ciues quidem et Burgenses Ciuitatum et Burgorum predictorum ac ceteri de dominicis Regis
congregati et super premissis tractatum habentes, considerantesque onera domino Regi incumbencia, ut premittitur,
eidem domino Regi vnanimiter concesserunt ob causas supra-
dictas Vicesimam partem bonorum suorum mobilium habendam, vt predictum est.

L.T.R. Memoranda Roll 77, rot. 22.

Adhuc communia de termino
Sancti Michaelis anno regni
regis Edwardi. xxxiiij^{to}
Adhuc Recorda.

Memorandum quod ad Crastinum Sancte Trinitatis proximo
preteritum prelati et ceteri magnates regni pro se et tota
communitate eiusdem regni concesserunt domino Regi tricesimam bonorum suorum omnium temporalium extra Ciuitates Burgos et dominica domini Regis et Ciues Burgenses et
tenentes dominicorum predictorum vicesimam bonorum
suorum tam ad Miliciam Edwardi filii Regis predicti quam
ad subsidium defensionis terre Scocie contra Robertum de
Brus et ipsius complices inimicos Regis etc., et forma con-
cessionis supradicte plenius annotatur in Memorandis anni
precedentis termino Trinitatis. Et subscripti venientes modo
hic concesserunt satisfacere Regi pro tricesima et vicesima
predictis ipsos contingentibus, vt patet subsequenter.

Here follow 3 entries concerning—

1. William de la More, Master of the Knights Templars,
who promises 700 marks.

2. The Prior of the Hospital of St John of Jerusalem, who
promises 700 marks.

3. John le Blound, mayor of London, who promises £2000.

III

ADDITIONAL NOTES BY G. LAPSLEY

A, p. vi, l. 27. It is of the essence of Dr Riess's argument that the words of the *confirmatio* which concede certain things to the church, baronage and *tote la communaute de la terre* were deliberately vague and cannot be taken as including the knights and burgesses. The suggestion gains support from the precise wording of the *de tallagio non concedendo*, which specifies knights, burgesses and other free men. This argument did not convince Dr Prothero, but he does not seem to have met it successfully. He urged in support of his position that taxation was the chief reason for summoning the commons, that they had co-operated in making grants on a number of occasions before 1297 and that the act of that year was intended to give the force of law to an existing custom. Of that act he wrote "henceforward the customs could not be increased, nor tenths or fifteenths legally taken save by the consent of the persons to whom the charter was granted, *i.e.* to the members of what became in 1295 the normal parliament, the representatives of town and country as well as the baronage[1]." But this appears to be assuming the point at issue, to say nothing of the assumption that the parliament of 1295 was normal in the sense of giving a model to which subsequent parliaments regularly conformed. The first point needs some discussion, the second has been sufficiently disposed of in Dr Pasquet's text.

The *confirmatio*, as is well known, is in the form of a charter under the great seal, and is accordingly addressed to "all who shall see or hear these present letters." The king states that he has granted that the charters shall be observed "for the profit of the whole kingdom." The sheriffs are directed "to acquaint the people" with what has been done. The critical passage is in the sixth clause where the king grants to "the archbishops, bishops, priors and other folk of holy church and to the earls, barons and the whole community of the land" that he will not take aids, mises nor prises "but by

[1] *English Hist. Review*, v, p. 150.

the common assent of all the realm and for the common profit thereof[1]." Now in the first clause the words "the common assent of all the kingdom" are applied to the king's reissue of the charters in 1217 and it is clear that the prelates and barons alone were concerned in that transaction. This is true also of the aid which was granted to the king in return for his confirmation of the charters in 1225, where the consent of the knights, free tenants and all men of the kingdom is specified[2], although there is no evidence that these latter were represented or consulted or given any opportunity of refusing. Moreover the aid referred to was in form, though not in effect, a feudal imposition requiring only the consent of the tenants in chief, and it was this "gracious" aid still feudal in form which is referred to in the *confirmatio*[3].

The words of the *de tallagio non concedendo*, whatever their origin, at least appear to show that a body of people capable of exerting some pressure desired the king to make the concession in the terms there used, *i.e.* to make the consent of the knights and burgesses indispensable for a gracious aid. If this is the case—and the fact that the chronicler thought it worth while to incorporate the articles makes it probable— then the king's choice of a vague rather than a precise form of words suggests that he did not intend to go so far.

The question of the maletote stands on a somewhat different footing. We know that the parliament of 1275, to which knights and burgesses were summoned, took part in the establishment of the customs, and it is possible that the words in the seventh clause of the *confirmatio*, "granted by the community of the kingdom" and "their common assent," may refer to the grant and assent of future parliaments so con- stituted. On the other hand, one of the two surviving official documents consequential on the act of 1275, states that the grant was made by the council, while the other suggests that it had the authority of the parliament[4]. In view of these facts Dr Prothero's assumption is scarcely warranted.

---

[1] Stubbs, *Select Charters*, p. 490 ff.
[2] *Ibid.* p. 340 ff., 349 ff.   [3] See below, note C.
[4] See Gras, *Early English Customs System*, London 1918, p. 64, 223. The first document is given here and the second in Stubbs, *Select Charters*, p. 443.

It is not of course denied that the previous consent of the commons, however obtained, facilitated the levy of a tax nor even that it was becoming increasingly frequent and necessary. There is a sense, therefore, in which the question of taxation was closely bound up with Edward I's policy much more closely, I think, than Dr Riess would allow. But it was not yet the constitutional sense. The real issue is whether the king meant to constitute a representative parliament as a permanent part of the machinery of government and to endow it with the right of granting or refusing taxation. The balance seems to me to be against such a conclusion[1].

B, p. 7, l. 10. Much new light has recently been thrown on the subject of the internal development of the *curia regis* in its administrative and political aspects. See T. H. Tout, *The Place of the Reign of Edward II in English History*, Manchester University Press, 1914; *Chapters in the Administrative History of Medieval England*, vols. I and II, Manchester and London, 1920; *Some Conflicting Tendencies in English Administrative History during the Fourteenth Century*, Bulletin of the John Rylands Library, vol. 8, no. 1, January 1924; J. C. Davies, *The Baronial Opposition to Edward II*, Cambridge University Press, 1918.

C, p. 11, l. 30. The treatment in the text of the problem of scutage and the beginnings of the principle that corporate consent was required before certain forms of taxation could be levied needs to be somewhat modified and supplemented in view of recent work. Three points have to be cleared up: how did scutage take on the aspect of a tax, what ends were clauses 12 and 14 of the charter intended to secure and why were they dropped in reissues of the charter after 1215?

During the first half of the twelfth century social and economic changes in the middle ranges of feudal society produced what has been conveniently described as the "ruralization" of the tenants by knight service. The number of such holdings increased and the tenants in many if not in all cases ceased to be professional soldiers. As they all owed to their lords either military service when the king required it of him or a money composition in lieu of such service, and as in many

---

[1] But see in the opposite sense, Hatschek, *Englische Verfassungsgeschichte*, p. 109, n. 1. Munich and Berlin, 1913.

cases a given lord had more tenants by knight service than he required to perform his *servitum debitum*, it is evident that there was a margin of profit here which might be claimed by the king. What Henry II did, in view of the changed character of the sub-vassals, was to get this right of the crown firmly established on the basis of the number of knights of old enfeoffment, *i.e.* before the death of Henry I, where that number was greater than the *servitum debitum*. Before the century was over, however, certain changes had occurred tending to obscure the character of scutage as a composition for military service and to present it, when seen from a certain angle at least, in the light of a tax. For one thing scutage had ceased to be the only form of composition for service, and under Richard I the king had begun to take from the tenants-in-chief fines *pro passagio* or *ne transfretent*, when it was a question of foreign service. Then the treasury, finding it impossible to secure either the full amount of service due or the corresponding scutage, had been driven to compromise and accept the service or scutage of a smaller number of knights than was actually due. Also the rate of the scutage had not changed, although the cost of hiring knights had risen considerably. Thus "at some point in the feudal ladder every fee in the kingdom was held by a man whose tenure was military yet who did not...perform military service except by paying scutage." To such men the scutage appeared to be a tax and indeed a tax of a feudal character, that is an aid. The new taxation of movables introduced by Henry II and the new system of the taxation of the land devised in Hubert Walter's régime, were actually aids of this sort. And apart from the three appointed cases such aids were, according to the feudal law, "gracious," *i.e.* they required the individual consent of those who paid them. Scutage, on the other hand, was really a composition, though it looked like an aid, and John's manipulation of it increased the resemblance. Briefly stated, what John undertook to do was to make scutage a true composition by rejecting the old compromise and demanding payment on the basis settled by his grandfather, by raising the rate to meet the increased cost of hiring knights and by himself determining—not always honestly—the occasion for levying a scutage. These principles would apply to the three courses which apparently were still open to the tenant-in-chief, *i.e.* to appear in person with the full quota, to pay a fine which would include the scutage and subsequently obtain the king's leave to recoup himself from his vassals or to pay the scutage. It will be seen that John's policy raised some difficult questions of law and right and these were answered in the great charter. The 12th and 14th clauses treated the scutage as John had imposed it as a gracious aid, although it might well be argued that, apart from the king's abuse of his rights, it was not that, and established the necessity of corporate as opposed to individual consent to all gracious aids. It would seem that this was accepted by the crown after John's death and that the scutage therefrom was put back on the basis of the fixed rate and the partial service or composition. There was no necessity therefore to insert clauses 12 and 14 in the reissues of the charter. The question of the right of the crown to a scutage that should be a real composition for military service was raised again in Edward I's time but with no great success. Meanwhile the old rigid forms of contribution, the scutage on fees, the tallage and the donum which covered indeed most of the property in the kingdom, had given way to the carucage and the tax on movables. These were flexible and based on a new assessment made on each occasion. They were national in substance, but the barons had seen to it that they were feudal in form, in the sense that they were treated as gracious aids requiring the consent of the tenants-in-chief.

See S. K. Mitchell, *Studies in Taxation under John and Henry III*, Yale University Press, 1914.

H. N. Chew, *Scutage under Edward I*, in *English Hist. Review*, XXXVII, p. 321 ff.; *ibid.* XXXVIII, p. 19 ff.

D, p. 21, l. 7. The influence of the church on the development of representative institutions in England has recently been discussed by Professor H. J. Ford in his *Representative Government*, New York, 1924. He holds that "the evidence now available warrants the statement that in making its start representative government got its mode and form from the church" (p. 88). It does not seem to me that the evidence warrants quite so much. No doubt "there was a real representative system in ecclesiastical assemblies earlier than in

L   16

civil ones " (the phrase is Freeman's, see p. 104–5), and the development in England could have been influenced by this fact, but it remains to be shown, I think, that it was so.

E, p. 24, n. 2. Documents of this sort have recently been discovered and published by Mr Hilary Jenkinson, *Plea Rolls of the Medieval County Courts*, in *The Cambridge Historical Journal*, I, no. 1 (1923), p. 103 ff.

F, p. 30, n. 1. This incident has been discussed by Professor A. B. White in an article, already cited in the introduction, *Some early instances of concentration of representatives in England*, in *American Hist. Review*, XIX, p. 735 ff.

G, p. 77, n. 3. Professor Tait has discussed the significance of the words *villa mercatoria* in an important article, *The study of early municipal history in England*, in *Proceedings of the British Academy*, X. He believes that the point of the writ was to get representatives from important places. There might be towns which, owing to the absence of burgage tenure could not be styled boroughs, but still had a considerable volume of trade carried on in fairs of more importance and general resort than the weekly market.

H, p. 80, n. 1. This whole matter has recently been discussed from the constitutional as well as from the economic point of view by Professor Gras in his *Early English Customs System*, Harvard University Press, 1918, to which reference has already been made[1]. The exact share of the parliament in the establishment of the customs and the measure of its authority in the matter are left in some doubt by the conflicting terms of the two surviving documents.

I, p. 109, n. 2. The interest of the towns and not the barons was involved in the tallage. The towns had not paid danegeld but instead a lump sum of varying amount supposed to be determined by arrangement between them and the king; this was called donum or auxilium. The arbitrary contribution which the king demanded from his demesne was called tallage. After 1168 it seems that royal boroughs were reputed to stand on ancient demesne and their contributions were treated as tallages. They were not helped, therefore, by clause 12 of the great charter, which spoke of aids only,

[1] *Vide supra*, p. 238.

and they never got free from arbitrary taxation until they secured parliamentary representation.

See C. Stephenson, *The Aids of the English Boroughs*, in *English Hist. Review*, XXXIV, p. 457 ff.

K, p. 119, l. 10. It should be remembered that customs duties were levied at a fixed rate. Any temporary increase of the rate if sanctioned by parliament or the magnates or the merchants would be called a subsidy, but if exacted by the king without such sanction it was described as a maletote. See H. Hall, *Customs Revenue*, II, p. 169 ff., and Gras, *op. cit.* p. 77 ff.

L, p. 122, l. 4. The community in Scotland would mean the minor tenants-in-chief. See R. S. Rait, *The Parliaments of Scotland*, Glasgow, 1924, p. 3 and *passim*.

M, p. 149, n. 2. Nevertheless it seems pretty clear that the actual election took place and was intended to take place in the towns. Riess, *op. cit.*, has brought some interesting evidence as to the first point. As to the second, a passage in the well-known writ of summons in 1295 seems to be conclusive: it runs as follows:

ita quod dicti milites plenam et sufficientem potestatem pro se et communitate comitatus praedicti, et dicti cives et burgenses pro se et communitate civitatum et burgorum praedictorum divisim ab ipsis, tunc ibidem habeant ad faciendum etc.

Stubbs, *Select Charters*, 9th ed., p. 481–482.

It is difficult to see how the citizens and burgesses whom the sheriff was to cause to be elected should have full powers to act on behalf of their cities and boroughs separately from the knights of the shire unless such powers had been derived by election in the cities and boroughs themselves.

N, p. 154, l. 7. This is perhaps too strongly stated: see M. McKisack, *Borough Representatives in Richard II's Reign*, in *English Hist. Review*, XXXIX, p. 511 ff.

O, p. 174, l. 12. So much has been written in praise and more recently in disparagement of this famous citation and the inferences that may be made from it as to Edward I's policy that it is interesting to take account of a gallant but not perhaps very successful attempt to support the old interpretation. P. S. Leicht shows that the maxim as it stands in the Codex applies to private law only, but its appearance in a decretal of Innocent III, subsequently incorporated in the canon law, brings it fairly within the sphere of public law. There it answered to existing political theories on the continent and the rise of the towns to political power, and was often cited by theorists and practical statesmen to show the necessity of the participation of the people in government and the validity of the theory of popular sovereignty. It was used by the supporters of Philip IV against Boniface VIII, and by Edward I in his letter to the pope with regard to the Scottish affair. The theory of popular sovereignty later known in England might thus have found its way there at this time.

The argument is not convincing. It assumes a similarity of conditions in Italy and England, which as far as one can see, did not exist in the thirteenth century, *e.g.* it neglects the fact that Edward I was dealing with country gentlemen as well as burgesses. It assumes that as the *confirmatio cartarum* gave something less than appears to have been demanded by the *de tallagio non concedendo*, the middle class was aiming at political power and had secured its position and forced itself on the king in 1297. Finally it infers a general policy not supported by other evidence from the use of a commonplace quotation in a controversial document and a writ issued in a moment of political crisis. See P. S. Leicht, *Un principio politico medioevale*, in *Reale Accademia nazionale dei Lincei, Rendiconti*, XXIX, p. 232 ff.

P, p. 174, n. 3. See an interesting and instructive discussion of this subject by F. Kern, *Recht und Verfassung im Mittelalter* in *Historische Zeitschrift*, CXX, p. 1 ff.

INDEX

For EU product safety concerns, contact us at Calle de José Abascal, 56–1°, 28003 Madrid, Spain or eugpsr@cambridge.org.

www.ingramcontent.com/pod-product-compliance
Ingram Content Group UK Ltd.
Pitfield, Milton Keynes, MK11 3LW, UK
UKHW020319140625
459647UK00018B/1935